# FIRST
# CAMERAMAN

.

# FIRST CAMERAMAN

**Documenting the Obama
Presidency in Real Time**

## ARUN CHAUDHARY

Times Books
Henry Holt and Company
New York

Times Books
Henry Holt and Company, LLC
*Publishers since 1866*
175 Fifth Avenue
New York, New York 10010

Distributed in Canada by Raincoast Book Distribution Limited

Library of Congress Cataloging-in-Publication Data

Chaudhary, Arun.
  First cameraman : documenting the Obama presidency in real time / Arun
Chaudhary.—1st ed.
      p. cm.
  Includes index.
  ISBN 978-0-8050-9572-2 (hardback)
 1. Chaudhary, Arun.   2. Photojournalists—United States—Biography.
3. Video journalism—United States—History—21st century.   4. Obama,
Barack—Friends and associates.   5. United States—Politics and government—
2001–2009.   6. United States—Politics and government—2009–   I. Title.
  E901.1.C47A3 2012
  070.4'9092—dc23
  [B]

                                                              2012014019

Henry Holt books are available for special promotions and premiums.
For details contact: Director, Special Markets.

First Edition 2012
Designed by Meryl Sussman Levavi
Printed in the United States of America
10 9 8 7 6 5 4 3 2 1

*To Laura, Leo, and Advance Staff everywhere*

# CONTENTS

## PART II GOVERNMENT FUNNY

## PART III HISTORIAN IMPERFECT

# FIRST
# CAMERAMAN

# THE FINE AMERICAN ART OF SAYING HELLO

Barack Obama didn't think about it too long before shaking his head. "No, I don't want to do that," he said.

I was a little surprised. It was October 21, 2008, and by that point we'd done a lot together. We'd visited hundreds of diners, state fairs, parades, and high school gymnasia, and let's not forget the factories. Together we'd inhaled the fumes of a thousand factories. (Traveling press secretary Jen Psaki always said that she, the president, Reggie Love, and I were all destined to die of some mysterious disease caused by a toxic mixture of glass, metal, and drywall particles.)

So I was slightly taken aback by Obama's refusal. Surely my question hadn't been *that* intrusive. Besides, the junior senator from Illinois was used to my intrusions. I'd already ruined plenty of amazing moments, like right after the nomination speech at Invesco Stadium, when Barack was hugging his VP nominee. I'd had to clear my throat: "Uh, hey, guys, could you and Senator Biden just quickly look into the camera and . . . I know, I know, it won't take long."*

I'd given no end of confusing instructions: "I'm going to need you to take this mic off before you start speaking into your actual mic-mic up there, okay?" eliciting nary a word of complaint.

This time, though, he was firm, and so I sank back in my seat on the bus with a pastrami sandwich left over from our stop at the Deli Den in Fort Lauderdale. "It's just that I don't want to fake it," he said. "Let's just wait until I really do it naturally, okay?"

I nodded, and I got it. What I'd asked him to do was a big deal for him. "Senator, would you mind looking out the window for a minute so I can film it? The guys doing the thirty-minute commercial have been asking if I would shoot some out-the-window-thoughtful kind of stuff."

It was a little inconvenient for me, but Obama's reluctance to put on a show makes for good politics as well as good policy. Americans detest inauthenticity above all things, whether in a job interview at an investment bank or at the neighborhood saloon of a gold rush frontier town. And there's a deep truth in that Head & Shoulders ad from the '80s—you never get a second chance to make a first impression.

We Americans are hand shakers, huggers. When we greet one another, we meet as equals. We're likely to use first names. There are no inscrutable titles or castes, and certainly no cap-doffing or bowing. We base our introductions on who we are and where

---

* This was, of course, not as bad as that November night in Grant Park, mere seconds before the just-elected next president of the United States was about to go onstage for his victory speech: "Congratulations, sir! Now, if you could just stand there, I already have the camera in focus. We can knock this thing out in two takes, get you right out there!"

we're from, what we do, what we're about to do, or maybe what we just did.

This frank and egalitarian manner of self-presentation dominates our cultural landscape, from the poetic boastings of Jack Johnson and Muhammad Ali ("I am the greatest, I said that even before I knew I was") to the humble biographies of Bruce Springsteen and Loretta Lynn ("We were poor, but we had love") to those who would be our presidents, be they from a log cabin or a town called Hope.

The first—and, I think, in many ways the hardest—step in running for president is the cold opening, the pitch, that initial handshake, done over and over again over the course of a campaign: *My name is so-and-so and I'm running for president. How are you doing and what do you do? This is what I've seen, this is what I've done, and this is why you should consider getting to know me better.*

These days, of course, many of these introductions are taking place on screens, and more than ever online (and not just on Match .com). In a remarkably short span of time, really just since 2008, it's become standard practice for presidential candidates to announce their campaigns and introduce themselves to the American electorate on YouTube, in videos that, intentionally or not, reveal a good deal about who they are and what type of campaign they'll be running.

My favorite from the run-up to the 2012 election was Jon Huntsman's announcement video, which showed the former Utah governor (or a devilishly handsome stunt double) on a motorcycle, cruising past the gorgeous rock formations of Monument Valley while a semi-funny reference to his long-ago rock band Wizard scrolls across the screen. But they are now a staple, from the fake-handheld look of the first online appearance of candidate Hillary

Rodham Clinton in 2008, who just wanted "to start a conversation," to Mitt Romney's out-of-the-package windbreaker on a hillside above the University of New Hampshire.

Interestingly, Obama for America's reelection video didn't show the president at all: it was a roundup of various supporters' reasons for getting involved in the president's campaign, followed by the words "It begins with us." This approach made sense, since the sitting president of the United States doesn't need an introduction; the goal was rather to relaunch a movement.

I think all of these intro videos are useful, revealing, and—for lack of a better word—*true*. Pretty much everything you need to know about the candidate you can deduce from a two-minute video. The Huntsman one speaks of a candidate who wants to be a little edgy, but is simply not suited to the more conservative elements of the Republican base. Romney: competent and unobjectionable, but also uninspired and uninspiring. Not comfortable in that windbreaker. (Also check out his brand-new NASCAR jacket at the Daytona 500; it's become a habit of Giulianiesque proportions.)

I should say that I have more than a passing interest in how political videos work because I spent four years filming Barack Obama pretty much around the clock. As the first Official White House Videographer, I was sort of like President Obama's wedding videographer if every day was a wedding with the same groom but a constantly rotating set of hysterical guests.

If there's one thing I learned over those years, it's that videos don't lie—on the contrary, they are the most reliable gauge of truth we have.* The basic narrative told in a shot is true, despite the ease with which some elements of motion picture can be manipulated. No one can deny the power of editing to influence a viewer.

---

* Jean-Luc Godard said that "cinema is truth twenty-four times a second." Now that I've gotten that out of the way, I swear I won't mention him again.

Way back in 1918, Soviet filmmaker Lev Kuleshov famously demonstrated that an audience would ascribe emotion to a neutral face based on the preceding shot, for example, a shot of a bowl of soup makes an expressionless actor look hungry. We're talking basic stuff here. But the great big personalities who vie for the American presidency are hardly expressionless or neutral. Just look at the cutaways in the debates, when the candidates are supposed to be at their most controlled. A bowl of soup plus Michele Bachmann or Newt Gingrich is just a bowl of soup plus Michele Bachmann or Newt Gingrich.*

In our age of media supersaturation, videos have an ever more direct impact on how we judge and elect our politicians. This, at the end of the day, may be a very good thing. Given enough screen time, all candidates reveal who they really are. No matter how carefully scripted and choreographed their media appearances and stump speeches, no matter how skillfully edited their official videos, eventually—for better or worse—the camera will catch them out. It didn't take long for Mitt Romney to announce that he was "running for office, for Pete's sake" and that he "likes being able to fire people." Or for Rick Perry to forget why he was running at all ("oops"). For many candidates, the video camera is a trap just waiting to spring open; for a rare few, it's a golden ticket.

Let me repeat: the camera doesn't lie. It may sound simplistic, but this is the chief reason I know, without a single precinct reporting, that Barack Obama will be reelected president of the United

---

* And the real tragedy here is that Newt didn't even know what flavor soup he was. In his announcement video, the former Speaker stands way too close to the camera and reads out a speech against what looks like a Sears Portrait Studio backdrop. But the thing that Republican voters like about Newt, and the reason they gave him three comebacks and a handful of states despite obvious and obviously fatal flaws, is his anger. Even *I* like Newt's anger. But his intro video, and in fact most of his campaign videos, were generic to the point of eccentricity, and just a real letdown for a guy with his own production company.

States on my thirty-seventh birthday, November 6, 2012. I know because I've seen the game tapes (figuratively speaking, of course; the White House has gone digital, like everyone else).

In fact, I've made a lot of these game tapes myself. I've filmed Barack Obama for thousands of hours, from a few months into his long-shot candidacy into the third year of his presidency. For four-plus years, I was responsible for capturing Obama's every move on film: first with political objectives, then for history. We'd progressed from greasy spoons and VFW halls to the Chilean presidential palace (where the famous progressive rock band Los Jaivas performed their signature classic "Mamalluca"), and, well, the White House. All along the way, I've also filmed the less public moments that in previous administrations only a handful of people—the ones right there in the room—had the opportunity to witness.*

Some of the moments were small: the president throwing warm-up pitches deep inside Busch Stadium in St. Louis before the 2009 All-Star Game while a touchingly concerned Albert Pujols gave sage advice. "It's a long way to the plate, Mr. President—throw it up!" Some of the moments were intensely affecting: POTUS (the president of the United States) comforting a grieving teenager whose father had died in the Joplin, Missouri, tornado two days earlier. And some were just plain scary: the then senator Obama's sudden appearance in Nick's Bar in Bloomington nearly inciting a riot among the college students far gone in their cups . . . at eleven in the morning. (I have to admit that at Nick's the survival instincts kicked in and I put my camera down and just started pushing through the crowd.)

Throughout all these changes of scene, and the dramatic

---

* As opposed to the hundreds of well-dressed midde-aged Chileans who rocked out to "Mamalluca."

transition from campaigning to governing, there's been one constant: Barack Obama. Over thousands of hours of filming him, not once did I spot Mr. Hyde offstage right. Republicans have repeatedly tried to paint Barack Obama as a scary outsider, but cameras have told a different story. Many Americans—myself and the electorate who showed up to the polls on November 4, 2008, included—recognize one of their own.

I certainly liked him as soon as he entered my radar. Though I'd been an interested American in 2004 when Obama made his famous convention speech, I wasn't interested enough to take the TV off mute before the headlining act.* (Watching the opening speakers was like watching whatever band was opening for the Flaming Lips who were opening for an actual band at Roseland in the mid-'90s.) I didn't really start paying attention until late 2006, when he made a satirical announcement video that aired during *Monday Night Football.* In the video, after a typically grave buildup, he talks about the big decisions facing America, and then finally commits to—supporting the Bears. The spot finishes with him putting on his Bears cap and breaking into his easy laugh. And try as I might, I simply cannot imagine this year's batch of Republican candidates—to say nothing of perennial non-runners like Sarah Palin—pulling off a fun spot like this; they simply don't have the foundation.

The authenticity that had grabbed me is one of the keys to political success, a phenomenon many observers have remarked on but I can empirically confirm. My 24/7 footage of Obama showcased that authenticity, that relaxed self-possession, and allowed voters to see him as he really is and judge him accordingly. All I

---

* I finally got to see him make that same speech at the rehearsal for his acceptance speech at the Democratic National Convention in Denver, where he delivered it to check the sound systems without revealing the text of the next night's address.

really did was hold the camera. Even so, many people have misunderstood my role, the first of its kind in Washington. I've been accused of turning the presidency into a reality TV show and of "mocking the free press" (this is a direct quote). I've been pegged as everything from the second coming of Leni Riefenstahl to a secret Pakistani militant tasked with doctoring images of a scar on the president's head to hide where special agents slip the discs in. That's right: the discs.

I try not to take these charges personally. No American president has had this type of videographer before, and I understand that people fear novelty, especially in a tradition-bound town like Washington. But there's actually nothing at all novel about recording the president for posterity. From the dawn of our great republic, artists have been capturing the presidential character in every medium. Before film there was photography, and before photography there was paint.* And with every technological advance, we get to know our leaders better. Since 1849, when James K. Polk's administration was the first to make official use of photography, the camera has played a key role in shaping how we understand our politicians, especially our presidents. In 1895, not long after the film camera was invented, Grover Cleveland—the first president to have an entry in the Internet Movie Database (IMDb), incidentally—agreed to be filmed signing a bill into law in what became *A Capital Courtship*, a one-reeler that was quite popular in its day on the lyceum circuit.

Different presidents have had different relationships with cam-

---

* A highlight of the West Wing Tour that staffers are invariably obliged to give friends and family is the famous picture of George Washington crossing the Delaware: "I'd like to draw your attention to six historical inaccuracies in this painting. First, George Washington *hated* water and would definitely have been sitting down. . . ."

eras and the people who operate them, though it wasn't until Lyndon B. Johnson that the president started appointing an official White House photographer, a position that comes with an unmatched level of access. Since LBJ, every president has had his own photographer—well, everyone except Jimmy Carter, who hated having his picture taken (and look how that worked out for him).

Motion pictures have had just as swift and deep an impact on the political landscape. From the moment Richard Nixon broke into a sweat on national TV during a 1960 debate with the debonair Kennedy, video has been central to the making and breaking of politicians, increasing our scrutiny of candidates, and stoking our appetite for intimate moments, especially from our president. This is because video leaves less to the imagination than even the most candid still photograph; whether consumed in a movie theater or on an iPhone, videos give us the sense that we're seeing our leaders at their most authentic. With every technological advance, candidates have had to work harder to appear confident, relaxed, and, at the same time, presidential—quite the command performance. Now that there's a high-res video camera lurking inside every smartphone at every fund-raiser, projecting that image is a 24/7 commitment.

Since the bar is so high and the cameras are always on, successful leaders' public images and performances must be grounded in their actual characters and personalities, which had better be broadly appealing . . . or else. Obama's relationship to the Internet is something like JFK's relationship to television—the right personality at the right technological juncture. And while there's no exact Nixon-Kennedy debate in the Obama narrative to mark the moment his triumph became all but inevitable, the personal appeal of both men played a big role in the success of their candidacies. I can say from my own experiences behind the camera that Obama is a dream documentary subject, able to create private space in public. It's his naturalness, his comfort in his own skin that made a filmed presidency possible.

There were other factors at play, of course, namely, new technologies combined with a new public appetite for history in real time. Just as FDR was not the first POTUS to use radio (that would be Woodrow Wilson) and Kennedy was not the first POTUS on TV (Truman and Eisenhower had made frequent appearances), Obama was not the first POTUS to use the Internet (that would be Bill Clinton, and George W. Bush maintained the practice). Obama did, however, have the broadest understanding of the Internet's possibilities and of his audience. The audience itself was just getting to know Internet video when Obama began campaigning; strange as it may seem today, YouTube has only been around since 2005, not exactly the beginning of human history. The precipitate rise of Internet video has been helped along by our incredible shrinking cameras, which, as they keep getting smaller, find their way into more and more hands and more and more places, including sewer pipes with deposed Libyan dictators. The Internet, or more accurately broadband, has given people the ability to reflect on events—that is, to make history out of them—while they're still going on. The Battle for Tripoli was being memorialized on Wikipedia even as the crack of sniper rifles sounded through the city.

Authorship is also important, and that's where I come in. Although none of what I, or other media innovators of the last election cycle, have accomplished would have been possible without Barack Obama, I don't want to sell myself *too* short. My personality was also a good match for my job, and for this particular president. I'm not a noodge, but I'm also not a silent observer: I'm a little neurotic and a lot chatty, often interjecting my opinions from behind the camera, a tendency that I think helped me build trust with both my subject and my audience. So much of political media is anonymous, institutional, and corporate, which provides a good veil for the all-out nastiness that often prevails in political advertising today. I hope I helped inject doses of humanity and humor into that toxic environment.*

Yes, I realize how naive my "the truth shines through!" brand of cinematic optimism sounds. Let me be the first to admit that negative campaigning works. Just look at how the Romney PACs (political action committees) destroyed Newt Gingrich in Iowa and Florida in the fall of 2011; Newt's lack of defense against the barrage of negative ads doomed him just as surely as his three wives and Tiffany's debts, to say nothing of his relationship with Freddie Mac and advocacy of a permanent lunar colony.† But curiously enough, when Gingrich had the money, courtesy of Sheldon Adelson, to crank out negative ads of his own and level the playing field, he won his first state in South Carolina.

But, of course, all that remains is scorched earth. A negative ad cuts both ways, tainting its instigator as much as its intended victim, as Romney's plummeting numbers in the wake of his negative-ad carpet bombing of his opponents demonstrated. And although, courtesy of Citizens United, we're spending more and more money on negative ads, the needle just isn't moving as much as it used to

---

* "You're just spitting in the wind, Arun," a Secret Service agent assigned to the campaign told me once as I tried to explain to some local police that I was allowed to walk behind the senator. This advice applies here.

† God, I just love Newt so much, I can't help it, I really do.

(or rather, it snaps back so quickly that the movement has no meaning). The problem is not just diminishing returns, although that's certainly part of it; it's scratching the audience's collective brain raw and senseless. Negative ads are like MSG: tasty and addictive, definitely, but also toxic, a poison that dulls our taste buds and deadens our sensitivities. That's the main reason I think the debates took on such unprecedented importance in the GOP primaries and why so many voters cited them as their main influence in determining how to pull the lever: What other opportunity did anyone have to evaluate the candidates as human beings?

Though I didn't begin with this goal, I like to think that the political filmmaking I did during the 2008 election and Obama's first term has served as something of an antidote to all the rampant negativity out there. The world certainly seems to be ready for it. After all, the most watched political video of 2011 wasn't Rick Perry's hateful (and hated) "Strong" ad, or even the hilarious star turn by Herman Cain's smoking campaign manager.* It was an impassioned defense of gay marriage given in an Iowa courtroom by a young man named Zach Wahls, who has two mothers and no discernible emotional scars. I hope the same can be said about the rest of us after being force-fed metric crap tons of MSG for so many months on end.

So just to let everyone know, the following pages won't be about what my lousy childhood was like or what the president eats for breakfast. I'm not going to complain about getting thrown out of Indian Parliament by my belt, or getting trapped in the White House library bathroom while POTUS conducted a forty-minute

---

* At NYU, my professor Paul Thompson always complained about American movies where people smoked wrong, "like they've never smoked a day in their lives."

YouTube town hall with Steve Grove on the other side of the door. (Curse you, noisy automatic toilets!) I'd rather explore the complex interplay of politics and media, and art and government, and audio and video, in the new millennium, and discuss what I've learned as the first-ever cameraman to train his lens on a president around the clock.

# PART I

# MIRACLE WHIP AND OTHER SURPRISES

# CHAPTER 1

# ORIGINS

*In which I offend America west of the Hudson, deal with the racial intricacies of cooking out, and make the unverified claim that I have drunk an entire gallon of milk in an hour.*

After a grueling day on the trail in mid-August 2007, we straggled off a bus in Atlantic, Iowa, population 7,257. I headed straight for the table of food a thoughtful volunteer had left out and bit into a chicken-salad sandwich, only to be overwhelmed by a sickly sweet, tangy flavor. I threw down the sandwich. "No one eat the chicken salad!" I cried at the top of my lungs, like it was bad acid at Woodstock. "This mayo has gone bad!"

The volunteer who'd prepared the food rushed over to the table and picked up the sandwich I'd flung down. "But honey," she said, "that's not mayonnaise. That's Miracle Whip!"

During my first months in the rural Midwest, there'd been many such misunderstandings. My political instincts were almost always wrong, and I'd been behind the wheel of a car approximately four times since passing my New York driver's test at age sixteen—a potentially huge liability given that I was slated to spend the next six months zipping back and forth between Des Moines and Chicago.

Even my sense of humor translated poorly to the political realm: Stephen Geer, the director of e-mail and online fund-raising, joked that I was rated PG in Brooklyn, R in Chicago, NC-17 in Iowa. Sometimes it seemed as if the candidate himself—who had awarded me the nickname Funny Man early on in our travels— was about the only one who got my jokes.* Far more often, my stabs at humor scandalized earnest young campaign workers: "Show me on the doll where you want me to touch the audience," I recall saying to an HQ staffer. The row of cubicles behind him went silent (except, of course, Geer's).

That long-ago summer of 2007, I wasn't yet tuned in to the sensitivities of a modern political campaign, especially one led by the first serious African-American contender for the highest office in the land. Soon after arriving in Chicago, I had unsuccessfully lobbied to have the name of an event changed from "Grillin' with Barack" to "BBQ and A" just because I (and, incidentally, the candidate) thought the new wording was funnier. But in questioning the original event name, I inadvertently set off a long e-mail chain about the class and race ramifications of dropping the final "g" in Grillin'. That was a good first lesson that I was out of my element, in a business where even if 99 percent is pitch-perfect, the remaining 1 percent will get blown out of proportion whenever possible.

This had not been the standard operating procedure in my previous work as a punk rock musician and filmmaker. And unlike many of the aspiring politicos I'd meet who'd begged for business

---

* But don't be too impressed; by far the best nickname was Special Forces for a particularly stern advance lead, and Twenty Clicks, which referred to the number of pictures in a photo line, not kilometers down the river, and a staff member who underestimated said "clicks" by sixty or more.

suits since early puberty, I had avoided formal wear well into my thirties. When I played dress up, I succeeded only on days when everyone else dressed down.* My markedly casual style of dress, even when upgraded, continued to attract attention through the end of my time at the White House. In a sea of high and tights and three-piece suits, I stood out for my shaggy hair, frayed slacks, and imitation Adidas shell-top sneakers. "Arun's a very cool guy, though I have to tell him to get a haircut every once in a while," the president told Ashley Parker of the *New York Times* in the Green Room of the White House.

Most of my new colleagues had worked on multiple campaigns by age twenty-five, whereas I, suffice to say, didn't have anything like the typical professional-Democrat credentials (and am in fact registered as an independent, which all independents mention constantly). And though I've been an Internet news junkie for a solid decade and a half by now, I remained so clueless about Beltway society that, even in January 2008, I didn't recognize Chelsea Clinton after chatting with her about Japanese literature for hours on a red-eye from Vegas to Charlotte.†

No, my path to politics had been very different, and far more

---

* Even years into my new life, I had trouble getting some of the sartorial details down. "Arun, c'mon, you work for the president!" Deputy Chief of Staff Nancy-Ann DeParle admonished me once as I crossed the street to the West Wing. A little hurt, I thoroughly examined myself in the mirror but found nothing wrong. I'd already gotten Obama's personal stamp of approval on the New Balance sneakers I wore with everything (all-black with tuxes, natch), so what could possibly be the problem? She was probably right, though. I remember my father observing as I adjusted a tie before some family event, "No matter what you wear, you always kind of look . . . like *that*."

† After our identities were revealed, we still tried to keep our exchange to neutral subjects. I had to stop a segue from a discussion about heart surgeons and other doctors to "That's why my mother stands so firm on health issues . . ." by protesting, "Please, let's just not . . ." This was the flight *after* the red eye, and before we both lost our luggage. I was not about to attempt a message-off with a Clinton. (See Land War, Asia.)

*On the tarmac at Andrews Air Force Base looking "like that."* (Photo by Drew Angerer)

meandering. For one thing, I was a whopping thirty-two years old when I joined the Obama campaign, having spent a decade as a struggling filmmaker, struggling musician, part-time teacher, even more part-time sound designer, and occasional belligerent film critic for some of New York City's smaller outer-borough newspapers. And, sure, working for a governor straight out of college is impressive, but *I'd* been a regional Student Academy Awards judge for two years running, and I'd also managed to book seventy-five shows for my band's seventy-day tour, which was no small feat. And once, at a VFW hall in Syracuse, I drank an entire gallon of milk in an hour. (That's a pretty big deal, too; lactose doesn't digest for ninety minutes or more, so peeing it out isn't an option.)

I'd also discovered the wonders of America well before joining the traveling road show that was the 2008 presidential campaign, having already visited forty-nine of fifty states (using the spend-at-least-one-night-on-the-ground rule) when touring with my punk band after college. The vast middle of the country wasn't quite "flyover" for me, but it was somewhat "drive-through." I saw a lot of crazy stuff on those trips, and it wasn't the endless gazebos and patriotic bunting that have dominated my last four years. I was surprised, on my first campaign trip to Elkhart, Indiana, to discover that everyone's neighbors' basement doesn't blow up regularly, and as for Las Cruces . . . let's just say there are definitely at least two Las Cruceses and leave it at that. But with the band I always met the same kind of people in every town, whereas on the campaign I was interacting with quite a few new types, from the members of the military to journalists, or at least interacting in new ways (see cops, local).

But for all my rock-and-roll bluster, I'd always been a politics nerd. Or at least since I was in junior high, when I finally gave up my childhood dream of becoming a paleontologist. (And a good thing, too, because they changed the names of all the dinosaurs for no real reason, and let's be honest, no one wants the same job as Ross from *Friends*.) The book that prompted this realignment of my ambitions was William L. Shirer's *The Rise and Fall of the Third Reich*, which is pop history at its finest. I remember being amazed by how brilliantly Shirer maintained the high-wire tension of the narrative throughout—even when readers knew exactly how the story would end.*

Over the next few years, I became so interested in studying history that most of my friends and family members assumed I'd eventually go into the law, politics, or some combination of the

---

* I don't want to spoil the ending, but—USA! USA! USA!

*The author during the "Rock and Roll" years
before a gig at SUNY Binghamton, in the mid-'90s.*
*(Photo by Morgan)*

two. Teenage cynic that I was, I had no interest in actually running for office, by the way: As I told my parents, how could anyone with such a funny name ever expect to be elected to anything? So however much I enjoyed following politics, I never considered it seriously as a career. I might even have told my parents that I was considering skipping college to play rock music for a living. (Luckily, the Chaudharys didn't have an official videographer, so there are no transcripts of this conversation.)

It was only when I saw *Roger and Me* late in high school that I considered another possible career path, a means of fusing my interests in art and politics. I'd liked spending my Saturday nights at the local multiplex as much as the next suburban kid, but I'd never seriously considered making movies. Then along came *Roger and Me*, which blew me away on several levels. In one scene, a worker is driving home immediately after being fired, and the Beach Boys' "Wouldn't It Be Nice" comes on the radio: an absolutely awful song at that particular moment. For the rest of the scene, Moore plays the song as his camera pans over one shuttered neighborhood after the next; this simple but powerful technique affected me deeply, even though (or perhaps because) I fully realized that I was being guided emotionally. Understanding the mechanisms of this technique—the contrasts between the images and the music—actually enhanced my viewing experience instead of detracting from it, reminding me of one of my favorite aspects of studying music: the deeper my understanding, the deeper my appreciation.* Sadly, fewer and fewer of these affecting human moments appear in Moore's later films.† As his career has evolved, he seems to trust himself more and the material less, a distinction I mention only because I've tried to take the exact opposite route in these last years.

I'd like to say that immediately upon seeing *Roger and Me* I packed my notions in a suitcase and knocked down doors to become a filmmaker working in politics, but that would involve an epic

---

* On a trip to Poland with POTUS, a Secret Service agent made this same point. Now that his son was studying film, he said, his whole experience of watching a movie was totally different, informed by all sorts of standards and rules that had never occurred to him before. I agreed, saying that it was similar to watching a football game when you're only vaguely aware of the rules versus watching it as an expert: enjoyable either way, but way better if you know what's going on. Immediately the site lead butted in and said, "Arun, you don't know crap about football—what are you talking about? Don't pretend that you've ever watched a single game in your entire life." To that, I'm afraid I had no rebuttal.

† For example, contrast "Wouldn't It Be Nice" with Moore's use of "Vacation" by the Go-Go's to play along the vacation sequence in *Farenheit 911*. While I mean no disrespect to the Go-Go's (and I never would), one is an emotionally resonant element from inside the story and the other is heavy-handed and manipulative.

edit, not worthy of this audience. The winding journey took fourteen years, during which I helped invent human bowling and then aged out of the cohort eligible to participate in this hazardous activity.* I overcame my cat allergies and developed a chronic colon condition. And through it all, I never stopped grappling with the torturous study of narrative.

---

* For those interested, all you need is a skateboard, an army helmet, and ten bowling pins. A couple of extra mattresses wouldn't hurt, either.

CHAPTER 2

# "WHERE ARE THE $@^#'N BALLOONS?"

*In which I quote dead European intellectuals, comfort Elliot after the 2004 Democratic National Convention, and throw Reggie under the bus (but only in a footnote).*

If, as Von Clausewitz would have it, war is politics by other means, then movies are also politics by other means—and not just because both start as concrete missions and quickly devolve into chaos. Whenever called upon to compare film to politics and vice versa, I often mention that moment in the great *Dr. Strangelove* when the Sterling Hayden character quotes another European thinker to Peter Sellers:

> MAJOR JACK D RIPPER: Mandrake, do you recall what Clemenceau once said about war?
> CAPTAIN LIONEL MANDRAKE: No, I don't think I do, sir, no.
> MAJOR JACK D RIPPER: He said war was too important to be left to the generals.

*The president turns the tables. Was the camera on? Wait until 2016 to find out! (Official White House Photo by Pete Souza)*

I feel the exact same way about movies—they're far too important to be left to the politicos, or even to the presidents. Some presidents have liked the movies more than others: Woodrow Wilson loved movies; many of his doctors and his wife, Edith, credited this pastime with improving his health, if not his chances of passing a certain treaty. Camera-hating Carter* watched more movies than Reagan—again, you never can tell—and Ike loved westerns. (Okay, you could've probably guessed that last one.)†

---

\* Not just still cameras. Veteran documentarians D. A. Pennebaker and Chris Hegedus described an unusual amount of paranoia from President Carter and staff when they made their three-part series *The Energy War* on Carter's energy efforts for PBS in 1977.

† It was a pain in the neck to watch a movie in the White House until they added the theater in 1942. In 1929, the engineer-in-his-former-life Herbert Hoover had many trucks' worth of cables dangling down the residence steps so that a talkie could be shown at the White House in 1929.

This POTUS is very fond of movies. He's always been very conversant in them and has correctly answered some high-level, on-the-spot film trivia questions at town halls. And once, while taping an introduction to TCM's showing of *Casablanca*, BO gave a stirring, spot-on, and well-put analysis of the film: "Rick isn't just an American, he is America, confronted with a choice." I was obviously impressed. "Did I pass, Professor?" he asked with a grin.

My own interests in film and politics had intersected and overlapped from the very beginning. In college, I'd intended to major in political science but switched to film theory, which didn't turn out to be that much of a leap. I soon discovered that many classic movies—everything from *Birth of a Nation* and *Citizen Kane* to the less obvious *Invasion of the Body Snatchers*—were heavily steeped in politics, and films, as much as or more than any other type of art, tend to embody the political discourse of their time. As I started to make movies of my own, first in college and later in film school, every script I wrote had a pronounced political subtext, mostly intended and often clumsy.*

Since the invention of moving pictures a little over a century ago, movies and politics have constantly fed off and informed each other. They also share some striking baseline similarities. For one thing, both are grounded in "reality" in some form. Politics is fundamentally built upon the dynamics between real people and the institutions they create to manage real life, even if these often get abstracted. (We often complain that politicians are beholden to ideology rather than conditions on the ground, a perfect illustration

---

* Or maybe that's putting too kind a spin on it. Too often, I clumsily confused political text with political trappings. I should've paid more attention to Boris, my favorite stern ex-Soviet directing professor at NYU. He watched another student's pan from a homeless person sleeping on a bench to an American flag and dismissed the entire project in three words: "Ideology is boring."

being John McCain's resolve to stay in Iraq a hundred years if necessary.) Film, especially documentary film, is unique among the arts for its use of "reality." It's the least abstract of all the arts, by its nature leaving little to the imagination. For that reason I'd argue that it's also the most absorbing art in that viewers sometimes forget that what they're experiencing is not unmediated reality.* By dramatizing the abstractions of politics—the formation of a union in *Norma Rae*, say, or the consequences of industrial pollution in *Erin Brockovich*—film can lend ideas a certain reality and immediacy.

Similarity #2: To a great extent, narrative determines success in both film and politics. Though dependent on modern technology, movies are an obvious offshoot of the oral storytelling tradition that's as old as humanity itself. True, the nice, dark, warm cave where people would gather to hear a story and gnaw on some rotting wildebeest has been replaced with an air-conditioned theater and extra-buttery popcorn, but the basic idea is the same. Coming together to hear stories unites us.

People have understood film's unifying qualities from the beginning. Countries like Russia and Canada, geographically sprawling places with disparate populations and little interaction between groups, provide a great example.† In fact, our more unified American culture can be traced at least partially to our early adoption of motion picture technologies, which we also put to widespread narrative use before any other culture. That's just one

* As Roman Polanksi put it, "Cinema should make you forget you are sitting in a theater." (Last mention of him, too!)
† In contrast to Russia and Canada, America is one of the few developed nations without any sort of national film board, but then the very success of the American film industry is the reason that no organization like that has been necessary. It won't necessarily always be that way, though. As Hollywood languishes, the same technologies that have made what I do possible are opening up filmmaking in countries all over the globe on a scale previously unimagined.

of the reasons I'd argue that the movies—even if they were officially invented in France—are, along with jazz, the consummate
American art form of the twentieth century. Plus, film is also a
mechanical art, and we Americans love all that whirring and clicking stuff.

But let's be clear. American or otherwise, film is by no means
the most efficient way to communicate information, even or especially among the arts.* I'd say that honor goes to the novel, or on
a much smaller scale the joke (cf. Freud), or even, see below, the
comic strip. I definitely learned more about the Spanish Civil War
from *For Whom the Bell Tolls* than from my advanced placement
European history course in high school: as with *The Rise and Fall of
the Third Reich* (not quite fiction but highly dramatized history), I
got a rewarding emotional experience that helped frame and fix
my facts.

What film lacks in efficiency it makes up in immediacy. Film
lays it all out in front of us, especially images of people who are
just like us, or not. And people just love looking at people; we can't
help it. I think the single best illustration of film's power comes in
a *Far Side* cartoon that shows people fleeing a city as a nuclear
bomb explodes. Almost unnoticed, in the corner of the frame, a
dog in a car is staring at . . . another dog in the street. We are all, to
some extent, just like that dog in the car, fascinated with one
another's lives and stories even in the face of much more exigent

---

* Forget the arts; the fastest way to transmit information is to tell it to Reggie Love.
When my wife called me to say she was pregnant, the Democratic National Com-
mittee (DNC) had just started and I was in a press file in a Montana hotel. "Don't
tell anyone," she made me promise, "I only just took the test." But then, before we
hung up, she agreed that I could share my excitement with Reggie and Reggie
alone. Or wait, a revision to my first statement: the fastest way to transmit information is to tell Reggie Love while he's in a room with twenty bored journalists.
Within three minutes, the entire press corps had come up to congratulate me on
the week-old zygote.

matters. We don't reflect as we watch a film; we are absorbed into the experience, for better or worse.

As the *Far Side* cartoon proves, even the single drawn frame of a comic strip can convey a large, complicated idea much more succinctly than a film: the dog is a symbol, a humorous stand-in for a big idea. No movie can say so much in a single frame, but then that isn't really the point. Movies aren't really about transferring information; the goal has never been to force-feed facts *Clockwork Orange*–style into people's brains. Whatever "information" a film conveys should slide down the throat agreeably, like an ice-cold beer in the hellacious DC summer.

Needless to say, this isn't an either-or dichotomy; you can obviously pick up some facts while watching a movie. You need only watch the title screen of *1492*, for example, to learn which year Columbus landed in the New World. But if you think back to the educational films of your youth, the facts you remember are tied into something else. I like to call it a notion: emotion inflected by some light information. Film is all about forging an emotional connection with the audience. You can be terrified by a movie, or you can laugh uproariously at it, but in the end you don't necessarily take away strict ideas from it; you take away feelings.

Politics operates on similar lines; one of the big appeals of President Obama going into the 2008 race was his "story." Because that's the thing: politics isn't always just about the facts, it's about presenting them in a helpful narrative framework (and of course this is much harder to do when your facts are wrong). Most of us just don't have the attention span or the interest to follow every twist and turn of Washington's latest budgetary crisis or would-be shutdown (believe me, I glazed over a lot). And more often than not, we vote for candidates, sometimes even against our own best interests, because something in their story appeals to us, or is us.

And though this isn't always the case—Rick "son of a tenant farmer" Perry did a fine job of beating his primary biographical strength within an inch of its life—the failure of storytelling can often presage electoral failure. Even before his alleged sexual peccadilloes brought him down, Herman Cain made the mistake of downplaying his absolutely incredible life story—the son of a housekeeper and chauffeur to the CEO of Coca-Cola—and instead leaned too heavily on some seriously shaky math. Maybe in this respect (and this respect alone), Herman Cain is in 2012 what John Kerry was in the 2004 cycle: someone with a pretty decent life story that he nevertheless, woe is him, failed to figure out how to promote.*

The 2004 election snapped me into focus and realigned my priorities from the reverie of fiction to the "real life" of politics. My wife, Laura, and I spent that August cat-sitting in a three-story penthouse on Central Park West, and one night we invited Elliot Greenebaum, a good friend and fellow filmmaker, over to watch Kerry accept the Democratic nomination on our borrowed big-screen TV in our borrowed gigantic living room. We were feeling optimistic through sheer square footage. (Anyone out there from NYC?)

The instant Kerry did his military salute and kicked off his speech with the words "reporting for duty," Elliot jumped off the couch and screamed, "Oh my God, he's lost the election!" Meaning: This guy is having a *hard* time up there—how's he supposed to take on an incumbent president? The best story in the world (which Kerry's wasn't, but a Vietnam vet turned antiwar protester

---

* Of course, while this notion is interesting for our discussion at hand, it was different and far more unsavory issues that led to Herman Cain's downfall. But I do believe that when you are not articulating your story correctly you inevitably leave that task to others: friend and foe. Truth and lie. And there did seem to be an awful lot of baggage on the Cain train.

is pretty good) didn't matter if the campaign didn't know how to capitalize on it.

I wasn't as panicked as Elliot, at least not until the customary shower of balloons didn't fall after the speech. And that wasn't the only technical glitch: on the CNN broadcast, a production mic was left on, and when the balloons and confetti didn't appear, DNC director Don Mischer freaked out in front of millions.

> Go balloons, go balloons! Stand by confetti! Keep coming, balloons! More balloons, more balloons—bring 'em! Balloons, balloons, balloons! C'mon, balloons, tons of 'em, bring 'em down! Let 'em all come! No confetti yet, no confetti yet. Go balloons, go balloons—we need more balloons! All the balloons should be coming down—c'mon, guys—where are the balloons? We need more balloons! I want all balloons to go. Go confetti, go confetti! I want more balloons. What's happening to the balloons? We need more balloons! We need ALL of them coming down! Balloons—what's happening, balloons? There's not enough coming down! All the balloons—where the hell? Why aren't they falling? What the fuck are you guys doing up there? More balloons coming down, more balloons, more balloons . . .

After this singular fiasco, I understood that Elliot was right. People expect a certain amount of razzle-dazzle, in visual or narrative form, and if they don't get it, they tune out. Kerry never managed to make his story compelling to voters, a failure most excruciatingly exhibited by his initial refusal to engage with the Swift Boaters, who used motion pictures to transform the heroism of Kerry's past into something shameful. I like to think that film is an inherently optimistic medium, but that appears to be just one of my notions when you look at the power of this type of destructive negative media.*

Immediately following the 2004 washout, I decided to get more involved in politics. I was tired of watching the world march by on someone else's flat-screen; it was time I put my skills to use inside an actual campaign. A number of my friends were working on documentaries around this time, most of them focused on the election or the deeply unpopular Iraq War; a classmate from NYU, Mora Stephens, made *The Conventioneers*, a fiction feature about the unlikely relationship between a Republican delegate and Democratic protester during the 2004 Republican National Convention in NYC. But however much I enjoyed them, these movies, just like the ones I'd made myself, seemed distant from the world where things actually happened. These were more People's Choice–type projects than real-life election changers—efforts that the real people in power could, and did, all too easily ignore (think *Fahrenheit 911*).

I wanted to work *directly* in politics, but how? Many filmmakers faaaaaar more talented than I—John Ford and Frank Capra and suchlike—had served their country to great acclaim, but to do so they had to enlist in the armed forces, which didn't seem like a good fit for a guy who'd never even been a Cub Scout. (What can I say? Uniforms make me nervous.) I debated going into political advertising, or joining a campaign, or . . . I didn't really know what. I basically had zero clue how politics worked—to the extent that I didn't understand why my total lack of experience might strike some as a deal breaker. Like everything else, politics has a

---

* Swift boating and birtherism are both classic examples of smear campaigns, which are far older than the presidency (only consider the legendary nastiness of a race like Adams v. Jefferson). But these tactics only really work when the candidate fails to fight back with evidence of his own authenticity, which is why swift boating sank Kerry while Obama survived birtherism.

track.There's a revolving door with certain industries, like journalism, but it's hard for people coming from most other professions to find a way in.* Fiction filmmaking turned out to be one of these "others." Despite my technical training and fancy academic background, I had absolutely nothing concrete to prove that I'd be an asset to a campaign. Apparently, having been part of the team that tried to brand a very rich venture capitalist's girlfriend as the "Hispanic Martha Stewart" wasn't enough to cut it.

Despite knowing nothing about media strategies, I felt confident that I could make good campaign ads, and the best route in, I decided, would be through local races.† And I am talking *extremely* local here, like much too local to appear on the radar of even the smallest political consultancies, local enough to advertise on Craigslist between missed encounters on the F Train and feel-good summer jobs that involved accosting pedestrians with clipboards. I didn't really care who I worked for; I just wanted to get my foot in the door.

Still, no matter how modest my targets, I kept striking out. Once, when pitching my services to the campaign manager of a micro-local New Jersey race, I suggested that if the commercial could only be thirty seconds, they should use only one shot to make it feel longer. If you could actually bore viewers for twenty-nine straight seconds, they might actually pay attention in the end. My idea had come from what I thought was an incredibly powerful Volkswagen ad that was on the air constantly around that time. In it, a man leaves his car and beeps the lock shut before walking

---

* The actual best route in is to volunteer when you are a young'un. Hear that, young'uns?

† This confidence is one of the most common problems in politics, the feeling that *you* need to be the one to do something, to save the day.

into the supermarket. The car sits tranquilly, filling the frame. We hear the rattle of a wobbly shopping cart just as it enters the screen, but before it can strike the car, the owner dives heroically into its path. I remember wishing I liked something enough to hurt myself for it—a reaction enhanced by the fact that, for the entire commercial, the camera never shifts its focus from the beloved vehicle. A few years later, the Geico ad with Abraham Lincoln used the same technique to great effect. It takes an interminable-seeming thirty seconds for Honest Abe to admit that Mary Todd might look big in her dress. I think this would've made a great campaign ad for Lincoln if only it had been produced in 1859.

At a meeting with another, slightly higher-level campaign, the campaign manager asked me to name my favorite campaign or advocacy videos. I started with the tried-and-true Hollywood script-pitching technique: start with two normal, obvious answers, then go for the unusual idea that actually excites you. Accordingly, I told him I loved *Roger and Me*, the LBJ daisy ad, and . . . the Beatles film *A Hard Day's Night*, which I described as "the best promotion film of all time."

"I believe I've seen the picture you mentioned," the grizzled campaign manager responded eventually.

Let's just say I wasn't picked for this position, either. But then and now, I reject the false distinctions between fiction and documentary, and between car commercials and political ads; at the end of the day, they're all the same things. They're movies.

Besides, I don't know many independent filmmakers in Brooklyn with the luxury of making these types of distinctions. Even with a rent-controlled apartment, I ended up working in all sorts of different capacities—as assistant director, sound recordist, and, of course, best boy. You name it, I did it—on a wide range of low-budget feature films, Eastern European music videos, TV commercials that were somehow always about coffee or pants, underfunded documentaries on a legion of subjects, Lifetime original movies, and TV shows with titles so unsavory, they seemed to have been customized to ruin my IMDb page, most notably *Indie Sex: Teens*. You hold up a boom mic for a few hours for an IFC show that has *no* sex in it (see documentary, basic cable), and the next thing you know the Special Agent in charge of your White House background check is investigating this not-so-dark secret on Google. "We did have a coupla questions there."

But however intermittently hilarious and/or embarrassing they may have been, the wide-ranging, anything-goes jobs I took in my twenties proved extremely useful when I shifted course. In politics as is in life, I discovered, versatility and adaptability win every time. I've drawn on these crazy filmmaking experiences constantly during the years I've spent in politics; no way I'd trade a single one of them in for some Senate internship. Okay, so maybe I could've done without *Indie Sex: Teens*, but everything else—absolutely essential.

In the end, it wasn't my know-it-all interview retorts that launched me into politics, but a re-acquaintance with an old friend. Remember I said I was a politics nerd? In 1992, I'd attended the Junior Statesman program at Georgetown University with one Kate Albright-Hanna, and we'd kept in touch ever since. (In DC, they'd call our level of contact "soft touch." Yet another reason nobody likes Washington.)

From our correspondence, Kate knew that, despite having chosen to pursue a career in fiction film, I was trying to get into politics. Sympathetic, she'd given me the e-mail addresses of several political-ad guys in DC, but those kinds of cold e-mails went straight to the dead e-mail pile. It was only when Kate became

Obama for America's director of video that I had someone on the inside who understood that underneath my manic, hard-to-follow notions lay an orthodox filmmaker.

Kate had come to the Obama campaign from a more traditional path—she'd been a long-format producer at CNN and was nominated for an Emmy for a documentary her team had made about the Howard Dean campaign.* When she took a job with the Obama team in early 2007, she introduced me to Joe Rospars, the OFA New Media director who'd gotten his start while still in college as a key member of Howard Dean's groundbreaking New Media team. After an elaborate game of phone tag, Joe finally called—on my wedding day, no less—to say that he wanted to hire me. I would help film the long-shot junior senator from Illinois on the campaign trail and post videos of his appearances on the Internet.

The job was above and beyond what I'd been looking for since that fateful night in August 2004, and the wife and I were up for a change, so we said why not? We left Brooklyn for Chicago two weeks after getting back from our honeymoon, on such short notice that we didn't even have time to run a background check, much less photocopy the driver's license, of the kindly-seeming woman who was the first to answer our subletter ad on Craigslist. "Her son was sweet to the cats," my wife reasoned, "and we live in the best school district in Brooklyn." She turned out to be a virtuoso scam artist. It was a good thing my future employer puts more thought into the big decisions than we did.

I was a little nervous about being hired as a "predator," then the popular term for producer-shooter-editor (now thankfully out of fashion). I'd spent a lot of time editing, directing, and sound

---

* The final scene with Joe Trippi and her driving alone in a car is one of my most enduring memories of that race. Haunting.

recording, but I was less confident about my abilities as a cinematographer. Though I had an uncanny ability to hold cameras steady in challenging circumstances (this was one of my big claims to fame in film school), I was not a natural talent and I'd mostly worked with outside cinematographers.* I also preferred old-fashioned film to video and had only picked up a video camera once or twice, but I was a quick study, or so I told myself.

I was thrilled to be getting a chance to bridge the gap between entertainment and politics—and almost as excited to find out what kind of apartment we could get in Chicago for the kind of money we were spending on our rent-controlled two-bedroom in Brooklyn.

---

* FYI, this wasn't always a compliment. I remember being very proud of some footage I'd shot and getting back the response: "Well, it's very steady." I got hip to it eventually.

# CHAPTER 3

# UPPING THE ANTE

*In which I talk an unusual amount about Phil Collins, pretend that I'm somehow emblematic of "professionalism," and drive up the word count by giving a quick summary of the entire history of political advertising.*

During my wedding-day conversation with Obama New Media director Joe Rospars, he told me that the campaign was hiring professionals from a wide range of fields to "up the ante" by bringing new skills to the political realm. Experience in politics was no longer the only experience that mattered; Obama's people were much more interested in expertise and innovation.

"The campaign made a very concerted effort to hire outside professionals, and not just in the creative fields but all over the campaign, from the administration staff down," campaign manager David Plouffe told me recently. A rare respect for the outsider perspective was one of the big reasons the campaign deliberately looked past the usual suspects from the political establishment and instead hired people who had been doing interesting things in the private sector. (Another reason, of course, was the fact that much of the traditional Democratic stable had already signed on with Hillary Clinton, the establishment candidate, or the then contender John Edwards.)

To me, this remains one of the most remarkable but not always remarked-upon distinctions of the 2008 Obama organization Plouffe assembled: to a much greater degree than any major campaign in decades, Obama's people understood that Capitol Hill and the corridors of K Street are not the only training grounds that count. Those of us raised on *Mr. Smith Goes to Washington* might assume that our government naturally attracts talent from a wide range of industries, everyone from tycoons to grassroots idealists. But in reality, it's usually an entrenched class of consultants that's running the show, which is why the electorate ends up with very bland politicians and a bland poll-savvy staff to guide them.

Because the thing about consultants is that they know everything about winning elections and almost nothing about anything else. Their staggering insularity is one of the main forces isolating Main Street, USA, from DC, and politicians from the people they're sent here to represent. I'm pretty sure it wasn't always this bad, but by 2007, there was no place in Washington for an outsider—like me—until Obama for America set up shop. The people doing the hiring for most campaigns would have ignored my résumé; even though I knew how to make films, I hadn't been making films in the right place about the right things. But when presented with a specimen like me by my childhood friend Kate, OFA was willing to take a gamble, trusting that we'd use our skills in ways that would serve and even invigorate the campaign.

Whatever the field, the campaign wanted the best of the best. Facebook cofounder Chris Hughes was one professional who joined and found ways to apply his expertise in social networks to the political realm. It was no accident that the most social guy at the world's largest social network succeeded brilliantly at making Obama for America the most social campaign to date. Later, Joe also hired Dan Siroker from Google to handle the website's analytics (the fancy New Media word for measuring and analyzing the activity of an online audience to see who is watching what).* They hired their graphic designers, people like Scott Thomas and John Slabyk, from high-end corporate advertising. Best of the best.

"The Obama campaign did bring in all kinds of new folks into the campaigning process—people like you and me," Hughes told me. "Both in Chicago and on the ground in the states, there was a great mix of political professionals—those who know what has and hasn't worked in campaigns before—and brand-new thinkers from unrelated industries. It meant the professionals always had to be on their toes and make sure they were thinking creatively, and it also meant that a whole lot of us non-consultant types got a crash course in how American campaigning works."†

The New Media component of a campaign was (and to some extent still is) so truly *new* that the pool of old hands was vanishingly shallow anyway. In that department, there was no option but to hire good people to make the strategy up as they went along. And though they're traditional media guys, Plouffe and David Axelrod had been thinking about this stuff from the start. Their determination to have a real in-house video team was just one example. Well before the announcement tour, before they'd even hired Joe or Joe had hired Kate or Kate had hired me, they'd brought

---

* Dan decided he wanted to work for OFA soon after sneaking into the talk Senator Obama gave on the Google campus in the fall of 2007. (I was there and it was the best: I uploaded his speech straight to YouTube from a massage chair while sipping homemade kombucha.) Dan was working on the launch of Chrome, so Google was pretty eager to have him finish his work, but in the end they let him follow his dreams—provided he return in time for the Chrome launch.

† The instructors of this course were campaign veterans like Joe Rospars and Scott Goodstein, the campaign's mobile-messaging expert and a DC institution.

*The old job was a lot like the new job. (My former sound mentor Charles Blackwell is kvelling somewhere. RIP.) (Photos by Christopher McEniry/Callie Shell)*

on two postproduction experts, Jessica Slider and Chris Northcross, to make sure the videos the campaign made looked good and were being posted on the Internet in a timely manner.

I'd always wondered why they'd hired a postproduction team

before a shooter, since production by definition precedes postproduction. David Axelrod told me the answer: "We knew we'd be generating a lot of content and that the most crucial tasks would be sorting and posting. We thought that video could be the life of the campaign online, an authentic mirror of the whole campaign." The fact that it was also so cost-effective sealed the deal. As in any good Internet venture—and it does seem peculiar to the online world—you set the mechanism in place before you know how it will end up being used or what will be interesting about it. You know there will be a lot of excitement that will generate "a lot of content" without knowing quite what it will be.*

When it came to film in particular, the open-minded, innovative outlook of those who ran the Obama campaign offered amazing opportunities. If you take a longer view, it's not all that revolutionary a concept to hire a fiction film guy to work outside the arena of pure narrative. Hollywood and Madison Avenue have always had an easy exchange of talent, with some of the most famous feature directors directing some of the biggest ad campaigns (like David Fincher, who directed *Seven* and *Fight Club* and *The Social Network* and also the Nike Instant Karma ad and the Coca-Cola Blade Runner ad). But because the political establishment tends to be more cut off from other industries, there's been a starker separation between—well, let's just call it "creativity" and politics.† A quick look at the history of Madison Avenue and Washington tracks the general rise and fall.

Remember that episode of *Mad Men* when Roger Sterling vies to make ads for the 1960 Nixon campaign? Back then, professional ad agencies routinely handled that brave new world of televised

---

* Twitter, anyone?
† This is not to blast the fine outsider art of Herman Cain's ad team, but that stuff belongs in the Whitney Biennial, not history class.

political ads, even if most of what they cranked out before the '64 election were cheesy cartoons of donkeys and elephants, accompanied by songs that did not preview the musical greatness of the decade with lyrics like "Kennedy, Kennedy, Kennedy, Kennedy, Kennedy, Kennedy."

In 1952, Eisenhower had been the first candidate to run TV ads—an operation headed by none other than Rosser Reeves, the Don Draper prototype who was behind M&M's immortal "melts in your mouth, not in your hands" campaign. Four years later, during his second unsuccessful campaign against Eisenhower, Adlai Stevenson equated his opponent's ads with an attempt to buy his way into the highest office in the land, declaring, "The idea that you can merchandise candidates for high office like breakfast cereal is the ultimate indignity to the democratic process." My dear grandmother was a huge Stevenson fan, so out of respect I'll let you draw your own conclusions about how deeply out of step with the times—or, at the very least, unimaginative—his decision not to play along was. Although his campaign ran television spots, Stevenson himself concentrated on a series of television speeches that aired at 10:00 p.m. (and I hear that people went to bed earlier back then).

High-minded qualms notwithstanding, television ads and admen seemed like they were here to stay, and, as usual, Richard Nixon was the one to kick it up a notch. In 1960, Nixon plucked "his people" from different Madison Avenue firms to form a sort of supergroup. He knew he needed the best ads possible, and so he assembled the best possible people to make them. Though this strategy wasn't quite enough for Nixon to overcome being, well, Nixon, or the sweaty on-screen persona he established in the first televised debate against Kennedy, you can see the glimmers of specialization in his Madison Avenue supergroup. At the same time, the people doing the work were, even if they were not at their usual desks, the vanguard of the advertising industry at a moment when it was going through a great transformation. They were no longer selling breakfast cereal: they were selling the cleverness of the ad for breakfast cereal, centered on the way breakfast cereal made the viewer feel, if that follows.

But sometimes a product sells itself. Kennedy's appealing personality and good looks (like Obama's) translated well into new audiovisual mediums. Lyndon B. Johnson and Nixon were, shall we say, less appealing, sometimes even off-putting, figures. LBJ is only a voice in the infamous 1964 daisy commercial, which juxtaposed a girl counting flower petals with a countdown to a Goldwater-induced nuclear Armageddon.

Daisy is still arguably the best political ad of all time. Though it only aired once in its intended format, news outlets replayed the spot endlessly in that election cycle, and then and now, scoring free airtime is the ultimate achievement of any paid ad. The agency that made the daisy ad, Doyle Dane Bernbach, did equally amazing campaigns for Avis ("We're only No. 2. We try harder.") and Volkswagen ("Think small"). These were smart people. The wounded Richard Nixon noticed, and he emulated this approach when he returned in 1968, tailoring his live image and choosing to appear mostly as a voice or a still image in the ads.*

With a crew that included twenty-eight-year-old Roger Ailes (yes, *that* Roger Ailes) directing "live spots" in which the candidate was coaxed into displaying acceptable levels of relatable emotion, Nixon's '68 media efforts were some of the strongest in U.S. campaign history. His TV campaign revolved around a series of spots depicting a country in crisis. The most memorable one was reminiscent of Marxist agitprop, with a series of still photographs of

---

* I love Robert Caro's account of LBJ in Los Angeles during WWII trying to figure out what his best side was. His best side turned out to be his Hill Country accent!

riots, bayonets, and guns, set against a soundtrack of creepy music and followed by the words, "Vote like your whole world depended on it." At the end, a disembodied Nixon voice declares, "We will have order!" This media campaign was so effective that people became aware of its effectiveness and that same year, Joe McGinniss wrote a book, *The Selling of the President*, about the techniques that helped the campaign succeed.

But it wasn't this awareness that prompted later politicians to move away from such extreme scare tactics. In 1972, Nixon was at it again, pushing these techniques even further with ads that ridiculed McGovern as an extreme liberal. Hands swept toy soldiers aside in an ad lambasting McGovern's weak defense strategy; in another ad, a voice-over suggested that 47 percent of America would be on welfare under McGovern. But, of course, it wasn't Nixon's cinematic impulses that were his undoing, but his criminal ones. After Watergate these were the actions that left Americans with less respect for the government, the presidency, and politics than ever before in our history, not exactly fertile ground for the type of media that had been so successfully employed previously.

The ads of 1976 continued the cycle of disillusionment. Voters just weren't in the mood to get jazzed up for their next president. Carter's ads were personal and biographical and a little bit boring, even as they used the candidate as a source of material rather than an obstacle to be avoided (in sharp contrast to both Nixon's and LBJ's ad strategies). On the Republican side, Ford comes across as exactly what he was: an incumbent in a lot of trouble. The Watergate hangover wasn't his fault, but it certainly was his problem, and he didn't know what to do about it. Also on Ford's side, we see the deepening of the consultant takeover. It was his advisers who came up with the not particularly creative or cutting-edge but by now extremely familiar ads of a man on the street sharing some "real talk" about a disappointing politician, in this case Georgians describing their governor, Jimmy Carter, or Californians describing their governor, Ronald Reagan. In her seminal book on presidential advertising, *Packaging the Presidency*, Kathleen Hall Jamieson also suggests that Ford started to simply sound like his slogans, rather than an independent-minded candidate.

In 1980 the Reagan campaign produced a similarly artless ad campaign (strange for a Hollywood entertainer, but perhaps smart when one remembers what an outsider candidate Reagan was in 1980). Moreover, his people used money from political action committees (PACs) to fund a big percentage of its ads, an indirect result of the campaign finance reform of the 1970s. One of the more memorable of these spots, credited to "Democrats for Reagan," showed Ted Kennedy shouting "No more Jimmy Carter!" during the primary. (In 1980, using a Kennedy was still a *very* big deal.) Art had been abandoned for other forms of manipulation, less creative but not necessarily more honest.

Four years later, as a popular incumbent, Reagan could afford to be bolder. In addition to hiring consummate adman Philip "The Choice of a New Generation" Dusenberry to produce several documentaries, he also enlisted Hal Riney who wrote two commercials that rank among the best of all time. People of all political stripes still mention "Morning in America" and "The Bear" when sitting down to brainstorm new ads. In 1984, this level of artistry was an aberration, or perhaps just the last gasp of artistry in presidential campaigns. (Interestingly, that same year on the Democratic side, the Mondale campaign came out with the original 3:00 a.m. ad—the brainchild of the same man who came up with the "Don't Mess with Texas" slogan.) That's mostly because Reagan and his wife, Nancy, took an interest in these ads; it didn't hurt that they had money. Republicans love inventing reasons to venerate President Reagan, but in the realm of political advertising, our first Hollywood president really did seem to know what he was doing.

Post-1984, it has seemed that every political ad is just a derivative of the last cycle's derivative ad, as exemplified by Hillary's unoriginal 2008 3:00 a.m. spot.* The problem, really, can be traced back to who makes the ads now—not professional admen or filmmakers, but consultants, those guys who know everything about politics and little about anything else. The hard-hitting and artistically compelling daisy ad was 180 degrees removed from the mediocre political fodder I recall seeing on TV when I was growing up in the '80s—but how exactly did the genius devolve into dreck?

Larry Sabato of the Center for Politics at the University of Virginia suggested to me that the change was simple and organic. Consultants, campaign managers, and political professionals paid attention to what worked. They learned from the successes of the campaigns that came before them and did their best to emulate those successes without the expensive intervention of outsiders. As a consequence, political ads suffered but poll numbers didn't: what they lacked in creativity they made up for in negativity. The ads are good enough when measured by polls, but they lack a certain something—soulfulness, certainly, and authenticity. This lack of vitamin X is a recurring problem in politics, and one by-product is a public that couldn't care less about the process by which they choose their leaders.

In his seminal book *The Rise of Political Consultants*, published

---

* These days, the film industry only gets involved in the convention videos, and sporadically at that. Al Gore's amazingly raw convention video was directed by Spike Jonze of *Being John Malkovich* fame, though weirdly, it aired in the middle of the afternoon, so only convention-goers and devoted C-SPAN viewers had the opportunity to see it. I actually heard about it in the NYU film school world, not in any political circles.

in 1983, Sabato argues that increased specialization and larger amounts of money led to the ossification of the consultancy class. It had been more free-flowing, less dominant, and less permanent—just one component of larger political organizations.* But by 1983, Sabato observed, the media/consultancy/PR factions of the modern campaign had started to crowd out more traditional and perhaps more democratic practices—you know, giving speeches and shaking hands and kissing babies, all those tricks Adlai Stevenson employed to so little effect. The importance of the so-called ground game—of having people actually going out into the community—diminished as the price of buying television airtime and, by extension, of winning an election, rose.

It's all about the "ad buy," that is, the price of TV distribution. Most consultancies will barely break even making an ad since so much of the budget goes into securing airtime, the first of many hard lessons I learned upon leaving the White House and failing to inquire who would be the purchasing agent on my first project. There's very little cash left over to put into the more creative aspects of the ad, which is one reason political ads are so uncreative.

Almost thirty years later, Sabato's depiction of the professional political consulting class remains shockingly relevant, and his cautions about the process overshadowing the people shouldn't be taken lightly. But for a campaign of its scale, I'd say Obama for America struck a uniquely good balance in that its leaders took both their media reach and their ground game equally seriously, proving the possibility (and I hope necessity) of emphasizing both, in even the most modern of campaigns. After the election, OFA has certainly done its part to continue this trend. In late 2011, as caucus season heated up in Iowa, the candidate with far and away the

* Not trying to make him sound old, follow him on Twitter! @larrysabato.

*On the set of an ad, this cycle. Generic, yes; dreck, no.*
(Photo by Arun Chaudhary)

most field offices and registered volunteers wasn't a Republican. It was Barack Obama. OFA's 2012 YouTube channel is already stocked far in excess of other candidates' channels, too.

Of course, the very structure of the system means that in many important respects political consultancies are the only ones that *can* produce campaign ads. Complicated and unfortunately mostly ineffective campaign finance laws present legal roadblocks that might prove too time-consuming and expensive for a nonpolitical operation to deal with. And, as a consultant at a start-up shop recently pointed out to me, Madison Avenue firms, while they're always willing to participate in presidential elections, will almost never get involved in smaller races, even at the congressional level. There just isn't enough money on the table, and so they never get the benefit of experience like a dedicated political professional will.*

And also, I was no clever adman, unless having recorded a couple dozen people in a diner chanting "TUM, TUM, TUM, TUM, TUM . . . TUMS" for a certain antacid commercial qualified me as such. Nor was I expected be one for the campaign; there were very qualified and experienced firms already employed. That was not the reason to employ a part-time teacher, an unsuccessful fiction filmmaker, and very far from what you would call an experienced political operative. When I'd interviewed with Rospars for the job, I knew little more than that Daisy ruled and Willie Horton drooled. And though I was a fan of Senator Obama, I was also a prisoner of the conventional wisdom of cable news. Way back in the spring of 2007, I just couldn't really see how he could win. When I left for Chicago, I told my friends to expect me back in New York the following February. We had such high hopes for our subletter back then!

Soon I found that, as hoped, my background really was an asset when it came to thinking "outside the bun,"™ and that the laboratory that was the New Media department in Chicago was the perfect place to work, one I'm finding hard to replicate on the outside. On one of my first days in the lab, Joe asked me to "kill" (he's gangster like that) a PowerPoint presentation on greenhouse-gas

* So it's not that simple. I have to confess that the first piece of political media I helped produce after leaving the White House, an ad that pretends President Reagan has beamed onto a cable news show to disagree with the GOP field about tax cuts, resembled the generic ads I remembered from my childhood more than a model for a better kind of material (though I believe the details were handled in a manner that would not totally disgust my former mentors at NYU). The final script was managed by perhaps too much careful back-and-forth by a few too many smart, talented people, so I think the process itself is at fault for some of the product, but each time since it has gotten better.

emissions. The not-totally-engaging data was about how, even though every president since Nixon had promised to tackle both our dependence on Middle East oil and the environmental pollution caused by greenhouse-gas emissions, the problem had kept getting worse and worse. The idea was to have the presentation open an energy speech in New Hampshire, so the senator could explain his plan without giving the exhaustive background facts himself (I also personally thought that taking on that many ex-presidents at once might seem more annoying than tough). It was my job to present the information in a nonboring manner.

I called upon the prodigious talents of Chino Wong, a volunteer and another "professional," whose day job was to make animations for clients like pharmaceutical companies. (In keeping with the ethos of finding outsiders who knew what they were doing, the campaign would later hire Chino. Talent before specialization every time.) Chino stayed up all night making really cool animation to liven up the slides while I focused on choosing some exciting music to accompany them. Alas, the campaign communications director (and later the White House press secretary) Robert Gibbs nixed my suggestion of "State of the Union" by DC's own Thievery Corporation: in this context, he said, the dub-acid jazz-reggae-Indian classical-lounge-aesthetic (as their Wikipedia entry would have it) song might sound cool, but it wasn't "presidential"—a qualification I didn't at all grasp at the time.* I was just as insistent that having no soundtrack at all would suck the life out of the presentation, and in the end Gibbs accepted my compromise of an experimental wood-block track my older brother had done, which was sort of halfway between silence and an actual song. (That, an unsympathetic Joe told me, was a mistake: never give anyone an

* Scott Goodstein, formerly director of Punk Voter, was a goldmine of music recommendations.

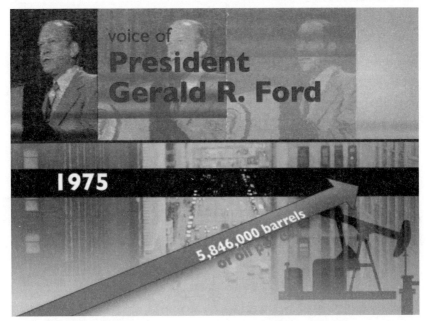

*This is total "us" style. Chino and I made a lot of things like this.*
(Screen Grab/OFA Video)

option, unless you actually like it.) Even without Thievery Corporation, we produced as entertaining a presentation as the material
would allow. Unfortunately, a last-minute kerfuffle with the numbers caused a panicked reedit in a New Hampshire bathroom and
soured the success of this moment. It was not an experiment we
repeated again, though the finished product was still quite good
(and relevant).

The film world has a few conventions about pacing that can
help politics with its sometimes not-so-sexy facts and figures.* In
thrillers as in educational videos, people actually *enjoy* being one

---

* By the way, when I talk about "film" or "the movies," use terms like "filmmakers,"
or the "film industry," or even "Hollywood," I don't mean the specific motion picture industry but rather the century-long practices of filmmaking technique, not
necessarily the (ruthlessly efficient but ethically questionable) studio system, and
definitely not its far inferior successor, the star system.

step behind the plot. Take it from me as a teacher—there's nothing more annoying than an overeager student who interrupts you with the question that you are about to answer while the rest of the class is patiently waiting for the explanation, having correctly assumed that you were just about to get there. Political media has a tendency to be like that one loudmouth student: too on the nose, completely oblivious to the possibilities of subtext. All viewers, even if they're unaware of it, love subtext, and all great or even halfway decent works of art directly or indirectly address that craving. Some classic examples: When the reticent father in *The Bicycle Thief* tells his son to put on his jacket, we understand, and feel proud of ourselves for understanding, that he's really saying "I love you." And while the text of *Lolita* is about a pedophile, its subtext is about the clash between the old world of Europe and the new world of America, even if you read it in Tehran.

The best of the old political ads also made skillful use of subtext, which helped them work on two levels—either you missed the subtext and absorbed the message, or you perceived it and got to pat yourself on the head.

Text served without subtext can be jarring. In Film Editing 101, you learn to avoid cutting a shot exactly when one character ends her line, or right when she begins. Instead, you lead one or two words of the line so that the actual cut isn't as obvious. Hearing the new shot before you see it is so standard a technique that when you don't do it, when you do cut at the beginning or end of the line, the audience snaps back a bit. So for maximum effect, you save the hard cuts for moments best served as emotional sashimi, lines like "Well, that's because I'm a spy and I never loved you! Our entire relationship has been a lie!" But such aggression must be used sparingly or we become numb to its effects; only a master crafts-

*On the streets of Bethlehem, Pennsylvania. Shooter/editor is not quite drummer/singer. (Photo by Scout Tufankjian/Polaris Images)*

man like Phil Collins can regularly get away with this kind of sustained crescendo.

With apologies to the legendary drummer/singer/songwriter, Christine O'Donnell is sort of like the Phil Collins of politics, minus all the talent and success. In her 2010 Senate campaign in Delaware, she put it all out on the table in her TV ads. I'm thinking especially of her "I'm you" spot, a response to her own earlier avowals of youthful experimentation with witchcraft (people of the future, this happened!). Dressed head to toe in black, she stares directly into the camera and declares, "I'm not a witch. I'm you." This bold move sort of felt like "Throwing It All Away" on the B-side of *Invisible Touch* to me, but these kinds of comparisons have gotten me into trouble before. (See Aldrin, Buzz.)

As the early weeks of the primary wore on and I adjusted to my punishing schedule, to the endless plane terminals and lost GPS chargers, I was starting to become convinced that I'd signed on to a special campaign, one that might actually be going somewhere. I can't really pinpoint the specific moment when my expectations first started to shift, but the atmosphere changed that fall, and it was coming across in our footage: the tectonic shift that was under way read on video. We in the video department were extremely lucky to have this visual evidence, for it would be many long, long months before any votes were cast, and BO spent most of that time with fairly stagnant national poll numbers.* Campaign workers had to dig deep to persevere for so long without tangible encouragement of any sort. (The notable exception to this was online fund-raising, which was unprecedentedly kick-ass, and a very powerful indicator of success to the New Media team in Chicago.)

The more time I spent around Obama, both in person and on my laptop, the better I understood that I was staring at history in the making. I felt really, really lucky to be the one who got to film that history, however logistically hard it was to do when, in those early days, the campaign plane was still too small to hold a camera-man and his gear. Then again, the frequent flier miles were plentiful and I was sleeping like a baby for the first time in years.

---

* This was of course back before you could rent a billionaire and start a Super PAC.

# CHAPTER 4

# WHAT STICKS TO THE WALL

*In which I manage to squeeze in bits about Charlie Sheen and Lyndon LaRouche, ruin several American-made compact cars, and introduce the "Is the candidate urinating in public?" test.*

I was still a bad driver—really, really bad. My early trips to Iowa were a succession of Avis incident reports that tell the story better than I can: "scraped in parking lot leaving," "abandoned in snowy ditch on I-80," "scraped in parking lot returning," and so on.

But, as with so many other aspects of my job, I was learning by doing, figuring it out as I went along. I made the 5.5-hour drive between Chicago and Des Moines so many times in 2007 that I became, if not a skillful, then at least a non-homicidal driver.* I also had many 5.5-hour opportunities to make sense of the bewildering new business I'd entered, and how it did or didn't resemble the job(s) I'd left behind in New York.

---

* It wasn't all smiles and sunshine from then on, of course. A few months later, I backed a rental Jeep into a ditch outside the home of Alice Waters while Kate was riding shotgun and frantically jotting down questions for an interview for the epic *Women for Obama* movie.

The similarities between making a movie and running for president turned out to be even more striking than I'd anticipated:

1. Campaign events and movie sets are both temporary structures designed to look solid and impressive for a day (though the grandeur of the former doesn't always translate to TV, since television cameras only show two feet around the candidate's head, much to the chagrin of all the people who work hard to make these sites great).*

2. Both are run by busy, high-strung Type As wielding walkie-talkies, and both are organized into hyper-specialized departments that adhere to a strict hierarchy. Though the "director," some "producers," and of course the leading man may show up only moments before the event starts, the trip lead (a campaign's answer to the assistant director) is on the ground well in advance to ensure the show goes off smoothly. Members of the press advance are analogous to the camera department that sets up the shots for the day, the "site team" are the art directors/gaffers, the "crowd team" are part casting directors/extra wranglers . . . I won't belabor this; you get the idea.

3. Both have food *everywhere*, crammed on every available surface, though film sets tend to skew more toward organic low-fat yogurt while campaign food is heavier on the meatballs, which are served *without* spaghetti or as a sandwich in several parts of the country. This is true. Sometimes with BBQ sauce.

4. Both are big on acronyms, though they don't always stand for the same things. MOS means "man on the street" in politics and journalism; in movies, it refers to a movie shot without sound.

* An example—and probably the least telegenic two feet in the country—would be the UN General Assembly chamber. In an average TV shot, you see nothing of the grand room, just a swirl of extremely ugly green marble behind the head of whoever happens to be speaking.

*On the ground in Wisconsin, ruining a perfectly good shot for someone. (Photo by David Katz/Obama for America)*

Luckily, I only messed that one up once. "You're sure you want this whole thing MOS? Fine, but only if you're totally and completely positive . . ."

But for me, the differences between film and political media were even more profound, if less superficially obvious. To wit: unlike a film set, a political event was not created in service of making a film but rather to serve a candidate and promote his message. It's like a film where the actual production comes second, or like making a documentary on a heavily armed soundstage. Well lit, but hard to get around.

Politics and art have vastly different goals, which necessarily inspire different approaches and spawn different machines. Put crudely, in art you can start with anything—a location, a funny overheard conversation, a traumatic childhood experience—but in politics you must start with a message, or at least a deep-seated conviction about how the world could or should be. (I'm *sure* someone told Rick Perry that at some point, less sure that he listened.) In art you can proceed without necessarily taking your eventual (should you be so lucky) audience into account, whereas in politics you'll get nowhere if you can't sell at least some measurable portion of the electorate on your ideas.

It took me several round-trips to Des Moines to understand the far-reaching implications of this difference, and some of my early experiments reflect my initial confusion. For example: When I was young, I loved those travel bingo cards—you know, the ones with the translucent red doors and pictures of cars and bison and whatnot. So in between the Quad Cities and that turnoff where the Amish stuff is, where there's no NPR station or anything, I had a brilliant idea: Why not make a global-warming bingo-game video? It'd be a nice tweak to the greenhouse-gases slide show we'd done over the summer, and a cinch to pull together. I'd just substitute the bison and Falling Rock icons with pop-art images of imminent climate destruction: polar bears in sunglasses, CAUTION EXTREME WEATHER signs, melting ice-cream cones, that sort of thing. The intended takeaway was that, just as you're sure to see a dead skunk on a long stretch of highway if you look hard enough, you can actually *see* global warming taking place if you pay a little attention.

It's important to note that there was no mandate for this video; I just thought it was a fun idea. So I enlisted Melissa Dean, an amazing and overqualified volunteer with serious graphic-design skills (Chicago HQ's proximity to the Art Institute was a constant

boon), to do the illustrations; threw in some creepy music (as a matter of fact, we used the nineteenth-century American classic "Daisy
Bell" as an homage to the LBJ daisy ad); and last and definitely
least, sent an e-mail to the environmental team asking for a message to tack on to the end. They suggested forming a green council
to combat climate change or somesuch, and voilà, just like that,
we had a rabble-rousing video.

Except the rabble weren't roused, and however cool-looking
the prop, the video all but vanished on our YouTube channel,
ranking far below the most-viewed ones; any random speech or
town hall usually got exponentially more views than a flop. So
why didn't my global-warming video set the world on fire, so to
speak? Quite simply, because it didn't fulfill a need, and that's the
key to all political media: the content must be need-driven for it to
work. In politics, an unasked-for video often turns out to be an
unwatched video. Other experimental videos I made early on that
drove that point home included a steak-fry video with an O-shaped
BBQ brand and a sci-fi Get Out the Vote video that featured an
LCD digital message belt.* (This last one turned out so weird that
I didn't even show it to my wife.) For a few months, I just kept on
spinning my wheels, making a torrent of videos on spec, including a sarcastic account of a volunteer meeting with narration like
"Many of these New Yorkers had never seen a movie for less than
thirteen dollars," which was sort of funny (see Government Funny),
but again . . . no point. I kept making the mistake of trying to
anticipate how I could have an impact rather than simply asking
how I could help. Over time, I also realized that I didn't personally

* The slogan of this one was "It's 2008—vote like it," slight shout-out to Nixon's
"Vote like your world depended on it." With a bigger budget, I definitely would've
used a higher-tech-looking prop than the LCD belt, and I probably would've made
the whole ad a person taking off in a jet pack. 2016!

have to respond to every single thing that ever went on in the world.

The failure of these videos also pointed me to one of the big lessons from my campaign experience and highlighted one of the chief differences between entertainment and politics: the audience. Political media campaigns and, say, Bravo reality TV shows (to name a personal favorite) just aren't targeting the same groups. That's not to say that the audiences never consist of the same people—they sometimes do. Fans of The Real Housewives of Atlanta may or may not also vote, but the overlap is more or less irrelevant. And let's be honest: lots of folks who are into politics are also into entertainment, but the reverse is not as true. I can make a Venn diagram here if it's helpful. An audience comprised exclusively of political junkies isn't the audience you're trying to reach, or at least not the only audience; there just wouldn't be enough votes to win an election, or even get on the ballot in some places. A campaign's target audience should be people who didn't follow politics closely but might have a particular vested interest in a specific issue, whether it be the cost of Medicare prescriptions or the legality of carrying a concealed weapon into Walmart. Those were the people we needed to engage.

Another point along similar lines: political media, unlike entertainment in the age of three-hundred-channel basic cable, must cater, for better or worse, to the greatest number of people. The equivalent of niche shows and art-house films just doesn't carry over into the political realm (or it answers to the name Lyndon LaRouche). Politics is all about plurality—appealing to the greatest number of people the greatest amount of time—and my funny videos didn't even try to hit more than one demographic. The 8 percent of the population you can drum up to watch almost any weirdo show on hoarding or Polynesian street food is more than enough to justify a cable show, but maybe not a government, and definitely

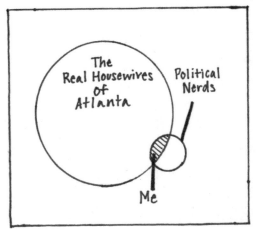

*Venn diagram. Entertainment, politics, and
me. (Drawing by Erin Eastabrooks/Courtesy of
Revolution Messaging)*

not our government (although, to be fair, the niche approach seems
to have done wonders for both Dennis Kucinich and Ron Paul).

Tailoring a message to multiple groups of people with different
priorities seems like a noble enough goal, but it's also one that's
incredibly hard to achieve. Attempting to appeal to everyone at
once often leads to lowest-common-denominator pandering.
(Entertainment-industry people do this all the time, too, though it
usually makes them incredibly successful—cf. the entire Adam
Sandler oeuvre. Let's run him for something.) The alternative—
making a million different things for a million different people—is
equally fraught. Many campaigns take micro-targeting to crazy
extremes to the point of sending dozens of differently worded
mailers to different addresses within the same zip code, but that
only works with fliers, analog and digital. You couldn't make movies in the same way, and I for one definitely wouldn't want to try.

As Lincoln famously said, "You can fool all the people some of
the time, you can fool some of the people all of the time, but you

can't fool all the people all the time," to which one wise man cynically added that, in the United States, "you just have to fool 51% every 4 years." But how do you even figure out what people want—how they want to be fooled—in the first place? This remains one of the chief mysteries of politics, as the arc of a politician like Mitt Romney's career demonstrates. Striving to be all things to all people is a fool's errand.

Granted, polls are as important to Washington as test screenings are to Hollywood, and the chance to test a product—be it a candidate's foreign policy views or the cinema experience *Ishtar*—with the public before it goes public should never be squandered. Neither polls nor test screenings offer absolute truths, though, because, as my NYU editing teacher Carol Dysinger always said: audience members can almost always spot the problem, but they almost never suggest the correct solution. And our instincts about our own work are often too myopic to be reliable, so we often end up magnifying the problem rather than solving it. In moviemaking as in political messaging, it's far wiser to choose a test audience we trust—our own personal focus group—and go with it rather than gathering a range of different and likely divergent opinions from a random assortment of people. My ideal test audience is my wife because I can guess (almost always correctly) why she responds or fails to respond to a movie, and I know her hang-ups, likely better than she does herself.

It seems to me that to mirror the success of a great statesman rather than, say, the success of a new cooking channel in a world with too many cooking channels, a candidate needs a message that appeals to different groups of people, in most cases either to a loose coalition of groups with different priorities but a basic shared belief in the function of government (see Democrats) or to groups with borderline contradictory worldviews but a shared distrust of government (see Republicans). Since it's impossible in politics to play to everyman—to appeal to everyone all the time—it's important to listen to your own judgment or to a few good friends over the American electorate writ large. Attempting to embrace a slew of contradictory positions just because they test well with focus groups doesn't usually work out so well for the Manchurian Candidate in question. Better just to stick to actual convictions; if nothing else, they'll be easier to keep straight during the debates.

Here's an instructive example from the 2008 campaign. When *TV Guide* asked Senator Clinton about her favorite TV shows, she mentioned a convenient but improbable roundup of the most popular shows in the country, a neither-here-nor-there response designed to appeal to the greatest possible percentage of the electorate: "Ever the triangulator," a *New York* magazine preview read, "Hillary Clinton says she's a fan of Nielsen family–approved hits like HGTV makeover shows, *Grey's Anatomy*, *American Idol*, and *Dancing with the Stars*."

Obama had a different approach, born perhaps out of necessity (a fellow named Barack Hussein Obama couldn't so easily pose as anything but himself), but ultimately much more authentic and, by extension, effective. His answer to *TV Guide*'s question was *The Wire*—not so family-friendly, that one! Obama adopted the same strategy when walking into enemy stadiums with his well-worn White Sox hat on. Fans of opposing teams in the bleachers might hoot at him, but they'd hoot with respect. Obama had no choice but to play Obama, a truth wonderfully captured in that SNL Halloween skit in which he showed up wearing an Obama mask. (For the opposite extreme, try Mitt Romney's experience in coach on a Delta flight to Boston, reported in the *New York Times*. When a fellow passenger asked him for a Boston restaurant recommendation, he replied, "I can't give you any. You'll have to ask someone else.")

And that was what I figured out about audience and electorate over those early months of the campaign. There was no one-size-fits-all formula to decode what voters would like or how they would decide to vote (though a volunteer motorcade driver on a POTUS swing through Silicon Valley was part of a team that was working to determine party affiliation by analyzing brain waves. Whoa, right?). So absent absolute certainty, a candidate stood the best chance of winning just by showing voters who he really was. Of course, all of these speculations might be irrelevant if, as Malcolm Gladwell would have it, people are prone to snap judgments, and most of them have already made up their minds about a candidate before the first note of mood music plays in the first ad, which I believe he calls the Warren Harding syndrome. If that's true, we're certainly spending an awful lot of time and cash on a process that's better handled as a police lineup.

But I, for one, continue to believe that video is the most important barometer of truth we have in politics. Mailers certainly lie, but try as their authors might, movies just can't. Even when they're edited dishonestly, the individual components of a film, plucked straight from life, end up speaking for themselves. It's no accident that the most egregious political commercials—with the notable exception of Rick Perry's *Brokeback Mountain* moment—tend not to feature the candidate. Candidates would rather get someone else to do the lying and/or smearing for them; they don't want their image muddied by association with the falsities that keep most campaigns afloat. This is one of the worst aspects of the Super PAC system: a candidate appears in his own, mostly positive ads, while "outsider" PACs do the (increasingly brutal) attacking.

A corollary lesson from my early experiments in campaign video was that people weren't logging on to BarackObama.com to revel in my creative flights of fancy. They were logging on to see

more of the candidate and to get specific information about his policies, or to find out where their polling place was. They wanted to
know about *him*—they weren't particularly curious what I thought
of him.

This directive became clearer after I made a trailer to plug a
rally being held in Washington Square Park in 2007, then the biggest planned Obama event to date. My harrowing drives to and
from Des Moines had reignited my interest in those nostalgic
Americana postcards that were for sale at truck stops all along I-80.
Their bright and cheery Dick and Jane aesthetic had inspired me to
start making trailers to promote campaign events like the senator's Iowa Bus Tour in August 2007, and the Harkin Steak Fry a
month later. My coworkers kept requesting more of these trailers.
Like the climate-change bingo card, they weren't moving the poll
numbers much, but the campaign workers responsible for sending
out e-mails found that more recipients would open and read the
e-mails if they happened to have a quirky video attached. I remember Kate saying, "You've created an internal demand for these trailers," though at the time I didn't realize how crucial that observation
would be to my progress.

So for the Washington Square rally, I decided to make a slightly
different type of trailer, one that was a more direct takeoff of
movie trailers. I stuck with the old-school aesthetic, this time add-
ing the portentous "in a world without water/underwater" narration we associate with *The Day After Tomorrow*–type disaster
movies.* I employed the disjointed montage that's characteristic of
a movie preview, using footage of the candidate that the public

---

* Michael Slaby, who had the deepest voice in the office, did the narration. Unfortunately, the legendary Don LaFontaine, the *real* voice in all those commercials,
hadn't yet volunteered for the campaign. He did eventually offer his world-famous
voice for our cause, but sadly, he died just a few months later, in September 2008.

hadn't yet seen. There's been a huge explosion of this type of satire in recent cycles, most notably by 2012 GOP contenders Tim Pawlenty and Rick Perry. (Incidentally, it turns out the same ambitious twenty-three-year-old Canadian is behind both these campaigns. Lucas Baiano, you have a great future in front of you, but pick a side!)

But this time—unlike in my climate-change bingo card video—this time the stars were clearly Obama and his family. We broke several times into natural footage; after the narrator promised that the candidate would "ask the tough questions," we showed footage that Kate had shot some time before of Obama and his daughter Sasha in the campaign Winnebago. "Some people think your tiger is a little scruffy-looking," Obama mock-interviews his daughter. "How do you respond to that?" Kate and I had been looking for a home for this great footage for a while.

In another part, as the voice-over describes how Obama is going to protect our communities, the video cuts to the candidate walking around a neighborhood in Iowa and admonishing reporters, "Now don't be stepping on everybody's grass!" We even showed Michelle picking up a baby chick. The end sting after the graphics showed the senator standing in a field facing away from the camera and asking, "Is this someone's backyard? It's a nice backyard." (Get it? Hillary Clinton was a senator from New York, and NYC— and therefore Washington Square Park—is her backyard?) The joke was only okay (see again Government Funny), and Joe was concerned that the shot made it look as if Obama was urinating in the bushes, therefore not passing the crucial "Is the candidate peeing in public?" test, but to my amazement, the higher-ups didn't excise it—a lesson to me in never assuming that someone else would edit your footage for you. Things move fast; don't screw around! But actually, David Plouffe remembered thinking about that video from the opposite point of view. "Anything we did we

*What's the candidate doing? You decide.* (Screen Grab/OFA Video)

would be hyper-analyzed, parsed, and rejected by HRC's campaign anyway, so why not push the envelope when the opportunity presented itself?"

In the end, it wasn't my cutesy flourishes or all the picturesque gazebos of Iowa that made the video a success. It worked quite simply because the Obamas were such naturals, and people loved watching them do their thing.

From the beginning, Kate the documentarian had repeatedly advised me to trust the material rather than always trying to impose my will on it, a classic piece of advice that's so easy to give and so hard to take. After the Washington Square trailer, we finally started to make good on that understanding.* With such a compelling

---

* One example: Though I loved credits, I knew they weren't as important in politics. I've always thought that if you are going to do anything interesting or strange in a movie, you need to announce your intentions to the audience, and teach them how to react, in the opening credits. So, if the movie revolves around some cheesy gimmick like being shown backward or out of order, you should see backward or discontinuous images under the credits or in the words themselves, just to give

subject, there was no need to create fancy conceptual frameworks before or do an excessive amount of polishing after. My mother-in-law describes my wife's beloved and deceased Siamese cat as being "hand-painted"—that is, exquisite but individual, finely crafted, with slight imperfections, and rough where he needn't be fine. Kate and I both wanted our videos to be hand-painted in exactly this way. And this, I think, is the future, since technology has made it easy for just about anyone to turn out a crisp, slick product.* We are on the cusp of a 3-D printer revolution where simple objects can simply be "printed" in solid material. What does this mean? One, you may never go to a hardware store again but instead simply "print" a perfectly sized screw and, two, an authentic handicraft will become more appealing as an object. You think I'm kidding about that first part, but I'm not: this is really happening. Science!

So I heeded Kate's advice and resolved to trust the material more going forward, and to include more backstage footage in all the videos that we put out. Instead of trying to prove how hilarious and creative I was, I began to turn my attention to capturing what Barack Obama was really like behind the scenes, a practice I'd carry into his presidency.

---

viewers a fighting chance of figuring out the conceit later on. Or in a cartoon: If it were about a cat with an ax chasing a mouse, the title credit would likely have a cat and a mouse and an ax in individual drawings. I also think opening credits give the audience a chance to push the straw in the Coolata or unwrap the first half of that sandwich (or am I the only one typing on an external keyboard because my laptop has a week's worth of meals mashed into it?), but in this case, cool credits just didn't fit with the work we were doing. Starker is better, especially when streaming; all people need to know is where and when the speech is taking place, no fancy stuff thrown in for my own amusement.

* As Quentin Tarantino reportedly put it, "This CGI [computer-generated imagery] bullshit is the death knell of cinema. If I'd wanted all that computer game bullshit, I'd have stuck my dick in a Nintendo."

CHAPTER 5

# IT'S A FINE LINE BETWEEN A ROBOT AND DOING THE ROBOT

*In which I consider the second bite of the senator's torta, disparage the band-naming ability of great American novelist Jonathan Franzen, and attempt to walk the line.*

I met Barack Obama for the first time in July 2007, about a month after I joined his campaign, at the first-ever "Dinner with Barack," which was (and still is) an opportunity for low-dollar donors to have dinner with the candidate in a relatively casual setting. After a long hot day of touring Washington with the lucky donors, we all gathered in the featureless brick basement of a steakhouse in downtown DC, the kind of room those poker-playing dogs might choose for a nice long card game.

The senator showed up tired from a long day of campaigning and legislating, but he was gracious with everyone.* He and I had

---

* Or at least I assumed he'd been legislating: On these trips, campaign staffers couldn't get through the front door of the Hart Senate Office Building. We were, it seemed, legally barred from participating or even observing Obama's official duties as a senator. This was a rare occurrence, so I was pretty unprepared for the legal distinction between campaigning and governing when I got to the White House.

never formally met before, so we quickly shook hands and exchanged first names (you know, the way Americans do) as I put a microphone on his shirt. This was the first time I'd filmed Obama at such close range, and without legions of the press present.

The thing that struck me first about him wasn't his charisma or his even manner but his authenticity, and how he acted exactly the same both on and off the camera, in front of supporters and staff, which is a more remarkable feat than it sounds. He told his guests straight up how tired and hungry he was, but also how glad he was to see them. He then half-jokingly apologized for the presence of NBC's David Gregory, whose snarky comeback was something to the effect of "If you didn't want to do the interview, we could've had Mike Gravel on instead."

Obama replied pleasantly, "Well, I hope you have the time for everybody running."

The main purpose of Dinner with Barack, I was told numerous times, was for the senator to get to know his donors in a more intimate setting. Making a movie about the evening was a secondary consideration—a caution I took seriously. Since I was already worried about the comfort level of the guests and the general believability of the event, I tried to make all the equipment as inconspicuous as possible. Instead of wiring every diner up with wireless mics, I hid microphones in the plants and around the plates. I became a bit obsessed with this whole complicated mic-planting process; I remember Kate watching me scramble with a mix of concern and amusement.

In the end, my fears turned out to be groundless, and my elaborate preparations a complete waste of time. Though most of the guests had arrived looking as nervous as I felt, Obama immediately put them at their ease, over the course of the meal coaxing occasionally painful stories out of them and frankly discussing the not-always-positive impact the campaign was having on his family. You can *almost* hear the relaxed conversation through those lousy hidden mics I spent so many hours setting up.

For our next event like this, the controversial Grillin'—which I think we actually did end up spelling Grilling—we had no qualms about using a boom mic, which did a lot better job of capturing sound than my ridiculous hidden microphone setup. We now understood that the focus of these events wouldn't be our ragtag video team, but Barack Obama, whose presence made even the most intrusive sound-gathering equipment acceptable.

What exactly does that term mean, anyway, "authenticity"? It's hard to define, in politics as in life.

For example: An intern once asked me if I was going to see the "big show" in town that night. I assumed she meant music and when I asked her who was playing, she rattled off a long list of bands that I'd never heard of. Each band name sounded crazier than the last like, I don't know, the Cosmonaut Diet? Somehow, that doesn't sound like a real band (and it isn't), but even though the true band names were just as bizarre, I knew they had to be legit; there's a certain je ne sais whatever that separates the authentic from the artificial. Even one of the current masters of the English language, Jonathan Franzen, can't write himself out of this trap; in *Freedom*, his character Richard Katz's band, Walnut Surprise, doesn't sound much like a plausible band name. Meanwhile, Austin's own band, called And You Will Know Us by the Trail of Dead, is so absurd that it *must* be real. (I'll spare you the chapter I could write on political jargon that would make good indie rock band names.)

However vague the criteria, most of us recognize authenticity—among other things, many of them considerably less savory—when we see it. Assuming otherwise is a potentially costly error in politics in particular. On one video of the senator speaking at a rally, I ran out of sound to cover the fade-out (I'd hit cut on the camera too quickly, but it was like 2:00 a.m. and I'd been up twenty hours, gimme a break), and since it seemed weird, I looped some of the closing applause to cover the gap. Within hours, a YouTube comment popped up accusing me of looping the applause. I gave a rare response to this one, congratulating the viewer on his ears and explaining what had happened. In general, though, I *never* recommend responding to commenters; do *not* get out of the boat.

On a presidential campaign, you have to meet, greet, and eat some pretty strange things. (As long as I live, I will never forget that fair in Brownsville, Texas, when a suspicious local in the crowd demanded that the senator "take another bite" of his *torta*; he just wasn't convinced Obama had been enthusiastic enough about the first.) Candidates across the spectrum find themselves in deeply bizarro situations, some of which end up on national TV. Some of these are of their, or their advisers', own creations. One example springs to mind: On the night of Michelle Obama's convention speech, we were still on the road, campaigning in Kansas City. (The nominee wasn't slated to speak until the final night of the convention.) Rather than watch his wife speak from some anonymous hotel room, the candidate watched it with a family at their house. The organizers even wrote a part into the convention coverage in which Obama and his hosts appeared on a Jumbotron on the convention stage. It was a great idea in theory but on national TV the whole thing came off as just, well, weird. Though both the candidate and the Girardo family were bright and cheerful, the exchange was fraught with the awkwardness inevitable to a conversation conducted over a live, nationally broadcast satellite connection.

But that was before seven-year-old Sasha came rushing

*Brownsville Texas, seconds before the second bite. (Photo by Arun Chaudhary/ Obama for America)*

unscripted across the stage. "Hi, Girardo family!" she beamed up at them. "Daddy, what city are you in? I think Mommy did good," she announced. "I love you, Daddy." Just like that, Sasha's unrehearsed outburst turned what could have been cringe-worthy into one of the highlights of the whole convention. Normally, of course, kids and pets aren't so reliable at bailing you out of these well-intentioned stunts. (That's Film School 101.)

And that, over and over again, was the lesson. Spontaneity wins out over artifice every time. "I love the way he walks. I can't do it—he's a natural," said a member of the world-champion 2008 Phillies as the president was strolling out of a reception in their honor. In other areas, too, Obama just had that elusive *it* that, for want of a better term, I'm calling authenticity.

And so it seemed only logical that we should capitalize on that most valuable of political currencies in the films we shot. We realized that we could use not just his speeches and official campaign stops, but everything that took place behind the scenes. Many of us had already commented that the outtakes from the direct-to-cameras we were shooting for the Obama website were just as compelling as the explanatory material the senator was sitting down to record. And this is by no means a criticism of Obama's official performances; it's just tough to make five-minute explanations of policy dance, especially when you're recording ten in a row.

But when he was just relaxing and being his smart, calm, collected self, Obama was extremely compelling. However electrifying his speeches, official appearances tend by definition to be formal and formulaic; they allow glimpses of real personality only through the cracks, even when it seems they've fully steeled themselves against revealing anything at all. In this respect, BO's relative lack of Washington experience actually helped him.

During one of the zillion primary debates, when the candidates were asked to name their worst quality, Senator Obama, after honestly and awkwardly thinking about it, said his was being messy with paper in his office. Hillary Clinton said hers was working too hard. John Edwards said his was loving people too much (and how). Senator Obama cut in and asked if he could answer the question again, because he thought he'd been asked to name his worst quality. The audience cracked up, and Obama scored a debate victory. For all the talk of the packaging of the presidency and so forth, it's nice that these types of off-script moments still happen at debates. The 2012 GOP debates have been especially fun to watch for such revealing interactions. (OMG, did you hear that Romney *touched* Perry at one early on?)

Authenticity also scored points for our main primary opponent—most pundits agreed that Hillary's tearing up in New Hampshire contributed substantially to her unexpected win there. Voters liked seeing Hillary's vulnerable side. In person, Hillary comes across as much warmer than she does in official appearances, which is just one reason that she probably would've benefited from more back-stage video and quirky spots like her hilarious-because-authentic *Caucusing Is Easy* video instead of churning out so many attack ads and wonky summaries of policy positions.* She's funny, too, even in trying circumstances; as secretary of state, she was one of my favorites to shoot, always equipped with a small joke, an unfailing smile, and unflagging energy.

An especially fine example of authenticity's power is a Ross Perot ad from the 1992 election.† The ad starts at the end of a statement Perot is making at a debate. He stares directly at the audience and explains in a very matter-of-fact voice why he should be elected. He then looks up at students in the balcony and explains why the election matters to them, the next generation. Finally, even as the timekeeper badgers him to stop, Perot looks directly into the camera and says, "America, I am doing this because I love you. That's it." I remember seeing that commercial when I was sixteen years old and for the first time understanding the raw, down-home appeal of everyone's favorite third-party candidate. The ad is just as strong two decades later; it adheres to the three-act structure and everything. It's the candidate's authenticity that clinches it—the ad works in spite of, or perhaps because of, its complete lack of subtext. The ad's real strength is that Perot's debate performance was never intended to be an ad.

The list of politicians capable of forgoing self-consciousness in

---

* It's reminiscent of President Clinton's amazing video of his final days in the White House. (You know, the one in which he's biking in the Oval?) There's practically an entire subgenre of hilarious Clinton videos just like this.

† You can watch it on the excellent Living Room Candidate website: http://www .livingroomcandidate.org/commercials/1992.

public is short. Two examples that spring to mind are New Jersey
governor Chris Christie and Massachusetts Senate candidate Elizabeth Warren. Christie doesn't take the Obama approach; he's
more of an instigator, and people are definitely drawn to his in-
your-face rants on the subject of private schools and his screaming
matches with teachers' union members. The hollering works
because that's just who Chris Christie is—*not* the kind of guy you
want to confront about where he sends his kids to school: "I'll tell
you where, none of your damn business!" Warren is more like
Obama: no fireworks, just remarkably cogent policy explanations
and compassionate positions; she has a dash of frontier folksiness
for good measure. But whatever form it assumes, authenticity yields
popularity, and Warren would be hard-pressed to pretend she was
"severely conservative." Politicians really have no choice in the
matter, since the now-ubiquitous movie camera seldom lies (unless
you're counting the twenty pounds it adds to your figure, and yes,
we filmmakers made that one up a long time ago, you really look
like that).

You can never really tell in advance which candidates' personalities will translate best onto video, but you can be sure that the
ones who are the same on and off the camera are the ones who are
in it to win. Despite some early bumps, New York senator Kirsten
Gillibrand (even as a DC resident, I still consider the NY senators
my own and so take a special interest) turned out to be even more
publicly winning than the woman she replaced. Speaker Boehner,
whom I filmed about ten zillion times during that endless succession
of government-shutdown meetings, is also very comfortable being
Speaker Boehner all the time, really. Leader Cantor . . . not so
much. Senator John McCain was once celebrated for his no-holds-
barred honesty, but video is not especially kind to him (doubters
need only watch his notorious "green backdrop" speech for a

reminder). Like Nixon before him, JSM translates better into other mediums—print and radio spring to mind, maybe a blog. But perhaps McCain's marked discomfort on camera should've also tipped off 2008 voters to his deeper flaws, like his general lack of authenticity (is "soul" too strong a word?) and most un-mavericky embrace of extreme positions he'd rejected in earlier election cycles. His 2010 "Complete the Danged Fence!" ad perfectly illustrates this disconnect. McCain doesn't seem to believe in the convictions he's espousing, and the camera knows it.

There is also, believe it or not, a peril in seeming *too* real. I always think of the moment in Robert Altman and Garry Trudeau's *Tanner '88*, an HBO miniseries that followed the presidential campaign of a congressman from Michigan in a fictionalized version of the contentious 1988 election. The adman character leaves a camera running in a campaign hotel room and captures a moment where Tanner, unaware he's being filmed, speaks with honesty, passion, and eloquence. It's shocking because it's real, and the campaign decides to use the footage. The fictional pundits on the show stir up trouble when they question if Tanner really was speaking extemporaneously, or performing a stunt for the camera.

We had our own *Tanner '88* moment. When the senator was giving an impromptu pep talk to the troops during one of his rare appearances at headquarters, I was taking still photographs, so an intern grabbed a video camera and filmed the speech. It turned out to be so great that we posted the raw footage on the OFA website. At a talk I gave at NYU that summer, we were (good-naturedly) accused of having manufactured the whole moment just for a video; one audience member even suggested that I had deliberately shaken the camera to make the footage seem more "real." (Luckily, I didn't have to deny this charge too strenuously because I'm all over the video, running around snapping pictures.)

Seeming "too real" can detract from the credibility of the very reality you're trying to convey. For the final cut of *Night and Fog*, his 1955 Holocaust documentary, the director Alain Resnais left out the most extreme visuals for fear that they wouldn't be believed. In the years that I followed President Obama, there were a few moments when I, for similar reasons, recommended against releasing footage I had shot. Just a few days after the devastating tornadoes in Joplin, Missouri, in the summer of 2011, I ran into a grieving family on my way out of the restroom. We stood together in the hold, and they were very sad but still friendly; they wanted to make sure I'd be taping their meeting with the president. When he showed up, they just broke down. In the footage you can see the emotion that had been temporarily submerged by adrenaline just bursting out of them. To me, that moment was a strong reminder of the power of the highest office in the land, and the importance of a president's physical presence in the wake of a disaster. Though I wanted others to see the exchange, I worried that it might be considered "too real" and therefore somehow exploitative.

Another one of these moments took place the day before the 2008 election, when Senator Obama learned of his grandmother's death. As he eulogized her on a rainy evening in Charlotte, North Carolina, a few tears started trickling down his face. The moment was extraordinarily powerful in person as well as on tape, but we posted the speech without the close-up and didn't post the photos. It simply wasn't worth risking the suggestion that we were exploiting Obama's deeply felt sorrow.

I didn't come to the campaign understanding what I should or should not post; like so much else, I worked that out as I went along. Perhaps my first lesson in the difference between normal editing and editing footage of the candidate came when I started to edit *Dinner with Barack* back at Chicago HQ. I discovered that much of my job was about finding the line.

What line? The line! As hard to define as authenticity, and just as important. The line between acceptable and unacceptable, appropriate and exploitative, funny and un-presidential, powerful-real and painful-real. Step over the line and call some poor tracker macaca and people recoil; avoid the line altogether and people lose interest. The line shifts with the geography, too, making matters still more complicated. Shooting a coyote while you're out jogging evidently falls on the right side of the line in Texas (and Moscow), but maybe not so much in San Francisco. This matters because since the Internet has made local news national, these days the line is more universal: what plays in Peoria also must play in Provincetown. The farthest edge of the line, the frontier if you will—that crucible of everything American where the civilization of traditional media meets the wilderness of YouTube cat videos—is on the Internet.

And though I knew our work was supposed to be edgier than the more traditional media that was going straight to TV, I'd yet to determine where edgy ended and inappropriate began. Often, I found that the people who asked me to "make something edgy" usually meant the exact opposite. Someone who *actually* wants edgy material usually asks for it by name: "I'd like a video about Mitt Romney strapping his dog to the top of his car." Anyway, back in the summer of 2007, I had a good deal yet to learn about this line, or so I discovered when deputy communications directors Dan Pfeiffer and Bill Burton came over to the desk Kate and I were sharing to watch our quirky first cut of *Dinner with Barack*. While Bill laughed occasionally, Dan was dead silent from start to finish—a somewhat ominous good cop/bad cop pairing, I thought at the time . . . maybe I still do.

Their verdict ended up surprising me, though. This is cool, they said, *but*. They were concerned about the robot section. The part that showed Obama joking with a dinner guest who works in robotics about inventing a robot that would allow the senator to campaign in multiple places—that was okay. But a few seconds later, when he actually started *doing* the robot (yes, the dance) and repeating in a robot voice: "There are no red states, there are no blue states"—well, that part had to go.

"But he's being really funny!" I protested. *"This is my guy!"* Nope. It was un-presidential in the extreme, and therefore a non-starter.

You can constantly see the line shifting when you're playing with live ammunition—that is to say, footage that can conceivably blow up and alter the course of events in the real world. In theory, handling live ammo is any filmmaker's dream, but in reality it's a privilege that comes with fairly terrifying responsibilities. All of us aspiring filmmakers spend years making examples, models, scripts, but we very rarely get the opportunity to take on the "real thing." The vast majority of what we shoot won't make it into a movie at all, let alone be scrutinized by scores of scandal-hungry journalists. But this wasn't about getting a short identity film into Sundance; it was about helping to elect a president.

Here I was, confronted with the real thing every day. Friends and foes alike could (and frequently did) repurpose every single still image of the candidate, and that was nothing compared to what they could do with live-action footage. Repurposing Obama's every last utterance was another favorite pastime: the more successful his candidacy, the larger the target on his back, and the fun certainly didn't stop when he was elected. Just one of countless examples: in November 2011, when, on the subject of attracting foreign business, the president said, "But we've been a little bit lazy, I think, over the last couple of decades. We've kind of taken for granted—well, people will want to come here and we aren't out there hungry, selling America and trying to attract new business into America." Within hours Rick Perry used that line, shorn of all context, in an attack ad, and Romney pounced on it in a stump speech about Obama's anti-American leanings.

Political opponents weren't the only ones who wanted to have their way with our precious footage, either. After their first viewing of *Dinner with Barack*, Bill and Dan taught me to put footage through what they called the Daily Show Test. What would satirists like Jon Stewart, Stephen Colbert, and SNL do with this footage of Obama doing the robot dance? Nothing good, that much was certain. So Kate and I took a second crack at editing the dinner video with these constraints in mind, and this time we got an A+ . . . or so I thought.

A few days later, when I heard that Jon Stewart would be using footage from the meal on his show, I was incredibly nervous; it seemed I'd failed the crucial Daily Show Test on my first try. The segment was a mash-up of unflattering pictures of politicians eating messily on the campaign trail, but when Stewart got to Obama, he actually highlighted a section we had put in *Dinner with Barack* about the short-lived TV show *Lil' Bush* in which the senator was unaware he had been depicted. The joke was that no one was watching this show, not anything to do with our show. Phew.*

We always had to stay on the right side of "presidential," perhaps the most important line of all, however nebulously defined and arbitrary it could seem. For example, we'd done several "direct-

---

* The still photographer equivalent of this has to be the Drudge Report Test: How will my picture be interpreted when displayed on top of a jumble of provocative texts in "too casual" fonts?

to-laptops" with Plouffe, who would explain some of the campaign's strategic decisions directly into a laptop's camera, as if video chatting with the viewer. (The current campaign manager, Jim Messina, has done a great job with these in the 2012 cycle.) These videos were always successful in establishing an intimate, face-to-face feel with supporters, but when Joe broached the possibility of shooting something similar with Obama, the higher-ups nixed the idea. Speaking straight into a laptop camera just didn't qualify as "presidential," and it's true that if you study any direct-to-laptop recording long enough, the speaker starts to look a little ghoulish.

Belorussian president Alexander Lukashenko would definitely agree with this characterization. For him, not even touch-screen technology passes the presidential test, or so he explained to a group of reporters during a major news conference in Minsk: "I can carry those iPads with me, dabbing at them with my finger," he said, "but this is not worthy of a president." When the generation growing up in front of laptops and tablets ages into power, the rules will no doubt change along with the modes of communication considered authentic and natural. We now have a president who uses a BlackBerry, and as of 2010, Congress allows iPhones and iPads on the floor. Who knows, maybe we'll even have someone in high office doing the robot on national TV one of these days. We were only able to put the tiniest of cracks in that particular glass ceiling.

But is dabbing your finger at these devices worthy of anyone? I'm the first to acknowledge the unfortunate consequences of our culture-wide obsession with recording everything all the time, which is that people are often too busy recording events to experience them in the moment. I can't tell you how many people I've seen missing a chance to shake hands or have a quick hello with the president because they're preoccupied with their camera,

*Darrell Issa's said tweet.*

phone, or even iPad. Many of the poster-size pictures (which we call "jumbos") hung in the halls of the West Wing feature as many phones as people. It was during the marathon health care reform meeting at the Blair House when we first noticed how many congressmen were wielding iPads and taking photos. Congressman Darrell Issa even took a photo of Hope Hall and me during debt negotiations in the East Room with his iPhone tweeting it out during the meeting itself.

Because of the nature of my job, I've often had a camera rolling during moments that I should've been "experiencing" more directly. Before an education debate at Columbia University in September 2008, I was rolling on the senator when Reggie Love told him that my wife was pregnant. I had been waiting for the right occasion, but that's why we love Reggie! Rather than switch off the camera, I kept it rolling for the whole conversation: "Mazel Tov, you better

*Backstage at Columbia University. "Mazel Tov!" (Photo by David Katz/Obama for America)*

catch up on your sleep!"* As if any of us were sleeping much at that point.

Of course, I don't really claim to have the knowledge or authority to tell people when exactly they should be experiencing life and when they should be recording life and when they should be experiencing the recording of life. Let's leave that to late-night discussions at expensive liberal-arts institutions. But I can definitely tell you that when you are a professional videographer, your wife will expect you to take video of your child once in a while despite any protestations of the "busman's holiday."

---

* Linda Douglas, plane companion and fellow cat lover, also had some good parenting advice for me: "Don't tell your child he is related to your cats unless you're prepared to pay for therapy afterward!"

# CHAPTER 6

# "WHOA, YOU GUYS TAKE THIS SERIOUSLY!"

*In which I resist the urge to steal Jon Lovett's joke from a White House Correspondents' Association dinner and don't refer to the Jefferson Jackson Dinner as a big effing meal . . .*

**B**ecause my fear of driving was exceeded only by my fear of parking, I made a habit of arriving at events super early, when there would be more room for error in the vast lots of our nation's convention centers. Still, even if I'd show up three hours before the opening bell, I'd catch glimpses of the Clinton death star. The campaign workers streaming out of her buses looked as intimidating and organized as most armies. Most of them were wearing full-on business suits.

But until the Jefferson Jackson Dinner on November 12, 2007—the major event on the Iowa Democrats' campaign calendar before the caucus itself, which would take place in the first days of 2008—I hadn't gotten a good look at our opponents' video teams.*

---

* Actually, that's not strictly true: I did know John Edwards's videographer slightly. It was *not* Rielle Hunter, but rather Peter Cairns, the assistant of my officemate at

Given what I'd glimpsed of HRC's operation, I was surprised at how much better prepared, video-wise, we were than all our opponents that night; it was the night Obama's political fortunes shifted for good. "Whoa, you guys take this seriously," said Hannah Rosenzweig, my counterpart in the Clinton campaign. Though we were on opposing teams, Hannah and I had quickly become friendly. We'd been stuck on the video platform for hours, she with a can of Coke, me with a bag of trail mix. We eventually pooled our provisions to make it through the long evening. Hannah offered to watch my equipment while I left the platform to shoot handshakes on the rope line if I'd do the same for her. I agreed to guard her gear but said I didn't need to leave the platform myself, since we already had a camera in the rope line. We also had cameras stationed in the balconies.

All told, our campaign had five different cameras shooting in the room that night, and that's not counting Joe on his first-generation iPhone; no other campaign had more than one. Though Hannah was a legit filmmaker, there was only one of her. Some of the other campaigns' videographers hadn't even met their candidates; some had been hired just for the evening. It wasn't pretty. They were young kids from New Mexico or Connecticut or hired

---

NYU, Jay Anania, who also happened to be Elizabeth Anania Edwards's older brother. The Edwards camp was also taking video seriously, and not because of Jay but because Joe Trippi—architect of DeanTV—understood its power. Anyway, that July, I'd spotted Peter and Edwards walking through the backstage door at the National Urban League Conference in St. Louis. A few minutes later, the security guys ushered Senator Obama into the room but then body-blocked me out: "No one goes out there."

"No, no," I said, "you don't understand. Did you see that blond camera guy who just went in with Senator Edwards? I'm like him to Senator Obama. I think his name is Peter." The security guys considered that for a few moments, agreed that it didn't seem fair, then went into the auditorium and unceremoniously threw Peter out. Peter, I'm sorry, I didn't mean to narc you out in there. That's really not my style, ask anybody.

guns from Iowa not really equipped to "get in there," as Hannah had put it when leaving the platform to join the scrum of press photographers crammed into the buffer right in front of the stage.

From the beginning, Iowa had been one part theory lab and one part obstacle course. Its arcane cuisines and rituals—from butter sculptures of farm animals to deep-fried Oreo cookies to butter sculptures of the junior senator from Illinois—kept us alert and entertained (and artery-clogged, with chest pains, and barely breathing really), but the Jefferson Jackson Dinner was no mere sideshow. It involved an enormous amount of pageantry, with downtown Des Moines transformed into a battleground for visibility. The venue itself was decorated like a Friday night pep rally in a small Texas town, with each campaign scrambling to outdo the opponents with signs and banners. The goal was always to demonstrate the depth of each team's commitment and the size of its bench.

The dinner was a big deal for both local Democrats and national political observers, and therefore yet another challenge requiring us to try to target multiple audiences simultaneously. For Iowans, especially those who hadn't yet decided how to caucus, the JJ Dinner was the official opening bell of the caucus season; for the national media, it was a way to frame the whole momentum narrative: who had it, and who didn't. There was a third audience, too, perhaps the most important one of all: the internal audience. The whole dog and pony show is an elaborate form of psychological warfare within the campaigns. I remember feeling physical pain when I saw a gigantic HRC campaign sign brilliantly positioned on the most prominent construction crane in the dead center of Des Moines. Why hadn't one of *our* people thought of that? (There was a similar sign right next to the Manchester Airport that irked me on every trip in and out of New Hampshire.)

Another indication that the JJ Dinner mattered that even a novice like me could read: it was the first time I'd ever filmed Obama rehearsing a speech. We all repaired to the conference room of Chicago HQ, trying to anticipate when he'd have to pause for laughter or applause (sound effects he'd occasionally add himself). Meanwhile, the video team was working on figuring out how to package the event in a way that would appeal to local Democrats while intriguing national media outlets in search of those tell-all smoke signals.

The New Media video team took a multipronged approach: making a trailer before the speech, expeditiously posting a video of the speech on our website and YouTube video channel, and later doing a more polished wrap-up video of the speech plus other events surrounding it.

To make a trailer that stuck to the wall, I took inspiration from what has since become an obsession to me, the Prelinger Archives, which Kate had introduced to me. Rick Prelinger has spent over a quarter-century collecting old movies—industrial, educational, governmental, corporate, and home movies that fall into a category he's dubbed "ephemeral films"—and then posting them on the Internet for free use. Perfect for a little genre work.

By "genre," I mean a type of shorthand, a way of presenting an idea in a context that the audience will know how to process, without too much cumbersome background information. If we recognize that the genre of a movie is "thriller," say, we'll enjoy anticipating the danger lurking in every dark corner; in a romantic comedy, we know not to think too hard when the male love interest is a successful photojournalist who never seems to have a camera and is never called into work while the female love interest is a size-zero professional pastry chef who never makes pastries (and how did either of them afford that *amazing* apartment?).

In politics, and particularly in campaigns, newscasters often use sports metaphors that viewers can readily understand and digest—running out the clock, the horse race, inside baseball (the latter phrase used by Joan Didion about Dukakis's infamous pitch for the press), playing hardball, down to the wire, neck and neck, head to head, going one on one, throwing in the towel, in the catbird seat, playing defense, odds-on favorite, dark horse, long shot, coming down the stretch, jockeying for position, a marathon not a sprint, sprint to the finish, closing fast. The headline from the October 27, 2011, *Houston Chronicle*: "Is Perry's Tax Plan a Hail Mary?" Talking Points Memo the morning after the Iowa caucus: "EIGHT VOTES: Romney Wins in a Photo Finish." Clichés are powerful and enduring for precisely the same reason. For all their cheesiness and generalizations, they provide useful shorthand that helps us absorb and organize information.

For the JJ trailer, I chose a genre best described as "nostalgia," an old-timey aesthetic—aproned June Cleaver housewives, gigantic old TV sets and educational videos from the same era—that I thought would hit at least two audiences: young people because they would find it ironic and amusing, old people because they would find it comforting and familiar. The graphic-design team pitched in by creating an amazing cartoon of the candidate based exclusively on a vague directive from me: "like something out of the *Saturday Night Live* credits circa 1949." (Over the course of the campaign, the graphic designers would dig into nostalgic imagery repeatedly, and even more effectively than I could. They were creating images from scratch while I had to hope something appropriate would turn up as I trawled the virtual cutting-room floor.)

Minor triumph! In the weeks before the dinner, my trailer got some press from the most important audience of all, the local one—of particular weight in Iowa, where two dozen extra people can make a quorum. I think the use of nostalgia helped our cause, and nostalgia can be a powerful tool in politics, though usually not in a good way. Nostalgia, in many ways, represents the flip side of hope and, in celebrating a vanquished perfection that never existed, can be a major obstacle to any endeavor that looks to the future. That's one reason I tend to distrust candidates who substitute nostalgia for authenticity. In the hands of various 1950s venerators on the right, who're all so fond of spinning a beautiful tale of an America that never was, nostalgia can be a dangerous tool.

Nostalgia is like an empty box that can hold ideas that are true but more often than not false; it's not in and of itself an authentic artifact. Nostalgia often has, in fact, only the loosest connections to reality, as I was reminded when I visited my elementary school a few months back. The scene should've been perfect—it was late at night, and the building had barely changed in the intervening quarter-century—but I felt exactly nothing. My nostalgia for that long-gone time of my life was absolutely incompatible with the reality of the place. On the other hand, when I stumbled upon an episode of *Beavis and Butt-head* (complete with music videos!) on VH1 Classic a few days later, I came very close to weeping for all the memories that flooded forth. I've no doubt that the senses can trigger Proustian "involuntary memories," but for me, a screen can retrieve lost time as well as or better than any taste or smell. (Looking forward to the all-new season!)

But back to the JJ mania. When the night of the dinner rolled around, we had every reason to hope that our candidate's speech would knock everyone else's out of the water. So, in addition to building up anticipation, we were also in a race to post Obama's full speech on our website and YouTube channel as soon as possible. Speed was critical; the faster we put up the speech, the greater percentage of the audience we would draw to our website; once there, prospective supporters might start to explore other issues as well.

As I'd wheezed through Hy-Vee Hall with my camera the night before, I was once again reminded of my advanced years. Campaigning is definitely a young person's game, so it was appropriate that a bunch of kids were running the show in Iowa. Pretty much everyone was a full decade younger than me, which mostly rankled when I tried to draw examples from pop culture—none of these infants had ever seen the *Love Boat*! A few months earlier, twenty-three-year-olds had been visiting me for office hours; now they were diplomatically explaining where I could and couldn't stand based on whatever badge I'd been handed.

But my fatigue wasn't just a function of my age. Way back in the ancient history of 2007, posting a speech on YouTube was a lot more labor-intensive than it is today. (Why, in my day, YouTube was uphill both ways.) Though we had high-def cameras, we had neither the space to store large files nor the bandwidth for uploading in HD on the road, so we were forced to shoot on DV tapes. That's right, *tapes*, which sounds downright primitive now. (Don't look at me like I looked at Ken Burns's partner Duncan Dayton, who, upon examining the lightweight camera slung over my shoulder in the West Wing lobby one day, told me that, for campaigns in the '80s, he had to haul around a duffel bag full of telephones.)

Using tapes meant that, before posting it onto the Internet, we had to spend at least the amount of time we'd spent shooting the content playing the tape back into the computer. The whole process was as analog and time-consuming as making a mix tape for your seventh-grade crush (which, come to think of it, very few of my fellow campaign workers had ever done). We couldn't possibly compete with MSM's (mainstream media, in Washingtonese)

*Tripping up the stairs with heavy bags. Why in my day it took eighty pounds of gear to make a YouTube video!*

satellite trucks, which could post video instantaneously but at enormous expense.

We dealt with these limitations in two ways. First, we developed a practice of cutting the speeches while Obama was still talking, meaning we'd cut the tape, give it to an editor, and simultaneously start a new tape every, say, ten minutes if necessary. Perhaps more important, we made an effort to live-stream as many events as possible. Live-streaming technology was still fairly touch and go back in 2007, but it was a much more time-efficient alternative to posting the mix tape, and a necessary means of growing that elusive audience. When we live-streamed, we could just send out the images in one continuous file that could be captured directly by a computer without all the hassle of editing and transferring the tapes.

Obama's speech—and its reception—at the JJ Dinner was even more spectacular than we'd dared to hope, and overnight the media narrative transformed him from the lagging long shot to the man with momentum. After he totally crushed it at the JJ, we knew beyond all doubt that the best vehicle for Barack Obama's message was Barack Obama himself. Nothing could be as effective as just showing the man doing his thing. Before the JJ Dinner, I'd still been a little surprised that we consistently got the most hits not from the clever, artsy videos I had so much fun making but from the long, uncut videos that showed the senator talking in detail about the issues that mattered most to him and the country. (Perhaps just as surprising, the people who watched these videos came from a demographic that skewed much older—and less rich and white—than any of us predicted.)

Pretty soon we were live-streaming all the time, or as often as the technology would allow. Already fairly advanced in the fall of 2007, by the next fall, at the end of the campaign, live-streaming technology was ubiquitous. This is not to say that there weren't many, many glitches along the way. Perhaps the worst took place during that famous Berlin speech. While the senator was addressing untold hundreds of thousands, I was on my hands and knees power-cycling (or turning off and on, in IT-speak) the cheap Dell laptop that was sending out Obama's speech to the world. We were just getting too many viewers, and the server kept crashing over and over. People watching the speech at home suffered these interruptions every couple of seconds. Sharon Barnes, who was deputy New Media road director during the general election, got upset whenever a live stream had to be pulled down for some technical reason. "I've become passionate about live-streaming," she e-mailed, and I knew exactly what she meant.

Live streaming became crucial to our video strategy for several reasons. As I've already mentioned, we had discovered that the most important segment of the audience was local: even if the actual number of viewers was relatively modest early on, we kept at it, recognizing that luring even a few dozen motivated voters to watch the speech online—people who might tell their friends, forward links, post on Facebook—could make a huge difference, especially in the more sparsely populated early states. There was no better, more organic way to grow the movement. And we knew it was working because people would come up to us, asking if we were the campaign video team, and saying they had seen and shared a speech the week before.*

Watching a speech live, even if only on a computer screen, really did help voters feel connected: *Hey, I can't get off work to go down the street and hear the speech, but I still feel that this guy is talking to me, right here and right now.* The Internet could not quite generate that euphoric or manic unity that overtakes large crowds at everything from NASCAR races to Burning Man to Black Friday at Walmart; watching a live stream or clip of a speech hardly approximates the magic of attending an event in person. (I couldn't dispute the assessment of the blind man I chatted with after a rally in Norfolk, Virginia. "What'd you think of the speech?" I asked him. "It was really great," he told me, "*so* much better than on TV.")

---

* Not everyone was impressed. One old lady in Zanesville, Ohio, came up to me and asked, "Are you Obama's YouTube people?"

I nodded, preparing to accept high praise.

"Your stuff looks like shit—you need to compress it better," she said in her best "the coffee's burnt, hon" voice.

Still, we could remind voters that our candidate had come to *their* town, and spoken in the auditorium of *their* kids' school, and eaten a burger at *their* favorite restaurant. It was remarkable, the degree to which voters—especially those who hadn't been able to attend the event in person—appreciated having candidates spend time in the place where they lived. That's one reason the overflow room is ubiquitous at political rallies and large religious events. Even if the spectators aren't directly participating in the spectacle, they're pretty close, which feels pretty good.

Not that every event was a bursting-at-the-seams megablockbuster. I learned a lot about adaptability, about tailoring our approach to an event's specific audience and scale. Just as bands play stadiums differently than they play small clubs, Obama wouldn't address a screaming crowd as he would an old friend in a diner, and we wouldn't shoot a town hall the same way we'd shoot an Oprah-palooza.

"Just don't look up at it and you will be fine," several veteran network cameramen advised me before Oprah's big endorsement speech in South Carolina in December; they were watching me attach my little camera to feed into the Jumbotron. It wasn't until about halfway through the speech that I realized I was doing exactly what the guys had warned me against and was using the Jumbotron as my viewfinder, staring up at it to adjust my camera and in the process seriously distorting my lens's focus. Luckily, Oprah's ecstatic audience didn't seem to notice.

And whether it's the viewfinder or the event itself, scale does matter. An ant falling one hundred feet off a cliff will be better off than an elephant falling half that distance. An ant can lift its weight many hundreds of times over, while most humans can't lift even twice their weight, and I can't lift more than half of mine. In both cases, the ant seems to be doing well, but that's not the point; the point is that different rules apply to objects—and events—of different sizes.

On the road, it was Axelrod who was always thinking about these issues, asking us how different-size events looked on camera. The campaign tried to strike a balance between quality and quantity, to do both massive rallies that introduced Obama to the largest possible audience and more intimate sit-down gatherings that allowed him to really talk with voters, and we had to adjust our cameras accordingly.

After the tide-turning success of the JJ speech, our goal was always to add more (virtual) seats to the room where Obama was speaking. We started filming him all the time; we shot, and posted, everything from the speeches in minor-league baseball stadiums to the one-on-one chats in coffee shops. And we weren't the only ones who had noticed; the traditional media folks were also aware that our team was getting the kind of "in the moment" footage that was only possible when you trail someone all the time. By the morning of the Iowa caucus, when I was summoned to the Des Moines Hampton Inn so that I could film the senator's early-evening visit to the caucus that night in Ankeny, Iowa, everyone on the campaign had embraced this approach.

I'll never forget that amazing half-hour of following the hoarse candidate as he greeted caucus-goers of all stripes. I hustled back to Iowa HQ to post the incredible footage, but by the time I arrived, Obama was already projected to win Iowa, so I left the tape with editor Jessica Slider and raced off to the Hy-Vee Hall to film his victory speech. Both videos posted within a few hours. The victory speech got millions of hits, while the caucus-going video only got about sixteen thousand; it was totally swallowed up. In hindsight, I should have posted the next day or, even better, right before the

*The only time I've been summoned to the Oval to show POTUS a movie, it starred Marvin Nicholson. (Official White House Photo by Pete Souza)*

New Hampshire primary. But the innovative campaign I'd joined was all about learning as we went along, and the fact that Obama had welcomed the intimate coverage signaled that in the future I could go even deeper.

Incidentally, this is the only video I've taken of Barack Obama that he ever asked to see after it was shot. It's a special piece. In fact, David Plouffe told me recently that he and the president were talking about it on the way over to make a speech to the 2012 Iowa Democratic Caucus. (I somehow doubt he mentions others of our thousands of collaborations nearly as often.)

In the weeks after Iowa, with the higher-ups endorsing our decisions, we began to experiment with a greater variety of videos, and greater variety within the pieces themselves. We all, but Kate, in particular, started making "wrap-up videos," which would include clips from official campaign stops as well as funnier moments on the road: standing in line at fairs and parades and ordering eggs and playing basketball or pool (or even bowling, though BO generally prefers sticking to sports he can actually play). The goal was to show Obama in all sorts of different situations: some grand, most anything but. We considered these videos rewards rather than calls to action. Early on, we'd bust our asses to get these videos out overnight, but as the reward model became more prevalent, we started holding them for a day or two, and then longer.

Over time, our wrap-up videos became more intimate, showcasing quieter, more personal moments on the road. These backstage moments gave a new "voice" to the candidate. (It was convenient that they also provided an outlet for the backstage material that I was gathering in increasing amounts.)

In a literal sense, we all have different voices—indoor voices and outdoor voices, conference-call voices and cocktail-party voices. We all naturally employ different voices in different situations; using a whole range of them makes us more effective communicators by, among other things, combating "listener fatigue." Finding new voices is not, of course, the same thing as inventing a new genre or anything crazy like that.*

Politicians have about four voices in their public capacity: the speech voice, the interview voice, the press-conference voice, and the direct-to-camera voice. But there's a fifth voice, too, perhaps the most important one of all: the backstage voice, the one that can't be scripted or fine-tuned by consultants.† Most interested voters

---

* That would be like aspiring to move the ocean or invent a new color or something else very, very, very, very hard.
† MSNBC's Lean Forward promo campaign is an attempt to script that fifth voice,

were already acquainted with Obama the master orator, the collected interviewee, and the calm debater. They had seen far less of the funny, confident, relaxed Obama, or the road-weary family man who just wanted to see his kids every once in a while. By filming this "other" Obama, we were indirectly addressing one of his greatest perceived liabilities—the fact that he was relatively unknown, at least compared to Clinton and then McCain, who'd both entered the national consciousness years earlier. Again, we believed that the more voters got to know our candidate, the likelier they were to vote for him. We'd staked our jobs on it.

I loved helping to make these wrap-up videos, which shined a new, more personal light on the man I'd become so fond of. I shot one of my favorites during the loooooooong Pennsylvania primary, as we wound down yet another Keystone State highway. Senator Bob Casey and Obama were sunk deep into the pleather couches, chatting about how they'd met their spouses. And though I'd heard the story of Barack and Michelle's courtship in various speeches and interviews, the tone of a simple conversation between friends made it new.

If my access to these conversations made for some powerful videos, it also led to some accidental incursions from yours truly. Though I really do try my best to be a silent fly on the wall, I have this unfortunate tendency to enter the scenes I'm filming, given enough time. Just a few moments after the senators' affecting love-of-my-life exchange, I found myself divulging the horrible details of my evil subletter, whose misdeeds had finally resulted in our losing our apartment a week after Super Tuesday. Senator Casey's jaw dropped: "I'm sorry, man—that's awful!"

---

and it really doesn't work. Al Sharpton's is pretty good, but the rest of them sound totally fake, like something Aaron Sorkin pumped out in five minutes of meth-rage.

Senator Obama, characteristically, focused on the facts. "What were the cross streets again?" I told him, and he agreed that such a prime location didn't come along every day. "And it was rent-controlled, too?! Oh, no! That's *tough*."

Witnessing this type of intimacy, even through a lens, builds real bonds. I've actually felt closer to Bob Casey ever since that conversation, and we always hustle over to each other to say hello at White House events. Nothing about his casual chitchat with the future president, or any of the exchanges we filmed, was set up—people can smell artifice a mile away, and besides, Obama was never willing to put on that kind of show.*

By that stage in the primary, the spring of 2008, we'd established a frenzied pace of shooting, live streaming, and uploading. Because we had no competition from other campaigns, members of the video team were always competing with one another to post the most clips of Obama presenting his message day in and day out. Our work was sort of like what the president says about infrastructure: "crucial but not sexy." We were Eisenhower's Interstate system, delivering the candidate to every corner of the country. As the primary wore on, we kept posting our candidate's public appearances, every last one of them, and in May 2008, our YouTube channel had one thousand videos, a number astronomically larger than our competitors'. Even the geniuses who ran YouTube noticed.

As we moved from the primary to the general election, our maximum-exposure strategy continued to work because of who Barack Obama was. My goal while shooting was always to amplify Obama's strengths rather than to diminish his perceived weak-

* I was recently speaking to a group of South Korean students about my work at the GWU. One of the first questions was "How do you get Barack Obama to do all those things? What do you say to him?" I had to have this retranslated several times before realizing what they were asking and disabusing them of the notion that I was in any way the presidential handler/trainer.

nesses. So instead of videos that directly refuted claims that he wasn't experienced enough, we made videos that showcased his superior judgment, uniquely American story, and sharp sense of humor.

This approach wouldn't have worked nearly as well with McCain, whose online video content could best be described as "sarcastic." Because the Republican nominee's greatest strength as a candidate was the relative inexperience of his opponent, McCain was better off focusing on snarky spots denigrating Obama's "celebrity" (if only his handlers had been this clever when it came to choosing a running mate). Of course, if you live by the snark, you die by the snark, and this approach did open McCain up for an attack from none other than Paris Hilton, who was, in 2008, still our national emblem of useless celebrity. I think her hilarious and smart rebuttal to the celebrity ad—remember? when she gives a serious energy policy brief before signing off with "See you at the debate . . . bitches!"—actually raised her standing, in the process paving the way for the Kardashian era of even-more-useless celebrity.

But there were other options open to a man like McCain, even though he really didn't seem to seek them out. In any campaign, there are many crucial voices other than the candidate's, and we sought to capture those, too. We found that people wanted to see real people, and profiling them as we traveled was a welcome break from always filming strictly inside the candidate's campaign bubble. From an African-American grandson of slaves and Korean War veteran in Las Vegas to the proverbial sign changers—Team Iowa created a genre of videos that showed voters switching the signs in their front yard to register their shift of support from Clinton to Obama. But of course, sooner rather than later this became a frenzy that cut all directions with all campaigns soon trying to make these videos in every combination possible: The original sign changer switched her sign yet again, to John Edwards!*

Together with the live-streaming and up-close-and-personal wrap-up videos, these longer topical profile videos added bullets to our message-machine gun and put still more voices into the ongoing conversation about who should lead the country over the next four years. The traditional media arm of the campaign would use similar profiles to great effect both in the DNC video made by Davis Guggenheim and in the thirty-minute infomercial that aired immediately before the election.

And still more voices we can't forget are the voices of the famous. Because we were on the road already, Team Away frequently shot some of the highest-profile campaign surrogates, that is, politicians, big-deal businesspeople, or celebrities. One plum assignment I didn't expect involved flying to L.A. in the fall of 2007, turning my room in the Beverly Hilton into a makeshift studio with the help of some rented lights, and recording celebrity and semi-celebrity endorsements to rally the youth of Iowa to go out and caucus. (Note to self: You *really* need to Wikipedia the B-listers before they arrive because when you don't know who they are, they can sense it immediately. Also beware of the over-entitled delusional types. "I've actually decided to wait until there is a nominee to endorse," one minor WB star informed me crisply. I mentally advised them to wait by the phone for sure.)

Politicians and entertainers are very different kinds of celebrities, a point that was made best by then senator Joe Biden during a

---

* It's a matter of curation as much as creation. While it's true that everyone has a story to tell, it's also true that not all stories are created equal. Case in point: One of my NYU students made a documentary about two warring brothers who ran rival pizzerias across the street from each other in Staten Island. This rivalry was bordering on violent. You can't tell me that every pizza place in NYC has as compelling a backstory.

conversation with actor Tobey Maguire. "I'm a big fan," he told the *Spider-Man* star. "Me, too," responded Tobey automatically. Joe Biden was totally unimpressed with this response and said so: "Hey look man, I'm trying to have a conversation with you," the future vice president said. "I'm *actually* a fan. Nobody is a fan of a senator. C'mon!"

But more often than not, Hollywood is a scapegoat for Washington, something to score points against (the 2008 campaign made a dirty word of "celebrity") and a cash cow for fund-raisers. And though the Obama campaign was even more cautious than most in its relationship with Hollywood—and this was long before John McCain's Paris Hilton/Britney Spears ad—its leaders were also first and foremost practical. If movie stars could increase youth turnout, then they'd use those movie stars to increase the youth turnout, simple as that. Granted, showing up in Hollywood and ringing on celebrities' doors for endorsements isn't exactly revolutionary; every campaign does it in some form or another, while publicly doubting it works. But not every campaign has a completely mobile studio that can churn out dozens upon dozens of endorsement videos over the course of a weekend. As in so many other things, the Obama organization was taking it up a notch.

My three days inside the Beverly Hilton (I left my room only to get cheap sushi from the Korean guy on the corner and Coca-Cola from the vending machine) were surreal but satisfying. The utility of having a Robert Redford, a Warren Beatty, or even a Frank Sinatra on the trail with the candidate is now openly questioned. Most of the actors I met were extraordinarily nice, extraordinarily humble, and extraordinarily excited to be participating in the political process, many for the first time. They were also impressively adaptable. Take Josh Duhamel, the star of *Las Vegas* on NBC. After a few

*Operation: Beverly Hilton. Sleeping in the studio is a hazard in independent filmmaking of all kinds. (Self-portrait by Arun Chaudhary/Obama for America)*

minutes of chatting, he mentioned that he was from North Dakota. I gasped. North Dakota was a caucus state, too, with thirteen whole delegates up for grabs! We did one more take, this time subbing in "North Dakota" for every mention of Iowa, and voilà, just like that, we had a North Dakota caucus video ready to go.

We used the voices of Obama's celebrity supporters more directly, too, most memorably for me in the madcap road trip that was the All Actor All Iowa All Star Voter Education Tour in late 2007. Kal Penn, Olivia Wilde, and Megalyn Echikunwoke braved the dangerously icy roads of rural Iowa in deepest, darkest winter to encourage kids on college campuses to go out and caucus. (Having figured out the importance of targeting specific constituencies—seventy-five-year-old corn farmers weren't going to be interested in the stars of *House*—we stuck with the young people.) Though the trip soon devolved into a series of accident reports and near-death catastrophes, our surrogates ended up registering a *ton* of new voters and signing up almost as many volunteers. Actors are naturals when it comes to retail politics, particularly Kal, whom Obama accurately described as a "monster" when it came to recruiting volunteers; on a single night at the University of Iowa Field House, he registered a record-breaking two hundred.*

* And the movie we made was great. In the opening shot, Kal, busy chipping away at the iced-over windshield, asks, "So do you think it's going to be this cold on

Other efforts to speak to youth culture in voices they wanted to hear made me feel even older than usual. I remember once, Scott Goodstein asked me to post a video of the band OK Go on You-Tube. They had met the president at a rally in Wyoming, and Scott figured the best time for folks to see a video endorsement would be right after their concert as fans went home. I looked at him like he was crazy. To me, this assignment sounded like a colossal waste of time—I'd never heard of OK Go ("It's not like it's David Bowie or something," I said. "No, David Bowie doesn't vet," Joe barked out from his office), so how was I to know how powerful their You-Tube presence was? The success of their shout-out to Obama proved that the best way to reach young potential voters was to meet them on their own turf. In this case, that turf happened to be on YouTube, in a post-concert clip of a band that was completely unknown to my thirtysomething self.

Then, on the other end of the spectrum, you have a performer like Bruce Springsteen. *Everyone* has heard of the Boss, right? I mean, is there any more universally beloved musician alive today? Well, yes and no. OK Go has its constituency and so does Springs-teen, and the two groups seldom overlap.

Most members of the road team—and almost all elder members of the campaign in relation to the youthful median—were thrilled when Springsteen volunteered to headline a series of campaign rallies. The talented director of photography, Kat Westergaard,

---

caucus day?" Next to him, a chattering Olivia Wilde says, "Imagine settling Iowa!"

But, as happened sometimes, HQ soon had second thoughts about the wisdom of releasing an official Obama for America movie featuring the star of the *Harold & Kumar* stoner comedies. (Kal played Kumar, if you didn't know; the youth of Iowa sure did!) After much debate, and to my great frustration, they decided to release the video but with zero fanfare, just kind of post it on the Web and hope no one notices, which no one really did. And, man, did I mess up that van while parking it in the rental lot after dropping our cast and crew off at the airport.

expressly coordinated her schedule to be there whenever the "two bosses" appeared onstage together. Then again, we were all in our thirties, and many of the people running the campaign were even older. There was no ambiguity about what Springsteen brought to the table: enthusiasm, excitement, and a whole lot of rock.

But as usual, the fault lines were generational, even when it came to the Boss. At a particularly rousing event in Cleveland, while the strains of "The Rising" floated around the light mist and a crowd of nearly eighty thousand shrieked its approval, Malia stood backstage speaking quietly to her father.* At the time, I was taping just for the visuals and couldn't hear what they were saying until Obama burst out laughing and said, "No, no, Bruce Springsteen is *way* more famous than the Jonas Brothers!"

After the concert, when the senator relayed the story to Bruce, the singer just laughed and nodded. "Yeah, that happens a lot," he said. "I just try to explain that I'm Barney for old people."

I think it's a very good explanation; maybe some politicians are Barney for somebody, too.

---

* One of my team, Peter Rubi, made what was essentially a rock video of Bruce playing "The Rising" at that event, which garnered an unusual number of hits for a political video.

CHAPTER 7

# OLD AND TIRED WINS THE RACE

*In which I stay at that Super 8 Motel in Tacoma, vandalize a*
*much nicer establishment in Cleveland, and propose the "Slider*
*Principle" of YouTube Uploadability.*

In the spring of 2008, as the primary season heated up, Senator Clinton released the instantly infamous 3:00 a.m. ad that presented her as the only leader capable of handling an international crisis.

The Obama campaign's multipronged response to this ad revealed the growing relationship between the campaign's Old and New Media arms. Sorry, I was recently called out on this by David Axelrod, let's say between the campaign's *traditional* and new media arms. For all the credit given to New Media after the fact, we were still, essentially, the JV squad, the backup singers to the Diana Ross that was the established old, er, traditional media operation, the ad teams run primarily by the firms AKPD and GMMB, the best-case examples of media firms.

After the JJ Dinner the ad teams had wanted our footage right away for a national ad, the first time they ever made such a request, and later I was always hearing how our team "saved the asses" of the paid media team and so naturally assumed there had been a mistake or accident with a crew they had sent to the dinner. But David Plouffe recently told me that the decision to let the New Media team handle the ad had been both deliberate and contentious, since some of their "TV guys" weren't happy. It was a "real test" and an "important moment" in our working relationship.

Also after the JJ Dinner, we started getting the occasional request for a high-def shot from the ad guys. By this point, we were a fully functional mobile studio, so adept at cranking out content that, in addition to our ever-improving live-streaming capabilities, we could post clips of the candidate's speeches before he was even done talking. His visceral reaction to Senators McCain and Clinton piling on him in the wake of his ill-considered "guns and religion" comment was up thirty minutes before he'd even left the stage in Terre Haute, Indiana. After a rally in Colorado, we live-streamed (in high-res!) the senator addressing a church in Atlanta. By using our prosumer equipment—this term, for those unfamiliar, refers to that sweet spot between junk cameras for consumers and expensive gear for professionals—and broadcasting the tape (yes, still tapes!) halfway across the country, we'd saved the campaign tens of thousands of dollars. The accomplishment did not go unnoticed. Even BO was impressed, asking, "Has anyone ever done that before on a campaign?" When I told him I didn't think so, he was clearly pleased. "You're my guys!"

With just a camera, tripod, laptop, and trusty Verizon aircard, three of us (and later four) could make an entire movie from stem to stern in record time, and on the go, too.* We edited and posted

---

* I should make clear that we weren't editing these things on Dells. We used the newest Final Cut Pro software on high-end Macs. We were, in fact, the only

*Preparing to test the Slider Principle with Peter Rubi on a tarmac.*
(Photo by Katie Lillie/Obama for America)

videos from motorcades, buses, vans, and airplanes. (Our Slider Principle posits that you can upload video from takeoff to approximately ten thousand feet above the earth, depending on cloud cover.) In grad school, it had taken me a bare minimum of three months to produce a movie; by the end of my first summer on the campaign, I could do it in three hours.

HD footage still took up a lot of space and was challenging to upload, though by the fall of the general election, I had acquired some serious MacGyver capabilities. I was also willing to interpret the law liberally if necessary. One morning in Cleveland, while the senator was attending Congresswoman Stephanie Tubbs Jones's funeral, I came close to vandalizing a hotel business center in a

department on the campaign with Macs. That was all some people knew about New Media, that for some reason we all had Macs.

frantic effort to upload footage we had just shot. After giving up on my aircard and then the wireless on BO's bus, I reached inside the locked cabinet housing the hotel desktop's case, yanked out the Ethernet cable, and plugged it directly into my laptop. The cable was ludicrously short and nowhere near an outlet, and the whole scene must've looked strange to the young man who wandered into the room and asked me what I was doing. I had about three minutes to go on the upload.

"The WiFi is messed up, or the computer or whatever," I explained, which didn't stop the guy from staring suspiciously at the open laptop on the floor, tipped onto its side and flashing lights like a Christmas tree.

"I need to print my boarding pass on that computer," the guy said, moving toward the hotel desktop.

"Are you a guest?" I asked.

He nodded. "Are you?"

I paused a bit too long; then it was my turn to nod. The guy stared down at me, took another step forward. Two minutes to go on the upload.

"Just go check with the front desk, they can fix it—I mean, they are fixing it!" I corrected myself. "Will you just, I mean, just ask them why it's taking so long? Thanks." I knew I'd be gone before the guy had made the long trip to the concierge desk and back.

Whatever it took, we always got the job done.

But even well before that act of near vandalism, when Hillary's 3:00 a.m. ad ran in March 2008, we had all the technology, and discipline, in place to pounce. In the unlikelihood that you've forgotten, the 3:00 a.m. ad—an echo of a similar ad made for Walter Mondale during the 1984 Democratic primary—followed a standard formula, with shots alternating between a phone ringing in the middle of the night in the Oval Office and angelic sleeping children. The ominous phone rings on and on as a creepy voice conflates national security flashpoints with the safety of "your children" safe and snug in their beds at home. The ad's implication was perfectly clear. Who do you want to answer that phone when the bombs begin to fall, the experienced Hillary, or the untested Obama?

Our campaign wasted no time in responding to these charges. First, the traditional ad guys made a smart response ad that used the same imagery of the sleeping children and the Oval Office, but in the Obama ad, a voice-over calmly made the case that Barack Obama had the judgment to lead. And then something interesting happened.

One of my favorite teachers at NYU always said that you're only allowed one moment of magic in your movie. And here, finally, was that small moment that rewarded our months of ceaseless work. It turned out that Casey Knowles, the sleeping girl featured in the old stock footage used in the ads, was now all grown up, old enough to caucus in Washington State. In fact, the seventeen-year-old happened to be a dedicated precinct captain for Obama. The day after her brother first recognized Casey in the ad, she was on local TV in Washington State, explaining the irony of her appearance in a pro-Hillary ad.

Anyone could see that this material was too rich to leave alone. I flew to Seattle, and within twenty-four hours we had a written, shot, edited, and posted counterattack ad starring Casey as herself. The whole production cost no more than my plane ticket to Seattle, a one-day rental on a domestic compact, and a super-luxurious night at the Super 8 Tacoma. (Yep, the one where reception is shielded by bulletproof glass—you've been there?) I woke up, spent an hour and a half shooting Casey, and drove right back to the airport, where I edited for another hour, uploaded, made it "less weird" per Joe Rospars's instructions, and uploaded again, all before boarding my plane back to Chicago.

The hardest part about making the ad wasn't the script, which, once I was presented with the concept, pretty much wrote itself: Casey begins by explaining how negative ads work, with scary music and scratchy voices accompanying the shots of her sleeping, and then declares that she's choosing hope over fear by supporting Barack Obama. The far bigger challenges had been getting everyone at HQ to decide whether such an ad passed the "presidential" test—oh, and the small matter of convincing Casey's dad of my legitimacy. "How do I even know you work for the campaign?" he asked me when I called to set up the meeting.

"Um, hmm. Because I have a BarackObama.com e-mail address?" He still wasn't satisfied when I offered to scan a copy of my business card. It took a phone call from Joe for him to green-light the expedition. The wrangling at HQ about the appropriateness of another response had actually taken longer than the production, Casey's father included.

Clocking in at about a minute, the finished ad demonstrates a real advantage of Web video—the absence of time limits. I asked Axelrod whether we should try shaving it down to thirty seconds for television; he said to try but his instinct was that it wouldn't have the same impact, and he was right. You could tell the story of the 3:00 a.m. negative ad, or of the girl, but not both, in thirty seconds. On the Web, content determined a video's length. And in the end, TV picked up the ad anyway; cable stations across the country essentially gave us free advertising by showing our Casey Knowles counterattack ad in its entirety over and over again.

Though the Casey Knowles ad brought our traveling video team to the attention of the traveling press corps for the first time, we still had a long way to go.* John Del Cecato—the "D" in AKPD, Axelrod and Plouffe's media conglomerate, and a very funny guy—always let us know where our videos stood in relation to other cultural phenomena. He would e-mail us when the Philly race speech surpassed an Amy Winehouse video or would approach the latest YouTube scandal of Britney or Lindsay—ever-humbling reminders of where even the most famous politicians stood in comparison to actual celebrities.

Most of all, the Casey Knowles experiment showed us how the Old and New Media branches of the campaign could work together for maximum impact. Even without taking the traditional media pros into account, the division of labor within the New Media department was already complicated enough, with our video team eventually splitting into two divisions (a source of constant confusion to outsiders and occasional competition among ourselves)—the Road Team, which I led, and the HQ Team, led by Kate Albright-Hanna.

As the primary turned into the general, the campaign "staffed up" to prepare for the long-haul marathon to November, with many of Hillary Clinton's former staffers joining our ranks. For the traveling video team, I assembled a group of formidable film-makers who could all write, shoot, edit, and, with any luck, not spazz out too much on the next president of the United States. We also added a still photographer, the multitalented David Katz, who had been Obama's body man, or personal assistant/everything else, in the Senate and had just graduated from Stanford business school in June. He'd vigorously question the future plans of our volunteer motorcade drivers: "I'm not sure I understand—what's your business model for that?"

---

* Until then, the press had only really noticed that the Internet got really slow when I was around. Uploading in HD took up all the bandwidth we had and some of theirs, too!

With this team in place, we were able to send a steady stream of material to our traditional media guys, who'd often identify part of an upcoming speech that they wanted us to shoot for a future commercial. We'd roll our cameras and upload the footage by any means necessary. And the more we collaborated, the better the results.

"At the beginning of the campaign," Del Cecato told me, "we had a pretty clear division (in our minds) about what was appropriate for the Web, which allowed us to be edgier with our message, and what could be used in a TV spot. But as the campaign progressed and we saw the great unscripted moments that you and your team were able to get, we decided to try using some of that footage in our TV spots. As the New Media team more regularly got good placement for their cameras, shot crisper footage, and quite frankly just captured that genuine, authentic Barack in a way that could only be done through shooting almost around the clock, we came to see the New Media footage and our footage as all one thing. In fact, in a great many instances, we totally relied on New Media to get the shots we needed from the trail."

For my part, I found that our team did its best work when the experienced political hands conferred with the techno-pros and us artsy types, and Plouffe and Axelrod and those folks deserve a tremendous amount of credit for seeing the potential of these collaborations long before most in their realm. (And while we're on the subject, I should apologize for always saying Plouffe and Axelrod in the same breath—they are totally different guys, for instance, you'd only lend your MacBook charger to one of them . . . )

Perhaps our most successful collaboration came a week before the general election, when the campaign broadcast a thirty-minute infomercial on all the major networks right in the middle of prime time. The infomercial's director, Mark Putnam, wanted the road

*OFA New Media bringing a touch of class to the Élysée Palace. (Photo by Peter Rubi/Obama for America)*

team to continue shooting the candidate on the campaign trail, but to increase the volume of HD and do it all in slow motion. And so we did, returning to our cameras with renewed vigor. We "did our thing" filming Obama riding the bus* and shaking hands in rope lines, footage that was mixed with an interview with the candidate and some nice voter profiles before cutting to Obama giving his "closing argument" live on the campaign trail in Florida. Buying such a huge chunk of prime-time airtime was seen as a ballsy move. Maybe it was, but for the video team, it marked the formal culmination of everything we'd been doing since Iowa.

---

* Only looking out the window when he did so naturally.

But long before the thirty-minute ad, I found that the more directly the New Media team interacted with the Old Guys, the better the ideas we came away with. It's no accident that one of my team's most successful gambits—what we referred to as the "walk-out" video—originated in Old Media. At the height of primary mania, we harnessed the excitement of the campaign trail by having the senator make an impassioned appeal directly to camera just before stepping onto the stage at every big campaign event—yet another way to target interested local voters who might be unable to attend the rallies in person.

Del Cecato had had the idea after watching a video of the senator wishing traveling press assistant Katie Hogan a happy birthday. "I just thought it was so cool of him to take a moment to connect with the junior campaign staff. It gave me the idea of doing a totally different type of ad—totally unscripted, that managed to capture the energy of the rallies for those who weren't able to attend in person, show the viewer something truly authentic and never-before-seen, particularly since one of our strengths was the fact that BO was the same person on- and offstage—in contrast to, say, John Edwards, who was able to turn it on and off depending on whether there was a camera and/or crowd present. The walkout videos were specifically supposed to target young people, who kept saying things like, 'I will vote for Barack in November.' We were like, 'Shit—you gotta do it in January or there won't *be* a November!'"

In a standard walkout video, Obama leans in close and looks right into the camera. Then he raises his voice over the roaring crowd to say, "Hey, North Carolina, you've got a chance to make some history with us," before going on to explain exactly how the early-voting process works in the Tar Heel state. Before long, every state director wanted one of these videos, so we started pumping them out like episodes of *The Hills* for every state in play.

*In North Carolina with Barack Obama, Joe Biden, and "late campaign" Arun. (I'm fat.)* (Photo by Callie Shell)

We shot the first one in Austin, Texas, with the help of the trip lead, Brian Mosteller, who warned me that I only got one take: "I am *not* having him walk these stairs twice." Obama was great, speaking extemporaneously about how exciting people's voices for change were, and saying that if they didn't all get out there and caucus, the crowds meant nothing. When he was finished addressing the camera, I kept the audio on as Obama tapped the shoulder of a little girl in a BO T-shirt and cracked "Nice T-shirt" in an endearing nerdy-dad way.

After one walkout video in South Carolina that went so well that the senator gave me a silent "we nailed it" signal, we turned to walk out the "chute" into the main arena. About two seconds before he made it to the stage, when I could fade out of the shot, a large woman being jostled by the crowd fell over the barriers and landed right on top of several members of Obama's Secret Service detail. She was unhurt—if extremely irate—but the senator correctly guessed that I didn't have enough footage to edit out the blooper. He turned to me with a grimace: "Please don't tell me we have to do that again tomorrow." I'm sorry, sir.*

About a week later, at an LED factory in the other Carolina, a member of the Secret Service pulled me aside. "Hey, do you still have that footage of the woman falling out of the stands?" I nodded and asked if he needed to confiscate it. "Oh, no," he told me. "We just want a copy to include in a training video." To this day, this is one of the greatest honors of my life—and how I'm able to defend democracy.

By the close of the campaign, our walkout videos had come to represent a kind of institutionalized spontaneity. If they lacked the total rawness of unmediated backstage vérité, they still captured the genuine excitement of the moment and, more important, the genuine "voice" of the candidate. We even made one of these videos at Grant Park on election night. Before going onto the stage to give his victory speech, Obama looked down the barrel of my camera and thanked his online supporters for making history. I hadn't been totally convinced this was "presidential" and had wanted to film him watching returns instead, but by then the point was pretty much moot. The next president of the United States was doing a walkout, and therefore doing a walkout was presidential.

---

* It was a great lesson in the pitfalls of live video, one that I learned over and over throughout the campaign. Earlier, in New Hampshire, I was on the verge of capturing some brilliantly composed footage of the silent senator, beautifully lit against an all-black backdrop, looking concerned and, let's face it, eminently presidential as the medics brought in a stretcher to usher out an overheated audience member who'd just passed out. Suddenly, from the first row came the voice of none other than Larry David screaming, "Sinatra made them pass out, too!" Before I'd managed to press "record," Obama went from looking pensive and presidential to cracking a smile.

# PART II

# GOVERNMENT FUNNY

# CHAPTER 8

# GREG CRAIG'S PHONE

*In which I finally address the issue that readers want to know about the most: my radical weight gain. Plus, al-Qaeda also makes its first appearance.*

Closer to dawn than dusk on election night, after hours upon hours of congratulatory rope lines, I was straggling home down Michigan Avenue when my BlackBerry buzzed. It was an e-mail from Director of Scheduling and Advance (and general Obama nerve center) Alyssa Mastromonaco, asking me to report to some anonymous Chicago skyscraper off Millennium Park at eight the next morning—in just five hours. "Hey, I'm not sure if anyone talked to you about what you're doing next, but I'm going to need you to film the president-elect making a phone call to thank staff. Oh, and don't forget to call him Mr. President-Elect."*

---

* For the curious, before I'd always called him "Senator" or just "sir": lots of other staffers called him "boss." It wasn't that he would've minded if we'd called him by his first name; on the contrary, he always went out of his way to introduce himself to people as Barack. But at least for me, the formal address served as a good reminder of what I was doing and what the stakes were. It was a good thing, too, because bystanders didn't always look on kindly at lapses in etiquette. Once, backstage at

Everything was different now. That much I'd known seconds after they called Ohio for the Democrats and just like that, an extra flank of men in black suits with various devices strapped to their chests had materialized out of the dark corners of Grant Park.

I probably got the first good look at them as I was positioned by the firework launchers waiting to get some serious (and seriously dangerous) backstage footage, when Marvin Nicholson, the trip director, tapped me on the shoulder and said, "Sorry bro, no fireworks." Folks correctly assessed the mood of the speech and the country was one more solemn than celebratory.

And though this was the moment we'd all worked so hard for, I was too exhausted to appreciate anything but the all too typical anticlimax that was waiting by the Porta-Potties while history unfolded a few feet away. As my BlackBerry buzzed with the well wishes of friends, acquaintances, and many of the people I'd profiled or filmed over the last few years, I just wanted to go to bed. Many hours and a seemingly endless series of rope lines later, after BO himself declared, "Let's go to sleep," I dragged myself to a victory party but left after twenty minutes, on my way out agreeing to post the victory speech video to YouTube, which in the rush of excitement no one had remembered to do. I got back to our small apartment to find houseguests sleeping on all surfaces, which left me no choice but to do the upload from the floor of our bathroom.

The next morning, I tried to take stock of the state of the world, but I was far too preoccupied with my wrecked body. Against the advice of my doctors, I'd been treating my ulcerative colitis (a chronic and fairly nasty GI disorder) with steroids for over

---

an event in NYC, BO was shaking hands with some entertainment-industry luminaries when Leonardo DiCaprio cried out, "Barack, buddy!" from the line. Fellow celebs all stared at DiCaprio with marked disapproval, and Usher offered a quiet correction. "It's 'Senator.'"

*Election night! That's a nimble and conscientious Dr. Jill Biden ducking out of the frame, bottom right. (Photo by Jean-Michel Picher)*

a year. That, combined with a deadly combination of stress-eating table after table of ranch-drenched turkey sandwiches, had caused my weight to shoot up thirty pounds in the same month that the stock market plunged nearly two thousand points. On the campaign trail, I'd paid so little attention to my deteriorating health that I found myself in a Portland ER on the eve of the Oregon primary. "It turned out to be some sort of abscess," I told the senator when I rejoined him in Florida a few days later for a taping.

"Glad you're doing better, but I'm going to have to ask you to stop right there—that's way too much information for me already," he interrupted, making an "icky" face.

I'd also developed a retinal complication and was having trouble seeing out of one eye. Since partial blindness was a serious occupational hazard for a man in visual media, I decided to deal with the eye before the colon or the weight and so, two days after the election, I landed an appointment with perhaps the only Obama-hating ophthalmologist in all of Chicagoland. As she lasered my retina, I could hear her angry clucks from above. "Congratulations," she grumbled. "But it's just these associations, you know? I heard he gave Louis Farrakhan an award, and frankly, that's a bit much."

That was it for my self-improvement course. If I'd been looking forward to kicking back and repairing my beat-up body during Transition, I had another thing coming. As was so often the case during this wild journey, I discovered what I was getting into only after I was shoulder-deep. The night before the election, I'd received a phone call: If in theory Obama were to win the upcoming election, would I in theory be interested in working on his Transition? I said yes, of course, having no idea what that would entail.

From that morning after the election, when I showed up to film Obama making his first phone calls as the next president of the United States—I flubbed his new title, incidentally, sputtering out "Good morning, Mr. Senator-Elect-President-Sir"—I was just making it up as I went along. Even more so than usual, that is.

If Election Day had marked the end of one narrative, none of us had learned the rules of the sequel. We just hadn't had the time. Most of us had never thought past the Armageddon that was November 4. I barely even knew what Transition *was* until that bleary first morning after. National Security adviser to the president-elect Denis McDonough had to lay it all out for us on one of our first days in our new offices in the Federal Building in Chicago, where we moved the Monday after the election.*

---

* Instead of going straight to DC like many soon-to-be presidents, Obama stayed in Chicago through the end of the year so that the girls could finish their semester at school. Oh, and there was also that small matter of President George W. Bush hav-

Temporally, Denis said, Transition was the two-and-a-half-month period between the election and inauguration; practically, it was the team that helped the president-elect and vice president–elect assign personnel and conduct business as they prepared to take office; and technically, it was some sort of nebulous pseudo-governmental organization. The goal of the Presidential Transition Team was to hit the ground running in January, Denis told us.

The Transition conference room where he was addressing us doubled as the vice president–elect's office. (The Chicago Transition office was so sparse that everything—both jobs and spaces—had a singer-slash-songwriter element, though the space certainly beat the Transition headquarters in downtown DC, a labyrinthine structure more suited to a sci-fi film than serious work.) We were all learning basic facts and protocol like when we did and didn't have to stand for the president-elect, when the president-elect himself walked in. In our confusion, roughly three-quarters of us catapulted to our feet.

"Oh, hey, guys," Obama said, looking a little confused himself. "I was just going to grab my lunch, which, uh, doesn't appear to be in here, but, er, while I'm here, let me just say something. . . ."

These encounters were fairly common in Chicago. We were a skeleton crew compared to the robust operation in Washington. The Chicago Transition staff was so small—just about twenty of us—that I sat directly next to Denis while he conducted some pretty high-level conversations on behalf of POTUS-E. Denis always remembered to get off the speakerphone just in the nick of time: "Oh, hey, the president-elect wants you to be CIA director—you

---

ing given up Blair House, the residence across from the White House where most POTUS-Es live right before inauguration, to former Australian prime minister Kevin Rudd.

up for it?" (Among other overheard gems, I learned the definition of a Delta Bravo, military alphabet for "douche bag.")

Sharing a cubicle with the man responsible for vetting some of the highest-level appointees in the next administration also meant I had to be on alert to stand up anytime Obama wandered over to consult with Denis.* "Arun, your desk is getting pretty messy," he said, appearing behind me one afternoon. "Or not messy actually, and not getting, it is a little crazy."

Of course it was crazy; how could it *not* be crazy? My team was down from six to one (me), and I'd foolishly agreed to take on two more-than-full-time jobs simultaneously.† I was officially the video lead, but because I was the only New Media guy in Chicago, I more often than not found myself in the role of still photographer as well—positions that turned out to be remarkably incompatible for a person with only two arms, though on a few occasions I did make it work, taking serviceable photos and video at the same time. (When the octopus act was totally impossible, I'd get an intern or press staff Ben Finkenbinder and Katie Hogan to shoot stills for me.)

Once, I ran the teleprompter while simultaneously filming an early *Weekly Address*. "Are you sure this is the best way to do this?" asked a skeptical president-elect. Lisa Kohnke shook her head no: she was serving as both deputy director of scheduling and advance and my lightstand, literally holding a recalcitrant light in place as I filmed. Such are the perils of short staffing during the cruel Chicago winter.

* Official etiquette dictates that you're supposed to stand when POTUS enters the room and sit again when he indicates. Following these rules was important to everybody except BO, who'd always either tell us to sit down right away or forget and wonder why we were standing.
† Actually, there were three video people, but two of them, Hope Hall and Jason Djang, went straight to Washington.

In addition to challenging my already challenged organizational skills, Transition taught me about the vast differences between campaigning and governing, even pseudo-governing. The day he failed to find his sandwich in the conference room-slash-VP office, the POTUS-E had explained to us that as high as the stakes had been during the election, they were even higher now. We had to dig deep and remember that from that day forward, we were representing an office and the country.

We didn't really need the formal reminder. We could feel the weight of the office everywhere, in everything we did. There was now a room so secure that no cell phones or two-way transmission devices of any sort, not even Obama's, were allowed inside for the twice-daily national security briefings. (From the election through inauguration, the president-elect got the same briefings as the sitting president.) There had been nothing like a SCIF— military for "sensitive compartmented information facility"—on the campaign; acronyms had either been funny or annoying, but never scary.

"I'll let you shoot in there if you want," the GSA (U.S. General Services Administration) guy in charge of securing the room told me once. He meant stills, not video, but even so, the way he whispered it, you knew it was something awesome.

One day, as the chief counsel to POTUS-E, Greg Craig, was heading into the phoneless sanctum, he told us he was waiting for a call from a certain Mr. Fitzgerald. Would Carlos (who was working for Denis) or I mind terribly getting him if he called? Carlos gulped and nodded. Of course he was nervous. This was Chicago in November 2008, and "Mr. Fitzgerald"—a.k.a. U.S. Attorney Patrick Fitzgerald—was investigating Governor Rod Blagojevich for attempting to auction off the president-elect's Senate seat to the highest bidder. And so when Carlos waited all of twelve minutes before announcing that he was going to lunch (at about 10:25!), I took the phone with trembling hands.

The phone rang mere seconds after Carlos disappeared. I panicked and frantically tried to form a plan for getting the phone inside the no-phone zone. The trick, if you're having trouble with the riddle, was to bring Mr. Craig to the phone and not vice versa.

Over the next few weeks, I began to understand that I could never again just spontaneously decide to film Obama at the Texas Hot Dog in Altoona, Pennsylvania. (And never again would I be crushed next to the phone at the Altoona bowling alley, so close that I could hear the other end of the phone: "Are you all getting busted again?" the voice asked, "lots of sirens in your parking lot—I don't think I better come over there today.")* Now everything was more formal, less natural. The motorcades were longer, the freakout threshold lower. That wonderful gray area between the official and the ordinary was going to keep on shrinking, which presented new challenges to me as a filmmaker: the more artificial and controlled the environment, the more I had to count on the realness of the people in that environment.

The nature of my own job was changing dramatically in other

---

* Actually, even in Altoona, the full press scrum was in full effect. I think the last time I was actually truly alone with the president, not counting my departure in the Oval and our conversation about this book, was a few days before the South Carolina primary, right before the campaign got its own plane. I was deliriously tired as I climbed into a rental car to drive to the next event when Peter Weeks, an advance man, put his hand on the car door: "Axe says he needs you."

"Wait right here," Axe said, indicating one of those "rooms" created out of four curtains on campaigns the world over. And then he vanished.

A few minutes later, the senator walked in by himself: "Funny man, what's up? What are we doing?" I shook my head. I had no idea, and I really hated to be the one to waste his time, and in my extreme exhaustion I was almost on the verge of tears. "I'm really not sure, I . . ." I trailed off.

"C'mon, man!" he said, bringing me in for a quick hug. "It's no problem, we'll go figure it out."

*Uh, that's my photo. Al-Qaeda, my lawyers will be in touch. (Once I get lawyers.)* (Photo by Arun Chaudhary/Obama for America)

ways, too, though I was initially slow to see it. Here, too, the stakes were higher every time I clicked the shutter or pressed "record." *The Daily Show* was no longer my main concern.

"Hey, Arun, check it out—one of your photos is on TV!" someone called out one afternoon.

As a big fan of myself, I trotted over to the communications pen, in which Katie Hogan and Ben Finkenbinder sat surrounded by umpteen television sets blaring the news of the day. And there, front and center on CNN, was a photo I had taken of Obama at the Western Wall in Jerusalem on our swing through the Middle East that summer.

"Cool, what's this from?" I asked, fairly pleased.

"The new al-Qaeda video," Ben said, laughing.

Denis looked up. "I bet you could sue them—there's money there," he observed wryly.

And speaking of Denis's dry one-liners,* another sign of the raised stakes postelection was the new humor, or lack of humor. It had been tame enough in the Iowa days, but now even those rules—of funny versus inappropriate, down-home versus crude, edgy versus offensive—had shifted slightly, hardening into a genre of humor that I've been referring to as Government Funny.

Government Funny isn't a retreat from humor, or not exactly. It's more like a sharper delineation of that famous "line." As we settled into our new reality, the definition of "funny" kept getting smaller and smaller. Look, I'm no expert, but I've been fortunate enough to work with fellow bureaucrats Austan Goolsbee and Jon Lovett, both past holders of the Funniest DC Celebrity title. I may have to get their approval on this one, but here's an example of what I consider government funny but not actually funny-funny: "Volcker Rule? No, no, Volcker rules!" (Stop me if you've already heard the one about the deputy secretary of commerce who got stuck doing the census . . . )

Even in this straitlaced new realm, I knew it was still my job to push things as close to the line as possible without embarrassing the man the American people had elected to lead them, and without physically hurting anybody. (I set a high bar, I know.) Easier said than done, actually, since most of the work I was assigned bordered on the outright dull. I spent most days filming an endless series of rollout events at the Grant Park Hilton, during which the POTUS-E introduced prospective nominees for the

---

* Not that my one-liners to him were hilarious, they were more like: "Uhmm Denis, my friend [redacted] in 2000. Should said friend be worried that he can't work at the White House? My friend knows he should tell the truth no matter what . . ."

top jobs in government while sundry would-be cabinet nominees did their best silent "Stand Behind." (Standing behind the president while he speaks about you is easy to do, but hard to do well. Joe Biden does a solid Stand Behind; John Boehner does not. Watch the last two State of the Unions to see what I'm talking about.)

Although these rollouts soon got tedious, I initially enjoyed the process of introducing a new cast of characters. The campaign had been all about stars, the Obamas themselves mostly, but everyone knows that supporting roles are just as important (and that character actors are the real craftsmen). But now the ensemble had expanded, and the formality of the rollouts felt explicitly theatrical, like that part at the end of the play when one by one all the actors come out to bow.

My role in all of this was entirely passive; I just stood in front of the stage and photographed the never-ending sequence of Stand Behinds. And when I look back on it now, I think this passiveness is what I hated most about Transition. I spent most of my time on still photography; the video that I did was serviceable, not inspired. I did a lot of lurking backstage before the events and in Elizabeth Taylor's former suite at the Chicago Hilton, photographing and videoing nominees as they read their BlackBerries, talked on the phone, or schmoozed with Obama. (Depressingly, I bet more of the photos I took in this capacity ended up being displayed than anything else I've done.)

Probably the biggest takeaway from that time was never to try to shoot photos and video simultaneously. Once, on the campaign, I remember holding two still cameras around my neck while videotaping frantically, but when really trying to do real work, it's best to choose one or the other. Since Obama moved to DC and got a team of *real* photographers, I've never gone anywhere with both a still and video camera.*

Despite having no creative say in anything I did, I still sometimes caught the blame for unconventional visual details. A few minutes before the rollout announcing Senator Ken Salazar's nomination as secretary of the interior, the Coloradoan, famous for his cowboy hat, boots, and bolo tie, was backstage speaking with POTUS-E, Axelrod, and Rahm Emanuel with Gibbs chiming in on speakerphone.

"Do you guys think I should wear the hat?" Salazar asked. Axe paused thoughtfully, while a pregnant "ummm" came over the speaker. Obama was the only one who didn't hesitate: "Of course— you've *got* to the wear the hat, Ken! It's your thing."

Armed with my still camera, I couldn't film the moment to defend myself against the skeptics who would later accuse me of suggesting Salazar's signature accessory: "Why did you have him wear the hat?" soon-to-be White House New Media director Macon Phillips reprimanded me. "You need to take this seriously!" It may not have been my idea, but I was glad Salazar had worn the hat. Salazar's authenticity translates even into his Washington persona, which still features the boots and tie (though he does more often than not leave the hat at home these days, I'll admit).†

Our own clothing was about to change, too, or at least mine was. I remember after shooting a *Weekly Address* at DC headquarters, I ran into old campaign acquaintance General Scott Gration, who gave me a perfunctory military inspection in the hall: ill-fitting

---

* Granted, these days, for all intents and purposes, still cameras are all video cameras and vice versa, but my intent and actions are still purely one or the other.
† The same boots he said he would put to the throat of BP after the oil spill. This is a guy who gets to wear the hat!

*I was not in charge of the nominee's wardrobe. "The hat's your thing!"*
*(Photos by Arun Chaudhary/Presidential Transition Team)*

blazer, fraying khaki pants, and that tie that Reggie kept calling "the saddest tie I've ever seen."

"Don't worry," General Gration told me with only the barest hint of a smile, "suits are cheap in Washington." Ugh. I knew there was no way around investing in clothing I'd previously reserved for weddings, funerals, and the occasional *"that* kind" of party.

Another sign of the precariously higher stakes that characterized Transition (and everything thereafter) surfaced on the very social media platforms we'd exploited to such great effect during the campaign. In this new and unfamiliar universe, the tools that had served us so well were suddenly being turned against us, most memorably when, exactly a month after the election, the *Washington Post* circulated an unfortunate Facebook shot of speechwriter Jon Favreau "hanging out" with a cardboard cutout of Hillary Clinton. Subsequent to this minor embarrassment, we got an e-mail from Macon suggesting that we close our Flickr accounts; attached to the e-mail was a blog post featuring a photograph of Macon in a clown hat that had been lifted from Macon's personal Flickr account. So, yeah. The message was clear: no more clowning around.

# CHAPTER 9

# YOUTUBEOLOGY AND OTHER COLLEGE MAJORS PARENTS WOULD HATE

*In which I consider ursine-generated content, admit that I got a cell phone in 2004, and help score 120 million nonviral views.*

One of the first foreign leaders President-elect Obama met with after the election was Felipe Calderón of Mexico. They had lunch at the Mexican Cultural Institute in Washington while their respective staffs ate in the adjacent room.* As the meal was served, we all went down the line introducing ourselves and our positions: "I'm Robert Gibbs, the press secretary," and so forth. (Robert said that, not me.)

Then it came time for me and Hope Hall—who had worked on my team in the general election (and would later be my successor

---

* Calderón's photographer does not have it easy. His subject kept asking to see photos as they were taken, which Obama has never done (with me), except the shots for the inauguration invitation.

*A lunch at the Mexican Cultural Institute. I find it much nicer to film these meals handheld, but different strokes . . . (Photo by Arun Chaudhary/Presidential Transition Team)*

in the White House)—to explain our roles. "We work in the New Media department," I said. A strained silence followed.

"New Media?" one of the Mexicans echoed. Confused glances were exchanged.

"We film and document the president . . ."

"You are with a TV station?"

"No, no, we upload videos of the candidate for his and now the government website . . . you know, on YouTube and the Internet and stuff?"

Suddenly, smiles broke out all around. "Oh, Obama's *YouTube* people, I see," the mission head said. "We are very honored to meet you, please take my card . . . This was the key to the election, yes?"

Well, of course and not really.

I didn't want to give away too many spoilers before, but it's probably a good time to mention our channel got a *Lot* of hits, about 120 million total, or roughly the same number of people who went to the polls in November 2008. And that was through a lot of traditional hard work and with very few "viral" hits.

We've all heard about how the Internet has changed politics forever; a common bromide about the 2008 election was that "Obama won because of the Internet"—seemingly a successful continuation of the Internet revolution ignited in 2004 by Howard Dean's campaign manager, Joe Trippi, who, if accounts are to be believed, has been preaching since 1984 that the Internet or something like it would transform politics (the fact that it took till 2008 feels like further proof that it's the convergence of technology with personality that matters most, that is, will.i.am was not going to make videos for Howard Dean, no matter how easy it had become technologically).

In subsequent years, this trend of conflating social movements with the Internet has only gotten more pronounced. Social media in particular has received the lion's share of the credit for all sorts of political upheavals and revolutionary movements over the past year: each successive chapter of the Arab Spring kept getting reframed as the "real Twitter revolution," in contrast to the last "real Twitter revolution" that had taken place in a bordering country weeks earlier. But they can't *all* be the real Twitter revolution, can they? (To its great credit, Twitter has never made this claim for itself, and as former White House colleague and current head of international strategy at Twitter Katie Stanton always reminds me: "People drive revolutions, not technologies!" This will not stop some brilliant commentator from branding the next revolt as the "Four Square Revolution." Check in or drop out!) And in the wake of the riots that swept the UK in the summer of 2011, Prime Minister

David Cameron went so far as to propose banning suspected rioters from using Facebook and Twitter, since obviously without social media there would have been no social unrest.*

I'm not denying that social media is a real and powerful phenomenon—it is, very much so, and it has a decent name to boot. But it's important not to overstate its importance, in revolutions or elections. Social media is what it is: social. It essentially industrializes the cottage industry underlying all successful advertising: word of mouth.

That's no small thing. The destruction of the SOPA (Stop Piracy Online Act) and PIPA (protect IP Act) was so thorough, and the swift reversal of Komen on its Planned Parenthood so swift, it makes the letter campaign to save *Star Trek* in 1968 seem like a feathered arrow in comparison to the guided predator drone that is social media. If water cooler buzz spreads at the comforting pace of a mom-and-pop store, Facebook memes metastasize with the merciless efficiency of Walmart.

But it's important to separate the medium from the method of distribution. Just because a YouTube video can be seen millions of times within minutes of release doesn't mean the century-old traditions of filmmaking have changed. In fact, when it comes to making movies, there are few new ways of doing things, no matter how nifty the gadgets get.

Even more nebulous and grandiose is the rubric under which social media falls, New Media. Even as, with each passing day, the Internet's reputation for omnipotence grows—whether it's applied to toppling a dictator, destroying the record industry, or organizing a flash mob of New Yorkers to make one long Soul Train line in

* I read in Wikipedia that the Mexican Zapatistas were the first to harness the power of social media, over ten years ago, in the first-ever "social netwar." Like I said, I'm not an expert, and I totally didn't know that; thank God for Google.

Times Square—there remains a good degree of baseline misunderstanding of what the term "New Media" means (not to mention what its strategists—who've recently become among the highest-paid in the consulting industry—actually do).

"New Media" is one of those intentionally fuzzy and meaningless concatenations of concepts that are tacked on to experimental majors at liberal arts colleges. It is akin to the catchall phrases embedded deep in every Hollywood contract: "in perpetuity throughout the universe in mediums created and yet to be created." In other words, "anything else we haven't thought of yet."*

We should not be surprised, then, that confusion about the term runs deep. On her first day as traveling press secretary, I was introduced to Linda Douglass as the New Media road director, which was my title during the general election. My soon-to-be neighbor in the staff cabin of the plane immediately exclaimed, "Oh, great! I need my computer set up, and I've actually been having trouble with my personal BlackBerry—could you have a look?" Luckily, Linda and I share a love of cats, so we quickly moved past this awkward moment, which I blame entirely on my title.†

But how could it have been otherwise? New Media isn't so much a field as it is a collection of unrelated disciplines that have migrated from printing presses, screens, and canvases onto the Web. However innovative and effective OFA's New Media department was in

---

* In fact, as I write this book, the term "New Media" is teetering into obsolescence, pushed aside by the equally vague but more malleable "digital," as in a "digital-native magazine" or a "digital team." The basic concept remains faulty, but at least the language is a bit more descriptive.

† It was funny, too, since as green as I was at politics, I was even greener on most things Internet. Unlike politics, technology has never even really interested me much, outside of filmmaking, and even then I was the little old man cutting on film, when everyone else was "going digital." I'm not a Luddite, and I do possess a certain fearlessness when it comes to messing with electronics (that the wife abuses, in my opinion), but c'mon, I got my first cell phone in 2004!

2008, I submit to you that it's a myth that New Media got Obama elected president; it's far more accurate to say that the people who promoted his campaign's "digital strategies" and "online solutions" benefited far more from Barack Obama's candidacy than the other way around. (Speaking of which, I'm still hoping CNN will pay me obscene amounts of money to play around on that oversized screen and explain the latest Internet trend to baby boomers—I'm not sure why they outsourced that plum job to the UK.)

Granted, 2008 was something of a special-case scenario, as Chris Hughes, Obama colleague and, as you'll recall, a Facebook cofounder, pointed out to me recently. "New Media needed its own department," he said, "because, even though it's really just a new platform for field, fund-raising, and communications to play out, these technologies were and are still nascent. Creating an independent department that could interface with the more traditional functions of a campaign was much more efficient for the organization and gave New Media a strength of voice that I'm not sure it otherwise would have had."

True enough, but in future campaigns, as these technologies become more entrenched, I question the wisdom of walling the New Media team off from the rest of an organization; all that this compartmentalization does is add an extra barrier of management between creatives and senior staffers. Wouldn't it make more sense to get the oldest people in the room—the ones who have the deepest understanding and experience of the message—together with the youngest—the ones who tweet in their sleep? You need the kids because the old folks will never break or bend the tools new technology affords, particularly when it comes to the Internet (which more often than not reveals uses it wasn't designed for). But you need the old guys because they're the ones who actually know how to win an election.

In the crucial arena of fund-raising, the New Media department played an undeniably powerful role, harnessing the low-dollar donations that make any insurgency candidacy possible. Again, this wasn't entirely new; Howard Dean was good enough at it that they put him in charge of the DNC. But, as Stephen Geer, who ran online fund-raising for Obama, points out, "Al Gore's presidential campaign had something like sixty-five thousand total donors. Howard Dean and John Kerry had a few hundred thousand. Obama had more than four million. You just don't see that kind of growth without a perfect storm of medium, message, and previously unmet demand."

Our New Media team's real breakthrough was not simply applying new technologies to old problems (Karl Rove had always been pretty good at that), but rather bringing the idea of customer service to supporters and potential voters. And this was a directive that came straight from the top.

I remember Kate and me shooting an interview with Betsy Myers, then the COO of the campaign, and she said something to the effect that when she took the job, Obama had asked her to make customer service her number one priority. And the New Media team did an amazing job making the campaign accessible to people of all stripes, and being as responsive to its online audience as Zappos is at making sure your shell tops come the next day in the right size. The revolution may have taken place in 2004, but in 2008 we added that all-important personal touch.

OFA had used the Web to maintain a very high level of personalized service from the outset. The candidate and campaign leadership recognized that, while the Internet is a place people go to loiter and linger, they also go there to get things done. Giving people the information they needed, making sure they could donate and volunteer, organizing door-to-door outreach efforts, and individualizing fund-raising tools, all with maximum efficiency and minimal hassle—that type of convenience was extremely important to Obama. He understood how people crammed a million different tasks into their day, and the extent to which the Internet made this juggling possible.

But personality matters, and just as a pet resembles its owner, a campaign resembles its candidate. Senator Obama did *not* become President Obama because of some mysterious dark Internet powers that only his youthful supporters understood how to tap into. He won because he was the right candidate with the right message at the right time. The boundless, open-all-night Internet simply gave his team the space and freedom to present him and his message to as many people as possible, in more ways than usual. Somehow the causality always gets a little skewed when the Internet is treated as a sui generis movement—an instigator and not a mere platform.

We have a tendency to blame every new technology for killing whatever came before it, but that's not the lesson of the 2008 election. Photos didn't kill paintings, TV didn't kill movies, Hulu didn't kill TV, and the so-called digital revolution certainly didn't kill more traditional forms of campaigning, like knocking on doors and phone-banking voters, or, quite frankly, running television ads. If anything, the Web helped revive the boots-on-the-ground model by making it easier for campaigns to organize volunteers and resources. And I've already described, for instance, how Internet videos helped people who could not make it to speeches and rallies feel as if they had still somehow participated in the candidate's swing through their town.

Marshall McLuhan is widely credited with predicting the birth of the Internet way back in the early 1960s, when he described the inevitability of "electric media" eventually replacing

*Behold the Internet in the form of a Triumphant Bear.*
(Screen Grab/*YouTube*)

print media: "Instead of tending towards a vast Alexandrian library the world has become a computer, an electronic brain," he wrote, uniting disparate tribes all over the world into the "global village" in which we now live. He also used that wonderful lightbulb metaphor: "A light bulb creates an environment by its mere presence" and creates places to work where it was previously dark. And that, I think, is exactly what the Internet does: it gives us space, and a place to work. God forbid, the Internet itself were the message. What on earth would it resemble? A Russian a cappella cover of Mötley Crüe's "Kickstart My Heart" and/or a bear in a hot dog–eating contest. (The bear wins over world champion Kobayashi!)

The Internet may well be the biggest experimental laboratory in the world, but at the end of the day, it's also really just a place to put stuff, whether in the archival or community sense. So devoting more resources to fewer projects seems antithetical to the Internet's unique assets, which are breadth, variety, and just a huge heaping helping of information.* Our new media team capitalized on those assets early and often: The Internet offered us infinite room to grow, and we filled it better than any other campaign.

Movies, I'll grant, don't fit quite so cleanly into this model. Filmmaking was the least "new," and certainly the least interactive, of the tools at the disposal of the digital team. They were also too absorbing to be of much use as a fund-raising tool, as Stephen Geer pointed out to me: When people are watching movies, that's all they're doing. They are not simultaneously filling out a form or grabbing a credit card. But the power of movies—and the sheer volume of them we were able to make and produce—were key in making our full-court-press approach possible and effective.

But just as the Internet makes space for more movies, it's also easier for those movies to get lost. Not every video can be "viral," a term I quickly came to abhor. Early in the campaign, we'd get strange instructions to "make a viral video," which quickly became my litmus test for whether the person understood the first thing about Web video. Because that's like asking someone to "write a

---

* In *Crowds and Power* (1960), Elias Canetti assigns nationalities their own crowd symbols. In his scheme the British get the ocean, a seemingly infinite number of water drops that separate "home" from "over there." He chooses the forest for Germany, evoking their famous organization and uprightness. Though he doesn't mention the United States, I've always thought our crowd symbol should be the frontier: a line separating society from the wild unknown, where individual gumption is prized, neighborly cooperation is necessary, and rules are broken. It is not unlike that shifty line between presidential and unpresidential. And the place where we now have the freedom to go closest to (and even cross) that line is definitely the Internet, itself a direct symbol for the crowd.

I think there's a reason this new brand of online politics has developed in America, and not, say, in Japan or South Korea, which both have a more advanced tech culture and are rapidly replacing things like cash. I think those innovations will be a long time coming to America, where people like to have some cash on hand. But we *are* still pioneers of democratic discourse, and it's no accident that the people who brought you the town hall and the televised debate are engineering this new style of politics.

hit play" or "record a chart-topping song." Viral only describes a pattern of success after the fact; it's not a method of achieving success. Pinning electoral hopes on a video going viral would be as risky as sinking a studio's last $100 million in a "summer blockbuster." Our guys in both Old and New Media were far too savvy ever to make such a JV mistake.

When you can no longer rely on a passive audience trapped in front of the same three networks, you have to step up your game. It's on you to earn viewers. We could be a laboratory, like the research division of IBM (International Business Machines) or DARPA (Defense Advanced Research Project Agency). We could *never* have taken the same chances on TV, with its prohibitively expensive distribution costs. And while many are eager to declare the death of the American attention span, the metrics by no means prove that shorter is always better. As we saw with Casey Knowles, not every story is thirty seconds long, and the Internet has created not just a forum but an appetite for longer content: people just enjoy going online and watching other people doing stuff, however mundane. There is a live stream (two cameras to choose from) you can watch of the Big Texan Steak Ranch, a restaurant in Amarillo that offers a free steak if you can finish it in some amount of time. (Go ahead and tune in http://bigtexan.com/free72.html. It's safe for work, depending on where you work.)

The arbitrariness of length is one of the great gifts of the Internet—a realization that struck me on one of my many 5.5-hour drives from Chicago to Des Moines. (Five and a half hours became the exact amount of time I had to solve a problem, and even now I can do any activity for exactly 5.5 uninterrupted hours because I've taught myself that this equals a single serving of work, just like an entire pint of Ben & Jerry's Coffee Heath Bar Crunch equals a single serving of ice cream.) This freedom to let content dictate length is more revolutionary than it might sound (and probably the most significant departure from traditional filmmaking that I've encountered). Coming from the film world, I had trouble getting used to the idea that an Internet video could be exactly as long as I wanted it to be. Thirty seconds, a minute, ninety minutes: in film, there are many standards, but the point is that there *are* standards. On the Internet, videos can find their own length.

The Internet also allows us all to work smarter and faster by not having to reinvent the wheel with every project. Spontaneity and creativity are hugely important, yes, but so is familiarity with what others have tried before. The Internet is like a limitless lending library of information, about everything from the Zapatista movement to those vacuum-cleaner demonstrations from 1950s educational videos that Prelinger collects, except now we no longer have to bother with card catalogs and scraps of paper and mini-golf pencils and days lost in the stacks.

The flip side, of course, is the problem of permanence: for better or worse, the Internet is forever. Nothing slips through the cracks anymore. A mostly unnoticed story from the 2012 Republican primary highlighted for me the way the Internet–as–record keeper has changed politics in the span of just twenty years. In his 1990 race for Texas agriculture commissioner, Rick Perry's campaign ran a television ad that showed his opponent, Jim Hightower, arm in arm with Jesse Jackson, whom he'd endorsed for president in 1988. When the ad came out, critics all over the state accused Perry of race baiting.

I'd like to judge the commercial's racial undercurrents myself, but that would require flying to Oklahoma and convincing the curators of the University of Oklahoma's Political Communication Center to show it to me. That's because OU seems to hold the only existing copy of the controversial ad. This seems amazing to me, and far more interesting than the question of Perry's racial insensitivity (which the name of his family ranch pretty much settles). We're talking about a statewide election that took place only twenty-two years ago—and the only copy of this ad is locked up in some Oklahoma library? Like I said: amazing.

Not only is this no longer the case with material created in more recent years; it soon won't be the case, period. Organizations like CSPAN have spent the last few years digitizing thousands and thousands of hours of footage from past decades and making it available to anyone who has the patience to search for it. Before this last election, there could've been no Andrew Kaczynski, the twenty-two-year-old history major at St. John's University and amateur opposition researcher who between classes digs up long-forgotten—and often damning—clips of candidates and posts them on his YouTube channel for campaigns and Super PACs to feast on (including a famously sticking clip of Newt defending a health-insurance mandate in an appearance with Hillary).*

These days, and even more so in days to come, the Internet is our ever-present flypaper. *So* much goes up on the Internet, in fact, that much of it isn't properly edited or vetted first. Remember Herman Cain's sensational Web ad in which his campaign manager puffs a cigarette directly into the camera? This spot was obviously shot in under five minutes and cost less than a pack of Marlboros to produce and post—and it's a *perfect* example of a video that would never, ever pass muster on TV as an *ad*, but did so over and over again as *news*.

Not all outsider art is as primed for prime time. The best (and craziest) exemplar of an only-on-YouTube campaign ad was released by Mike Gravel in 2007—you know, the one in which the former

---

* He is now at buzzfeed.

senator from Alaska stares at the camera for close to an eternity before picking up a large rock, hurling it into a nearby lake, and then walking away as the "gravel2008.us" appears on the screen. That campaign classic (talk about viral!) clocks in at an excruciating two minutes and fifty-one seconds. Without the Internet, candidate Gravel could never have pulled off such a bizarro masterpiece.

And without the Internet, voters wouldn't be able to make their voices heard to the same extent—right? After all, if you asked a child to describe the difference between the Internet and TV, the first thing he'd probably mention is the interactive component of the Internet. McLuhan famously differentiated between hot and cool media, between those mediums like movies that command total absorption (hot) and those like comic books that invite participants to fill in the gaps on their own (cool). We like to think of the Internet as cool—that is, actively calling upon the viewer to determine meaning—but I'm not sure I buy it, especially when it comes to movies.

Just look at the YouTube comment wall (this is the opposite advice I gave POTUS on the same subject, by the way): Is that really proof of the Internet's interactivity? All over the Internet, comment boards are less town hall than urinal wall. The top comment on Gravel's rock ad, "I find this difficult to masturbate to," illustrates this more hilariously than most. Commentators aren't responding to the content at hand, and often not even to one another. They are just—emoting. Shrilly, and often obscenely, making their voices heard in a desperate bid for your attention. But heard by whom exactly?*

---

* I have to say, I find crowd sourcing invaluable in two contexts and only two contexts: Amazon product reviews and recipe websites, particularly the latter. If the consensus is that you need to add less salt, you'd better add less salt.

People on the Internet are "at home" on their laptops, sheltered and emboldened by their own anonymity: "It's okay if I put my feet up on your couch and it's okay if I call you a very, very bad word . . ." This type of vandalism is older than those Paleolithic bears that scratched up the cave drawings at Chauvet. (H/T, Werner Herzog.*) Criticizing YouTube videos or reviewing thrillers on Amazon à la Newt Gingrich is just another means of inserting ourselves into stories, without the usual risks. Or, it should be said, the usual impact. Commenting on YouTube is a form of pretend power: a negative review on Amazon might make you rethink the toaster you were about to buy, but will a YouTube (or blog, or nytimes.com, or Facebook) comment really compel you to shift your political allegiance? Beware the trolls!

Besides housing our access-granting videos and organizational tools, the Internet opened new venues for Obama's message—social networks and mobile devices (OFA had a Facebook app before anyone knew what an app was—I certainty didn't). These connected like-minded voters within even the most specific demographics and alerted supporters—over e-mail, text message, Twitter, whatever—of all activities and gatherings in their area.† Our no-stone-unturned outreach effort—knocking on every digital door—was just another route into communities across the country, a means of finding voters where they lived and providing them with relevant-to-their-lives information about the candidate and his

---

* "Who is to say, perhaps zee bears are zee real artists who we meet facing ourselves in zee dark"—not a real Herzog quote, but you get the idea.
† I'd differentiate this tactic from the rise of Rovian micro-targeting, in which a campaign presents one community of people with information that directly contradicts information they've sent to another community. This tactic is, for reasons I'll explore later, cynical, divisive, and ultimately self-defeating—and not just because of the fact-checking powers of the Internet.

policies. (Being able to figure out on the fly and target it in real time is the new technological frontier in 2012.)

And our team was superlatively smart about pressing on all fronts. It wasn't just the minutely targeted OK Go–type endorsements we posted; I remember the Web ad guys showing me a digital poster that was going to be hung on the virtual walls of a video game. Still, it bears repeating that connecting like-minded people is a very different thing than creating momentum in a vacuum. That was and is as impossible as leading a coup with smartphones alone. The Internet's most basic impact on politics, riots, and revolutions alike is that it can help build momentum for movements and ideas that *already exist*. But it's only a means, not an end. Before the World Wide Web there was the candlelight vigil, and if Twitter didn't exist, people would still be pitching tents and protesting corporate greed in Zuccotti Park. I really do believe that. The Internet has made it easier for people to disperse ideas, but it's still only the platform, not the message itself.

# CHAPTER 10

# THE HOLOGRAPHIC PRESIDENCY

*In which I mistake Davis Guggenheim for Charles Guggenheim*

*and finally get to talk about the "Double Rainbow" guy.*

**O**nce the motion pictures were invented, it was inevitable that the presidency would one day be filmed; this is America, after all, the birthplace of both modern democracy and Hollywood. Accordingly, just about every new technology has been pressed into the service of national memory, used to make records of presidents long before it has caught on with the mainstream.

But though presidents were photographed and filmed soon after cameras and video cameras were invented, the government itself is a notoriously late adopter of technology, and I'm not saying that just so that I can curse the Windows 98 ineptitude of most White House computers.* It actually makes sense. We've all seen companies get ahead of themselves technologically and then just fall apart, or just become victims of even newer technologies.

---

* The old joke is that in film, new technology—video, VHS players, even holograms—
  is always applied to porn first.

What happened to all the Smell-O-Vision theaters from the '50s, that short-lived fad that was supposed to deliver the scents of the cinema? The government is too big to withstand such whimsical experimentation. The same is true of the Super Bowl. The NFL, which has always been at the cutting edge of motion-picture innovation—they had slow-motion video before anyone else—live-streamed the Super Bowl for the first time this year, in 2012, long after that technology had become widespread. Why? Because you don't mess with those ratings unless you know *exactly* what you're doing.

And so naturally, it wasn't really all that revolutionary that we wanted to film Obama all day every day. The desire to film the presidency up close is as old as the medium itself. The real change was that, for the first time, the technology enabled us to do so fairly unobtrusively and for prolonged periods.

Film, like all technology, has a history of incremental progress, with each innovation standing atop the last. And since the debut of the Lumière brothers' *Workers Leaving the Factory at Lyon* in 1895, every advance has been aimed at making film more lifelike, "more real," as it were. Color is one example, sound an even more important one. Though the first "talkie" came out in the mid-'20s, recording sound in a documentary context was all but impossible until mid-century.

Before 1960, sound that could be synched to picture had to be recorded either in studios or with the help of enormous, cumbersome machines. But 1960 held revolutions in both politics and film technology. The same year Nixon and Kennedy faced off on television for the first time, filmmakers could make complete movies in the field, without having to rely on narration recorded after the fact.

The widespread commercial availability of these sound-recording devices triggered an explosion in filmmaking, spawning the cinema verité movement. American documentarians preferred the term Freedom Cinema—just kidding! The American version is called Direct Cinema, and is similar to cinema verité but a little rougher around the edges, less smug, more guts. The formal techniques of both include handheld cameras (made commercially available the previous decade) for mobility, longer edited takes to offer viewers a chance at real observation, and lots of attention to natural sound. The goal was to rely only on the elements of reality, incorporating documentary footage with synchronous sound to simulate a "fly-on-the-wall experience."

So what exactly does Direct Cinema have to do with twenty-first-century politics? Soon after his sound experiments proved successful, Robert Drew trained his focus on glamorous Kennedy duking it out against stodgy Hubert Humphrey during the 1960 Democratic primary in Wisconsin. As in the 2008 election, the behind-the-scenes footage of the two senators contending for the nomination helped one and damaged the other. Both men had agreed to have a camera crew present at their events, and also in their meetings, following them backstage while they heard about polls. The resulting movie, *Primary*, is fascinating. We get to see Kennedy delivering his standard stump speech, and Humphrey working over a group of farmers. We see the candidates work the crowds, shake hands, and ask that simplest but most crucial of questions of the democratic process: Please, will you vote for me?

When I spoke to vérité documentary veteran and *Primary* cameraman Al Maysles (*Salesman* and *Grey Gardens*), he told me that both Humphrey and Kennedy could immediately differentiate them from the journalists. "They look in your eyes," he told me, "and they see what you are doing."

The conventional wisdom about *Primary* is that Kennedy and his beautiful wife come across as glamorous and engaging; he represents something new in American politics. Humphrey, by contrast, appears old-fashioned and a little dumpy. While there's a lot of basic truth in these assessments, I think time has been kind to Humphrey because of how authentic he was. Maysles agrees. He thought both men were real, Humphrey as the man of the people and Kennedy as a man comfortable with his wealth and success, and in the end the people picked their preference for their time and their issue.

*Primary* is some of the first sound and picture we have of our highest elected officials in their less formal moments. And it wasn't just *Primary*. A few years later, for the documentary *Crisis: Behind a Presidential Commitment*, which aired on ABC in September 1963, Kennedy allowed Drew to train his lens on him once again, this time over a twenty-four-hour period inside the Oval Office as he made big decisions about the desegregation of the University of Alabama.

The Drew pieces, both on the campaign trail and in the White House, were made by multi-person crews with lighting technicians, boom operators, and cameramen (sometimes and in the right conditions, as small as two people)—in the case of *Primary*, pretty much the crème de la crème of the American documentary world, not just Albert Maysles, Richard Leacock (cinematographer who did *Louisiana Story* among other greats), and D. A. Pennebaker (*Don't Look Back*) shooting. As this dazzling list indicates, most of the major American documentarians of the next few decades came out of Drew's unit. The *Primary* crew was like a documentary film version of that Ramones concert in London where members of the Sex Pistols, The Clash, and the Damned were all present.

But no matter how prodigiously talented, an outside crew is still just obtrusively *there*, and it would be impossible to sustain such a multipronged cinematic assault for the duration of a presidential campaign. In 1960, even the most streamlined operation would've consisted of cameras running around the clock, which would've been prohibitively expensive, not to mention exhausting for the filmmaker and enervating for the subject. It's also important to remember that, however much access he was given, Drew was also a journalist. When he made *Primary*, he was working for ABC, and while he certainly provided a valuable backstage look at the political process, he was not on the same team as the people he was filming.*

For people who live a good deal of their lives in public, politicians have a distinct (and understandable) discomfort with the kind of permanent record journalists threaten them with—a discomfort that has become only more pronounced in this Internet age, where every awkward exchange with a waitress is preserved forever, and on thousands of websites. Gaffes are inevitable, of course, and the stress of performing 24/7 under the klieg lights for a bustling film crew would be too much for almost anyone. I think the only two living politicians who could tolerate the live-in-video treatment for any length of time are Barack Obama, because of who he is, and Ron Paul, because of the simplicity of what he believes. Even those two would lose patience sooner rather than later. In the spring of 2009, the White House invited NBC to shoot

---

* Decades later, when Pennebaker and Chris Hegedus shot *The War Room*, a documentary on the 1992 Clinton campaign, they decided that rather than fight through the impossible restrictions to access that Bill Clinton would have post–New Hampshire, they would focus on the communications staff of James Carville and George Stephanopoulos, filming them mostly in Arkansas without the candidate or his bubble to contend with. Although they had initially thought it might be the booby prize, the material with Carville turned out to be cinematic gold. Amy Rice and her team on the HBO documentary *By the People*, about the Obama campaign, took the opposite approach; after Iowa, where they shot tons of great footage, they tried to make every single aspect of the campaign all at once, and the final film suffers from the lack of selectivity, becoming disconnected and loose even as *The War Room* gets tighter and tighter.

*Keeping the setup simple in the Oval. (Official White House Photo by Samantha Appleton)*

on-site, and it was like an army had invaded. They were using small cameras, about the same size as mine, but there were just so *many* of them. The crews traveled in groups of three, with as many as six groups roving the cramped West Wing at once. Pretty distracting, to put it mildly. Just do it like you always do it, they told us as we taped the *Weekly Address*; be natural.

The presence of an internal camera crew—one retained by the campaign or political organization itself—should alleviate some of these difficulties, or so documentarian Charles Guggenheim reasoned when he decided to set up shop in DC in 1966. After starting his career at CBS, Guggenheim had shot typical political ads for, among others, the presidential campaign of the TV skeptic Adlai Stevenson in 1956, followed by a successful stint filming the governor of Pennsylvania. Once in Washington, Guggenheim worked as a media adviser to political campaigns, rigorously applying the lessons of vérité filmmaking to the political process.

In the 1960s, Guggenheim worked inside many political races, most notably RFK's. He won an Academy Award for the retrospective convention film shown after RFK's death. In the next cycle, 1972, when George McGovern ran for president, Guggenheim—by now an old Washington hand—tried to capture the populist nature of the campaign by making TV ads that chronicled the candidate's extemporaneous interactions with people he met all along the campaign trail. (Sound familiar?) But, alas, according to the Living Room Candidate, an excellent website devoted to presidential ads, the public viewed the candidate portrayed in these ads as compassionate, but not necessarily "presidential."* (There it is again, that inescapable line . . . ) Guggenheim himself thought the ads ended up being ineffective.†

Looking back on the McGovern ads, it seems doubtful if the

---

* I had serious Guggenheim on the brain once in Butte, Montana, while getting ready for a Fourth of July parade. After hearing that a famous filmmaker by the name of Guggenheim would be there to film material for the convention, I went around telling everyone how we should all be so honored and I had no idea he was even alive and did they even realize that this was like the original DC art crasher? I managed to work up a great deal of excitement within the campaign until Katie Lillie said, "Are you sure, he also directed that Al Gore movie." I said that wasn't possible, he'd be way too old . . . and then I saw him. So clearly too young. I soon afterward discovered that the Guggenheim in Montana that day was Charles's son Davis, who was still in the family business and had indeed directed the filmed lecture *An Inconvenient Truth* as well as the president's convention film *A Mother's Promise* and 2012's *The Road We've Traveled*.

† The 1980 presidential cycle, which we have previously described as a low point in political media, was the last go-around for Charles Guggenheim and his idea of Verite Politics. He was pushed out of Ted Kennedy's campaign in the primaries for more typical (and negative) styles of advertising.

public's tepid reaction can really be chalked up to problems with Guggenheim's technique. Rather, it seems to be a measure of the distance we the viewers have traveled in how we perceive politicians in particular and media in general. These days, we're used to getting an up-close-and-personal, around-the-clock look at our celebrities; we all but demand it. It could also be that there was "just something about McGovern" that voters didn't respond to; I believe FOX has trademarked this elusive quality the "X Factor." (Incidentally, we met McGovern at a campaign stop in South Dakota when he endorsed Senator Obama; I had a hard time passing up the serious steaks that they were serving in the press file and came out just in time. In his age and fragility, he had an almost ecclesiastical presence, though I admit maybe lacking a certain edge that people like in their POTUS.)

Another issue is money. Even when he was working on the inside of a campaign, Guggenheim couldn't cover his candidates around the clock for the simple reason that filming them all the time was just too exhaustive and expensive. Although the handheld camera and portable sound recorder had simplified the work, the cost was still prohibitive, with even the simplest shoot requiring a never-ending supply of film stock, someone to run and move lights, and possibly an assistant to change out film magazines.

Even in 2008, AKPD or GMMB had to pick and choose when to send their ad crews to cover an event. And it was precisely the expense of blanket coverage that gave us an opening to take advantage of the one-man-band alternative. Now, I'm not talking about my film school plot to tape microphones inside his shirt and try to sneak a 16mm film camera and sound system into Walt Disney World to make an unauthorized documentary about trash collection in the park—that was thwarted! But seriously, with the help of small but powerful video cameras, we could now record a high volume of material with minimal intrusion, using equipment so compact that it could all fit inside a single solar-powered backpack. The ability for a single person to cover an event as massive as an international peace treaty signing is evolutionarily new—and, incidentally, one of the big driving forces behind the explosion of reality TV. (In the case of the latter, the less obtrusive the equipment, the wackier the footage.) Curiosity was never lacking.

Though we were a lot less in-your-face than the NBC crews, I'm definitely not claiming that we were invisible or unnoticed; that was neither possible nor even really all that desirable. Even when his personality is a bit less boisterous than mine, a filmmaker is never a fly on the wall but rather an instigator, whose mere presence causes things to happen. This is the argument of French documentarian and anthropologist Jean Rouch. Rouch set out to prove this theory in his 1960 film, *Chronicle of a Summer*, in which he asks a wide range of Parisians a simple question, "Are you happy?" and then profiles several respondents as they show him their lives. Throughout *Chronicle of a Summer*, you can distinctly feel the camera's presence. That was Rouch's whole point. It feels disrespectful to call this wonderful film the progenitor of reality TV, but I'm afraid that's exactly what it was.

I'm always seeking out that line between present and absent, between noticeable and unobtrusive. Sometimes, when the stakes are high, I intentionally fade into the background, but far more often I've sought out a certain visibility. The size of the camera I use is appropriate for this balancing act. If my camera were any bigger, I'd be in the way; any smaller, and people might not see that I'm packing. ("What is that, your rifle?" Obama asked me once when I started using a strap for the camera, slinging it over my shoulder.) Given the situations I'm filming, I generally think it'd be unfair for people not to realize I'm filming them, but I don't exactly have the luxury of tapping everyone on the shoulder. So the solution is to carry a moderately conspicuous camera and never hide behind the curtains (or, you know, cut my hair all that often).

Lucky for me, we're now living in a Goldilocks era of camera size; they offer just the right balance between conspicuousness and convenience. Of course, given how miniaturized some A/V equipment has gotten, there's almost no justification for people's objections to filming trials based on the disruption a camera might cause in the courtroom. If people really want to see the trial of Saddam Hussein or Hosni Mubarak or Slobadan Milošević, or even the inner workings of their own Supreme Court, they shouldn't accept this flimsy argument. Fond of proclaiming on the stump that "sunshine is the best disinfectant," Obama made a firm commitment to this type of transparency. Posting meetings on the White House website has turned out to be incredibly difficult, and the obstacles are both human and technological. Despite leaps and bounds in date and access people have been cynical about this commitment, and I understand, as someone literally trying to make it happen, but the White House hasn't been the one throwing up roadblocks. (It's the people he's meeting with who tend to be more gun-shy, particularly the Republican leaders who didn't exactly benefit from their caucus's one spontaneous on-air encounter with the president.)

Of course, the further miniaturization of cameras continues at such an astonishing rate that we're now all walking around with HD cameras, most of them on phones. Our politicians' fear of being constantly filmed is fast becoming a reality. Who should be more worried: the politician with "macaca" on the tip of his tongue, or the professional cameraman whose job is being usurped by amateurs?

I would argue the former. Granted, these days, pretty much

*This monkey self-portrait is public domain, right? Can we ask the lawyers? (Photo by the Monkey/Caters News Agency)*

everyone can take a good picture, even if by accident; it's the contemporary equivalent of monkeys typing Shakespeare. In the case of this picture, it looks pretty good, but when you can't leave your images to chance, when you want to produce consistently good work and actually attract an audience, you have to rely on professionals.

Even in this lawless new medium, it's a mistake to throw out the old rules of art. I'm always getting technical questions from folks determined to make videos. Whether they are advocating for organic food, say, or excoriating the supercommittee's failure, they usually come to me with little or no background in film and zero preparation for the task at hand. And while I think it's great that technology has made filmmaking more affordable and "smaller," I do worry that those who don't respect the medium do themselves and their causes little good. Macaca-monitoring trackers definitely have their place on the modern campaign, but so should people capable of producing videos that others will actually want to watch.

Wherever you click, the Internet's Wild West atmosphere has given a huge lift to "unproduced," "raw," or "natural" material— terms that have lost all meaning by dint of repetition: from stoner guys exclaiming over rainbows to borderline-unhinged Alaskans walking sloooowly into the sunset. But regardless of its length, or how much it cost to make, an Internet video should share the same basic characteristics of any good TV segment—it should be well shot and carefully edited, possess basic entertainment value, and be worth viewers' time. Film grammar—the rules by which an audience understands a film—isn't changed much on the Internet, there's nothing *too* innately different about big screens and monitors when you're putting together a video.* Frame sizes have tightened to reflect the smaller screens of most computers; movies are all about wide shots, TV's specialty is medium shots, and the Web is primarily close-ups. But all these experiences have far more in common than their technical distinctions might suggest.

Even if the migration of content from TV to Internet wasn't an all-out revolution like, say, the addition of sound to movies, the way we consume Web video *is* different. For one thing, people consume more Web videos at work than at home, which completely changes the whole viewing experience. I can't give you a

---

* A great example is from that greatest of examples, *Citizen Kane*. There is a point where young Charles Foster Kane begins a sentence in the past and finishes it as older Charles Foster Kane in the present, thus taking the audience from one point to the other in time. Somebody had to think of that; it didn't just happen naturally.

behavioral study, but for me it means listening to a video with headphones on while simultaneously checking my e-mail and paying my wireless bill and reading about last night's debate, never with fewer than four different Web pages open on my browser. The experience is both more individualized and more schizophrenic than when I sit down to watch a preselected TV show at home in the company of family and pets.

Online video has to be twice as good as other types of videos precisely because the viewer is paying half as much attention. You have to work that much harder to engage the distracted viewer, making sure to keep all the important information in the soundtrack—and, believe it or not, pulling off a smooth audio track is actually much more technically challenging than a smooth visual track. At the end of the day, a movie is a movie is a movie, and you have to do whatever it takes to hold your audience.

# CHAPTER 11

# THE PRESIDENT'S WEEKLY INTERNET RADIO YOUTUBE ADDRESS

*In which I confess my ignorance of professional wrestling and name the last honest teleprompter operator in America.*

"Arun," I got used to hearing, "you have the best job in the world, you lucky SOB!" And I humbly acknowledge that official White House videographer—the first in history, thank you very much!—was definitely one of the top half-dozen jobs in Washington. Let's call it the third best at the White House. (Trip director Marvin Nicholson gets the number one slot, and chief official White House photographer Pete Souza runs a close second.) However exciting it is, though, to film history in the making around the clock, it's not all turkey sandwiches on private jets; and even when it is, those sandwiches can be pretty unappetizing. "There can be something very sad about a turkey sandwich," the president himself once said on a bus in New Hampshire.

But something actually worth complaining about were the tapings. Lots and lots and lots of tapings. We might look happy in that NBC special, just because NBC is filming us filming him. Most of the time, the scene was far less jocular. In fact, I'd say that the Friday night ritual of taping the president's *Weekly Address* and sundry other direct-to-camera messages was the biggest burden that comes with the privilege of being the presidential videographer.

This president does many, many more video tapings than any of his predecessors, who did them only for the occasional meeting or convention. We started doing them so regularly for several reasons: because we've gotten very good at them, they take up very little time and, since we figured out how to do them ourselves, they cost almost no money. When the threshold shifted from "we have to hire a studio" to "we have to go grab Arun," the spike in volume was all but inevitable. We were, in a sense, victims of our own success, but we repeatedly found that there was no faster way to communicate directly with the American people than to have Obama record an address (even if, as some have argued, the increase in the number of taped messages has led to a decrease in their rhetorical oomph).

The taping mania got under way fairly soon after the first primary votes were tallied. Since the campaign had a video camera (and me) within arm's reach, we did a lot of tapings, some on the fly, some on a whim. Sometimes both. On the campaign plane, I recorded BO delivering a message that was slated to play at the opening of a Grateful Dead concert. Whenever a message was too long for the candidate to commit to memory, we'd pay a teleprompter guy decent cash to come out to wherever we were and roll the teleprompter in front of the camera. After the taping Obama would pose for a picture with the teleprompter operator, who would then invoice the campaign for the honor. If we were pressed for time, or the teleprompter guy wasn't available, we'd sometimes try to make do without one, with mixed results.

Once, Jessica Slider and I balanced a burning-hot laptop over the camera lens, causing nerve damage to our fingers so that the candidate could opt out of public financing. Another time, in South Carolina (possibly, now that I think of it, the same day that the large woman fell out of the stands), we had to pull together an impromptu setup so that Obama could be beamed live into *The Colbert Report.* Gibbs took one look at the cue cards that an intern had scrawled out illegibly in Magic Marker on several pieces of poster board—the effect was straight out of an eighth-grade science fair—and said, "Arun is going to hold those up." And so I did, looking like a very JV Bob Dylan in the world's worst remake of the "Subterranean Homesick Blues."

We continued with these creative, ad hoc solutions for some months, until the fateful day at HQ when I asked America's most honest teleprompter operator (can we give Sean Graham-White a shout-out?) how much teleprompters actually cost.

The guy thought for a moment, then cited a staggeringly low figure: less than a thousand dollars or roughly three times as much as it cost to hire him for an hour. "Really?" I asked, completely taken aback. "So what's the deal—are they really hard to use or something?"

The guy shook his head. "Not especially," he said, "but you really do have to know your reader." By that point, I knew my reader very well indeed, and my only remaining question was whether we should buy one or two machines.

We settled on the smallest, most portable model and tossed it in with the rest of our ruthlessly efficient mobile studio. Within hours of its delivery on the day of our makeshift Passover seder in the basement of the Hershey, Pennsylvania, Sheraton, we started installing the necessary software on our computers (by which I mean I forced motorcade coordinator Herbie Ziskend's Windows

computer into service; people feared us slightly for sudden technological tyranny like that) and soon had our new setup in near-
constant use.

Despite the added convenience of our teleprompter, everyone
from Eric Lesser, the baggage handler, who might have to pull gear
off the plane at the last minute, to the candidate himself, hated
these so-called direct-to-cameras, which usually had an extremely
small target audience—"The Livestock Poetry Association of Ken-
tucky *really* needs a video message?" Obama would groan. I started
to notice him having a Pavlovian negative reaction to me in particularly direct-to-camera-heavy weeks. "Hey, man," he'd say, then
pause to look at me warily. "Wait, do we have a taping or something?"

It didn't help that the timing and setting of these messages
tended to be wildly, comically inappropriate. We once did a taping
for an Alaskan union from a Miami hotel while en route to Puerto
Rico. Another bleary afternoon, Marvin Nicholson noticed that we
were about to tape a message commemorating the Prague Spring
directly in front of a North Carolina flag. Needless to say, both
I and the National Security adviser involved were appropriately
embarrassed.

Direct-to-cameras were also fraught with annoying glitches so
wide-ranging we couldn't possibly catch them all in advance. At
our very first taping with our own teleprompter, for the World
Wrestling Federation, we scanned the list of wrestling stars and
found more than a few unfamiliar names. "I don't know much
about wrestling," I remember asking a Secret Service agent after the
taping, "Did we pronounce everything right?" He shook his head
sadly. In the end, we had to retape the message anyway, because
Gibbs thought it was too boring for the intended audience: "C'mon,
guys, this is professional wrestling," he said in his inimitable

Alabama drawl. But at least we didn't have to spend a single extra campaign dollar on extra takes or rewrites.

Months later, by which point we were all experts, we were in the same Hershey, Pennsylvania, Sheraton when we all just lost it. It was well after midnight, we'd been up since dawn, and with some half-dozen tapings to run through, Obama—and soon the rest of us, too—came down with a bad case of the giggles. Which gave us the giggles, which in turn gave him the giggles more.

"So, uh, did you see the game last night?" the unflappable Marvin asked in an attempt to distract the hysterical candidate.

"No, because I was busy," Obama said, rocking with laughter. "Running for president."

A full twenty minutes later, when he'd finally calmed down long enough to look at the script, Obama burst out laughing again. "Oh, man," he said, wiping away a tear. "It's also funny that no one bothered to spell-check this!"—setting off yet another explosion of contagious laughter.

On the tape you can clearly hear the director of advance barking "Arun!" as if the whole thing was my fault, but I swear, Emmett, he was making *me* laugh!

I don't mention this just as an amusing anecdote (which it is, I hope!) but as a stark contrast to the opening scene in *The Selling of the President*, where Joe McGinniss describes the dark paranoid atmosphere of a Nixon taping at the Merv Griffin studio in NYC. An account I hadn't read until after working with Barack Obama.

That was another thing. Because he does so much of his own writing and is a skilled speaker to begin with, the nonhysterical Obama could usually nail these direct-to-cameras on the first try, even when it meant improving the language as he went along. And when he didn't, he would often stop the take himself to fine-tune the wording. We knew he found the tapings to be a chore, though, and so whenever he asked for a second take on a message that seemed fine the first time around, we had reason to be suspicious.

"Let's just try one more, and really nail it," he said once to me and Denis McDonough after a taping about a rocket attack against Israel.

Puzzled, I shook my head. "Nah, no need—the first take was totally fine." Before I could say more, a staffer poked his head through the door to hustle the candidate out to debate prep. It was slightly heartening for me to realize that *something* was worse than direct-to-cameras on the "least desirable activities" list. He actually identified the "Shine Police," the half dozen of us who would remark when he looked "shiny" on camera and needed product, as one of his main pet peeves in the WH to the AP in July 2009.

But there was one kind of taping that was always great: those with Barack and Michelle Obama together. The couple was always extremely funny, cracking self-deprecating jokes and critiquing each other's performances. They were also always genuinely glad to get a chance to spend time together in the middle of a workday, even if it was just for a taping. We always looked forward to the annual Christmas *Weekly Address* for precisely this reason. "And don't go posting that!" the First Lady might say just as you were thinking, "I should cut something together out of this great footage!"

Another upside to these interminable tapings was that, by the time Obama got to the White House, his advisers understood how to use them as a policy tool. In 2009, around the time of the Iranian riots, the State Department decided that the president should record an address in commemoration of the Persian New Year that directly engaged with the Iranian people, without the interference of their repressive government. We were able to tape this message

*If it's Friday, it must be time for the* Weekly Address. *(Official White House Photo by Samantha Appleton)*

right away, and within minutes have it ready for the State Department to translate. The president has continued to tape these New Year's messages to Iranians, getting more attention than ever during 2011's Arab Spring.

Our familiarity with the daily grind of tapings also made it much easier, when the time came, to begin recording the president's *Weekly Address* to the nation on video and not just, as in administrations past, audiotape.

The *Weekly Address* has a storied history in American politics. FDR first started broadcasting his radio "fireside chats" in 1929, during his first term as governor of New York. He brought the practice with him to the White House. Every subsequent president has delivered such addresses to the nation, each in his own style. Clinton would invite visitors into the Oval Office to watch the recording, while George W. Bush would do them on his own, early on Saturday mornings. Until the Obama administration, they had one thing in common—they were always audio-only.

While in retrospect it seems inevitable that the *Weekly Address* would one day be videotaped, it wasn't at all clear how or when that would happen. We began recording the official Democratic response to President Bush's *Weekly Address* once Obama had accepted his party's nomination, but this, too, had been audio-only. After the election, we decided it was time to take it to its next level.

We shot the first video *Weekly Address* at Transition HQ in downtown Chicago, and it was, not to put too fine a point on it, a complete and total mess. Secret Service didn't want us to use rooms with any Chicago landmarks visible in the distance because people might be able to study the shots to determine exactly where we were taping. Instead we chose the most depressing, windowless room in the building. Ted Chiodo, deputy staff secretary during Transition and the man in charge of POTUS-E's extensive paperwork, diverted some gifts destined for the archives to give the set a homier look. We arranged books and various bric-a-brac people and a few stray family snapshots of Michelle, Malia, and Sasha. (One of these props, a family picture we'd hurriedly enlarged on a photocopier, sits behind the Resolute desk in the Oval Office to this day; pointing it out was one of the highlights of the West Wing tours I gave.)

Obama viewed the results of our interior decorating with marked skepticism. "That's a lot of wood," he said, indicating the faux wood paneling that failed to give the room a more executive look, "and a lot of weird stuff on my desk." Yep, it was.

A lot of people watched that first *Weekly Address*, and a lot of them criticized it. One website made a diagram of every single

*Recording the* Weekly Address *during Transition. "Is this really the best way to do this?" (Photos by Alexandra Eaton/Presidential Transition Team)*

object displayed on the screen and pondered the possible significance of each. I admit that the variety and just plain bizarreness of the assembled props made the room look more like a garage sale than a future president's office, but what could you do? The president's soon-to-be senior adviser, David Axelrod, put it perfectly; he said it looked like a "hostage video."

For our next *Weekly Address*, we tried to transform the soulless corporate skyscraper into a passable simulacrum of the Oval Office. There are only about three people alive today with the skill to transform the Spartan blinds of the vice president's corner office into the curtained splendor of the fake Oval, and I'd like to thank all of them for their contributions to our country. We did it, guys.

For all these art-direction difficulties, the advantages of having a video address became apparent as early as our Transition rollout events. For example, rather than hold yet another press conference for HUD nominee Shaun Donovan, someone suggested we have Donovan appear in the *Weekly Address* instead. When I expressed concerns that the Stand Behind would translate poorly to a seated *Weekly Address* (the Sit Behind is still years away from being perfected; I hear the Chinese are working on it as well), it was the president-elect himself who came up with an elegant solution: take some still photos of his conversations with Donovan that afternoon and insert them into the video while Obama described his strengths and qualifications. Obama even swung by my desk to see how the montage had come out: "I see we went with black and white . . . classy! Can we do the Ken Burns thing?" (While we snapped photos, Donovan had stopped me from recounting the sorry epilogue of my Brooklyn subletter fiasco. He was still the housing commissioner of NYC at the time, and didn't want any conflicts . . . likewise, very classy.)

Once we made the transition to the White House, the apparatus was all in place to continue filming the *Weekly Addresses*, with ready-made backdrops and military videographers and none of the improvising we'd had to do during Transition. On the day of inauguration, I'd scoped out the real Oval Office for possible angles on Obama's first *Weekly Address* as president. "Which angle do you think we should shoot it from on Friday?" I asked Robert Gibbs that afternoon, indicating the options inside the Oval.

"I don't think we're going to be shooting the weekly in here that often," he told me. "I mean, the Oval Office is kind of a big deal. It's the Oval Office, you know? Come find me later, and we can scout out more options." Gibbs was right. In the future, we'd shoot most weeklies on the first floor of the residence like the library or the Blue Room, which would be familiar to anyone who's taken the public White House tour, or just past the tour boundaries, in the Diplomatic Reception Room, where Roosevelt had recorded the fireside chats, or the Map Room.

Most of the challenges of the *Weekly Address* could serve as ciphers of the difficulties attendant on government filmmaking in general. For one thing, the script never got written until the very last minute—and by "last minute," I mean "ninety seconds before I hit 'record.'" It's important for the material to be current, relevant, and, most crucially, accurate. Navigating the line between the need to wait and the need to anticipate is one of the perennial tasks of journalism and government alike, and a thorn in the side of the filmmaker.

Updating the format has been an even greater stumbling block, and it's one of my big regrets that I left the White House before figuring out a way to make the *Weekly Address* more visually interesting—not just with b-roll or stills but perhaps with archival or, better yet, backstage footage. The *Weekly Address* is an institution for a reason, and it's the most-watched video on WhiteHouse .gov, but I still wish we could've made it more appealing to a wider swath of people. Alas, that's one of the many projects I left undone while searching for a means to satisfy my creative impulses within the confines of government. (Another is the stop-motion camera I left in the First Lady's vegetable garden, which I fear is totally overrun with insects by now.) Really should have cleaned that up before I left!

# CHAPTER 12

# THE HAIRCUT STRIKE

*In which I lurk around hoping someone will notice how hard*
*I've been working and "take a chance on the kid with half-tied*
*bow tie."*

On the evening of January 20, 2009, while the newly inaugurated president was preparing for the evening's balls, I was at a computer in the Outer Oval Office, half-dressed and frantically refreshing a YouTube video on how to tie a bow tie. Next to me, a concerned Katie Johnson, the president's personal secretary, was learning the phone systems, but the right phone never rang when it was supposed to. The so-called first New Media presidency wasn't getting off to a very high-tech start.

I didn't yet know my way around the White House, having only visited twice before. The first time was soon after Senator McCain announced that he was suspending his campaign so that he could fly back to Washington and fix the economy. While Obama and McCain met with President Bush in the Cabinet Room, the Democratic nominee's traveling press corps had crowded outside the West Wing entrance, jockeying for position with the

*Marvin takes pity on me before we head to the inaugural balls. (Photo by Jen Samawat)*

Republican nominee's traveling press corps and the White House press corps. Everyone wanted to be first in line to take notes on the statements that were surely forthcoming from the candidates.

The public may never see exactly how badly that meeting went, since there was no official White House videographer to document it, but it was bad enough that the anticipated statements never materialized.

"Hey, we're leaving!" Katie Lillie, our overworked and overwrought press wrangler, made a looping motion over her head, offering no further explanation. The reporters all murmured in confused disappointment, and for the first time I understood that the White House was also a sort of lightbulb, a permanent space that must either generate news or risk actively generating no news.

My second visit to the White House had taken place shortly

after the election, when President Bush gave President-elect Obama a tour of his soon-to-be home. (That day, Obama had with characteristic calmness observed, "Hey, Arun—these are some pretty nice digs, huh?") I was there strictly in the capacity of still photographer, and, in fact, Bush's people had reacted with a combination of surprise and horror when my name had been submitted for security clearance. "Why are you sending your YouTube guy as a photographer?" "YouTube guy" was pronounced in the tone usually reserved for "national security threat."

I was completely disoriented as I trotted down the colonnade after Bush's photographer, Eric Draper, passing the press's "remote" cameras that clicked as we went past. It wasn't until President Bush grumbled, "Hey, pal, close the door," at me that I realized we were in the Oval Office. During the private meeting between the president and the president-elect that followed, the rest of us paired off with our counterparts: Robert Gibbs with Dana Perino, Reggie Love with Bush's body man (and fellow Blue Devil) Jared Weinstein, and Eric with me.

Eric showed me the White House Photo Office, or rather the small portion of it that was housed in the West Wing: a room and attached closet that had been the White House barbershop for most of the twentieth century. "This is where you'll be," Eric said.

"I doubt that," I said, looking at the cramped quarters that could really only reasonably hold a single still photographer and his gear. "Where does the New Media team work?" I asked him. "That's probably where I'll be."

Eric wasn't really sure—maybe in one of the buildings across the street? "You know, the military do a lot of our videography," he said.

I'd heard this, but I had no idea what to make of it. That seemed to be pretty much par for the course during those confusing days.

*Couples. Incoming and outgoing. (Photos by Arun Chaudhary/Presidential Transition Team)*

As for Washington, well—what could I say about Washington? If you'd told me ten years ago that I'd ever live in Washington, DC, for an extended period of time, I would've ROFL-ed in your face. The District is physically cramped, architecturally unimaginative, three-quarters legit southern town and the remaining quarter overcrowded by government functionaries, sprawling over its too-tight borders into the otherwise reasonable states of Maryland and Virginia.

Washington's mean, too, meaner than Boston in a Ben Affleck movie. Once at the airport, I sat next to a soldier on his way home from Iraq and welcomed him back to Washington. "It must be a relief to be back in the District," I said.

The solider shook his head. "Nah," he retorted. "At least over there you get to shoot back."

DC is a one-industry town, but unlike the scrums of Hollywood and Silicon Valley, it has only two players. It often seems, in fact, barely big enough for one government and two political parties. Instead of building camaraderie, the competition and close quarters breed deep, deep contempt.

For all its geographic constrictions, DC is even smaller mentally, a town so focused on itself that it wouldn't be surprising to see the deputy director of the Department of the Interior reading a book about the former deputy director of the Department of the Interior. Jobs are often indistinguishable from, or equated with, the people who previously held them. "Who is Ray LaHood's Reggie?" I've heard time and again. And: "Oh, are you the new Scott?" strangers repeatedly asked me at the beginning of my tenure. Still haven't met Scott.

Everywhere I went, the learning curve was steep. By inauguration night, I was no more familiar with the labyrinthine corridors of the West Wing, and even after Marvin helped me get the bow tie in place, I was afraid to stray too far from the safety of the Outer Oval. We'd had Secret Service protection from the time I'd joined the campaign, and even more postelection, but the security level inside the White House was a different matter altogether.

Washington had been filled with many such surprises. A few weeks before the inauguration, we'd flown in from Chicago on what would've been Air Force Two if only Vice President Dick Cheney had been present. Aboard the government plane, we were served chicken parm with a side of pasta on real plates, with real silverware. After thousands of meals in foil and plastic, we were completely wowed. My intern, Alex, who'd been spared the soggy turkey sandwiches of O-Force One during the campaign, laughed at our over-the-top delight.

But despite the major menu improvements, the downsides soon outweighed the perks. I had trouble dealing with Beltway bureaucracy, like the necessity of acquiring what seemed like dozens of multicolored ID badges and pins for every function; I soon started bringing a special camera to work to give to all the people dropping by to borrow a camera for an ID photo. It didn't help that with each passing day, my role within the administration was getting harder to define. During Transition, I had repeatedly had the same conversation about the nature of my job, what it was going to be in the administration, and why exactly it was necessary. It first seemed logical that I'd take a slot in the New Media department, which oversaw the official White House website, but when I discussed this possibility with the director of New Media, Macon Phillips, we both kept coming up with reasons why it wouldn't be a good fit.

The New Media team was small, and its video director would be responsible for pretty much all the video content on the White House website—static direct-to-cameras, live chats with staffers explaining various administration policies, PSAs (public service announcements) with other agencies and outside groups. Not that I wouldn't occasionally be charged with all these tasks, but still, there was only so much I could juggle, and the New Media video lead would definitely *not* have time to traipse after the president all day. Since I was the only videographer who had the most established rapport with the president, everyone wanted me to stay in the bubble with him. They would say, "We want you to keep doing what you're doing," but the White House was a place that ran on precedents, which meant I needed an official title and slot in the budget. I didn't necessarily want to be just "the guy with the camera near the president"—I wanted to be creative, too—but saw no choice but to take a chance on "let's try to figure something else out." Sometimes you just have to leave that luggage set behind and pick the mystery behind door number two.

I soon got a shock when Macon asked me to meet with the visual information commander of the White House Communications Agency (WHCA), a part of the White House Military Office, which was formed in 1942 with service members from all five branches of the military who had been brought together to serve the president in various capacities, from running the White House Mess to providing secure communications with commanders in the field.

Why the military? Because their thirty-third commander in chief asked for film support. And since they'd provided this service to Roosevelt, they were prepared to offer it to others as the need arose. For instance, Commander Bean told us WHCA knew they would have to step up their game because from what they had seen on the campaign, the incoming administration would be asking for a lot of content and coverage.

Naval photographers had been assigned to the president since 1949, with film crews coming on board in 1960 (the same year Drew shot *Primary*). Later, President Johnson expanded the military's role providing audiovisual support and in fact considered tearing down the WH movie theater to make an in-house studio. I hate to suggest paving over history, but this really would have made a lot of things very convenient. Nixon slowed down the program and in the '70s the unit was codified and called White House Television Office (WHTV) to "provide videotaped documentation of the activities of the POTUS." These servicemen and -women normally served in combat camera units and rotated in and out of the White House. These were videographers with a ton of talent, not to mention guts, who knew how to keep their cameras focused over the course of firefights and covert missions. (Famed documentary cameraman Richard Leacock, who worked with Robert Drew to develop sound-synch technology in the early 1960s, had gotten his start as a combat cameraman in World War II.)

WHTV was responsible for filming official presidential tapings and public appearances, then readying the footage for the White House website, any press outlets that requested it, and ultimately the National Archives. The mission as I can quote it goes something like this: "This documentation of constitutional, statutory, official and ceremonial duties includes official functions at the White House, 'in-towners,' trips within the continental United States and to foreign countries, and as much of the president's personal life as he desires. WHCA Camera Crews cover . . . : events, speeches, public addresses and appearances, meetings with cabinet members and foreign dignitaries, weekly radio addresses, live and taped, on the eighteen acres and on the road, videotapings of PSAs, head of state visits including arrival ceremonies; official phone calls and tele-conference, media interviews for magazines and television, break-fast lunches, state dinners, holiday receptions, receiving lines, press conferences and bill signings."*

As this exhaustive list indicated to some extent, the military videographers were getting a lot of footage of the president—not

---

* Interestingly, I heard the same rumor from a number of sources that WHTV's actual purpose was to film POTUS for security reasons, and because of this they couldn't take shots that didn't have the POTUS in it because that would mean they'd be "taking their eyes off the ball." Turns out just to be a rumor, so take the damn establishing shots, guys!

just official phone calls but private moments with aides and family. When preparing a documentary on the national parks in the summer of 2009, I reviewed film that naval crews had shot over more than half a century and marveled at the evolution of American casual wear over the decades. A friend making a doc on Whitney Young recently e-mailed me to say she was looking at *LBJ's West Wing Weeks*, which she received from the LBJ Library, which had been shot more as a historical document for future generations.*

I myself didn't stumble upon this archival footage until long after I joined the White House, when a few career White House staffers, who'd been around since the time when "it all changed," pointed me to it. After several WHTV staffers were called in to testify about the Monica Lewinsky incident by the office of then Speaker Newt Gingrich, WHTV videographers were kept clear of a lot of nonofficial events, and had severely restricted access to just about everything else.

In spite of these institutional obstacles, White House TV sounded like the right department for me. The not-so-small problem with this plan was that WHTV was part of the military, with no spot for a civilian like me. In order to film the commander in chief, did I have to enlist? I had a bizarre conversation on this subject with Commander Bean, WHCA's visual information commander, who kept alternating between talk of "psyops" and the

---

* To this day, the military produces an amazing amount of footage all over the world, and while it's available to the public, it's not often packaged or presented with public consumption in mind. You'd have to do what my friend did and go to the relevant presidential library and know exactly what you wanted to find. I hope the George W. Bush Library will be the first to have most of these archives available in digitized form when it opens; his administration has had to do a lot of the heavy lifting of the transition to digital.

need to revive the "Barney-cam" video for the Obamas' as-yet-unchosen dog.* When I joked that I was considering joining the National Guard to keep my job, the commander sized me up, looked alarmed, and then shook his head sternly.

After that shaky introduction, and of course the inevitable culture clash between art school and the world's finest military, working with WHCA was my greatest learning experience at the WH, and not just because I got the inside scoop on all the interbranch rivalries, which reminded me of the mild racism of a good '80s comedy. Everyone agreed that I definitely looked like an air force guy because of my unruly hair. "Hey!" the actual air force guys objected.

But no better alternatives presented themselves, and as Transition wound to a close, I started to wonder if I was hanging around for a position that was unnecessary or undesirable. Inauguration day would resolve my misgivings.

The White House TV military videographers were shooting the main speech as they'd been preparing to do for weeks. Because of Capitol politics (I won't bore you with a lot of Article I stuff), I was mostly relegated to hanging out in one of the many kitchens in the vast Capitol complex that was serving as a staff hold. Of course, I was used to these, er, offbeat locations. For most of the nominee's convention speech in Denver, I'd been crouched behind a folding table backstage, preparing for that night's joint Obama-Biden taping. More often than not, there is an upside to these unlikely vantage points, and indeed, on the morning of the inauguration, through a small window in the kitchen, the waitstaff and

---

* Further evidence there's nothing new under the sun in politics or media: the Bush administration's Barney cam was but a pale shadow of the amazing six-minute one-reel film made during the FDR administration of the Scottish terrier Fala giving a tour of his master's executive residence.

I watched George W. Bush depart the Capitol for his last Marine One ride. It's great footage that I never could've shot from a more conventional location.

From the roof of the Capitol, where I eventually ended up surrendering my camera (I told you it was complicated!), I watched the military videographers filming Obama's speech. Later that afternoon, with my head sticking out of the sunroof of Axelrod and Valerie Jarrett's limousine as it rolled down Pennsylvania Avenue in the freezing cold, I watched these same videographers shooting the parade from the press truck. Later that night, they captured POTUS's remarks on the grueling circuit of inaugural balls, as well as his (many, many) ceremonial first dances with FLOTUS.

What'd the military team miss? Quite a lot, actually. They were eminently well prepared and professional, but their focus was different. They weren't there when the motorcade of golf carts ferried POTUS and FLOTUS to and from the different balls being held inside the cavernous Washington Convention Center, and they didn't capture the visual incongruity of tuxes and designer gowns sweeping into gritty freight elevators and past loading docks. They didn't film POTUS meeting his military aides, the officers who, among other duties, safeguard the "nuclear football" for the commander in chief. Those hands holding that bag—where was that close-up going to come from if I didn't shoot it?

It was the in-between moments that were left out, those same transition shots that are so often missing from an undergraduate student film. And transitions are often the most interesting parts of life, whether it's the chaotic change from water to steam or BO having a private moment by a monument in Berlin immediately before launching into a speech for an audience of two hundred thousand. These moments inform what comes before and after and in a situation like inauguration, you need a lot of access and a great deal of trust to fill in those blanks. But then, that's precisely what separates art from journalism or a documentary from reality TV. These moments aren't just transition shots that establish a location or ambience shots that establish a mood. They constitute both context and subtext. It's this material that gives the American people a deeper understanding of the presidency and the character of this particular president. My job, once it had snapped into focus, was to fill in the cracks, to find the proverbial line in what I saw and what I shot and how I put it together. It would require an artist's touch, and the kind of trust I'd spent the better part of two years building with my subject.

I'm not claiming that behind-the-scenes video footage was unprecedented in American presidential history—by no means. The navy has great footage of Warren Harding playing medicine ball with his cabinet. Lady Bird Johnson was an amateur filmmaker, and though her most-seen work is of her husband in his early years, she also filmed FDR in the late 1930s and early 1940s, when LBJ was a congressman. You can still see this excellent footage at the FDR Library.

A better-known look inside the Oval Office is *Crisis*, the film Robert Drew shot of JFK during the desegregation of the University of Alabama in 1963. This groundbreaking film blurs the line between journalism and intimate home movie. I got a chance to speak with D. A. Pennebaker, one of the cameramen for the project, about the experience and he said they always felt like they had complete access to anything they wanted, and that both Kennedy brothers were amazing subjects. But it's always funny when one of your subjects is the president. "I became very good friends with Bobby," he told me, "but the president is the president, he was totally relaxed with us, exceptionally so, but also totally inaccessible."

Drew was an outsider, yes, but Kennedy had come to trust him during the filming of *Primary* three years earlier. The president certainly wouldn't have authorized a total stranger to enter the inner sanctum of the Oval Office, nor would he likely have approved the project if he didn't have a strong sense that he was on the right side of history no matter how the "crisis" turned out in the end.

Once completed (the project is still on Kickstarter), super 8 silent home movies taken by several of Nixon's highest-level staffers between 1969 and 1972 will finally be seen by an unintended audience in a documentary that shows the WH in some of its final moments before the Watergate scandal. The Nixon footage, while intimate, wide-ranging, and "safe" (because shot by friends), is also amateurish, trading access for polish, without sound or purpose.

What I was proposing to do was exactly what I'd done since fairly early in the campaign. I wanted to show a side of Barack Obama that the American people might not otherwise see; to use the power of video and the freedom of my access to capture more of the American presidency than had ever yet been recorded, which was a stated policy goal of this administration, and one that I could actually help with.

With that higher goal in mind, I threatened not to cut my already shaggy hair until we'd figured out my position. (Or at least until the air force drafted me for my impressive mane . . . See now I'm doing it, too; sorry, AF!) My haircut strike wasn't as noble as a hunger strike, but in my own way I was fighting for what I believed in: the in-between moments that will give present and future Americans a sense of what their president was really like.

By February 28, I'd shot three *Weekly Addresses* on a volunteer basis. It wasn't exactly like enlisting in the navy in World War II, but hey, we all do our part. In recognition of my bravery, the president told an assembled group of armed services people observing a taping that he "didn't give a crap if Arun wears sneakers" when someone pointed out that I was profaning the White House library with my New Balance sneakers. (And I was wearing my dressiest pair!) By the time we all finally settled on where I should work—in the Photo Office, as Eric Draper had accurately predicted (and I had so vehemently denied), though not in the tiny closet attached to the ex-barbershop, now Pete Souza's office, that we affectionately refer to as the "hurt locker"—my hair stood a full three inches on top of my head.

"Your hair is really long," Eric Lesser said to me one morning in early March when we ran into each other in the echoing hallway of the Eisenhower Executive Office Building. I was on my way to meet with Commander Bean.

"I was on a haircut strike," I explained. "I wanted my job to be worked out before Laura gives birth."

"So did it work?" Eric asked dubiously.

I nodded. "Actually, it did. You're talking to the first official White House videographer."

Eric nodded blankly, so I decided to speak in a language Washingtonians could understand. "I'm like the Pete of video, and I'll be working in the Photo Office."

"So get your hair cut!" Eric's boss, David Axelrod, boomed from behind Eric.

And so I did just that.

# CHAPTER 13

# WHAT THE HELL IS THE WHITE HOUSE VIDEOGRAPHER?

*Which has a hell of a good opening line, and in which I get all*
*"science," endorsing the theory of evolution and then boiling*
*water.*

In August 2010, a few days before the end of combat operations in Iraq, I was inside the Iraqi defense ministry in Baghdad at an official good-bye ceremony for General Raymond Odierno. I desperately wanted to do a thirty-second pull-aside with the general for a scene in the movie I was making about the change of command. As the ceremony dragged on and on, I was getting nervous that the general would take off before I got a chance to talk with him. I kept glancing over at the general's formidable-looking public affairs officer, whom I hadn't yet met.

"Excuse me, hi," I said finally. "So, um, I'm Arun from the White House—"

She cut me off. "Hi, Arun. I know who you are and who you work for, and please believe that we're trying to get this moving along. But I have to say, I'm not entirely sure what the White House videographer actually does . . ."

She wasn't the only one.

To this day, I can't remember exactly how or when we decided that I belonged in the White House Photo Office. What little I knew about the department I'd picked up from Bush's photographer, Eric Draper, the guy who had shown me the barbering closet on our trip to the White House during Transition. The ever-indispensable Internet helped me round the sketch out.*

Since 1964, when LBJ appointed the first official presidential photographer, the purpose of the Photo Office has remained the same: to document the activities of the president for history. Even though I'd be relieved of my still-photography duties and returning to the video camera, as a member of the Photo Office my objective would no longer be to persuade voters, but to leave a documentary record for present and future generations. Every cabinet meeting, every foreign-dignitary grip and grin, every casual exchange aboard Air Force One—though many of the images they capture (as many as twenty thousand every week!) aren't released until after the president leaves office, White House photographers have access to it all and a duty to preserve it.

Still, early on, I had my doubts about working for the Photo Office. It seemed like a tight operation that could easily be overwhelmed by the addition of video. My soon-to-be boss and Obama's chief official White House photographer, Pete Souza—a White House photographer during the Reagan administration and sub-

---

* As did Janet Philips, a treasure of the federal government. Janet has been a White House photo archivist since the '80s and has seen every photo of every POTUS between then and now. She also told me that I caused quite a stir in the Bush WHPO when they scoured the live feed of BO's arrival for evidence of the new official photographer during our postelection trip and found me in sneakers and my "sad" tie (named such by Reggie Love).

sequently a photojournalist for the *Chicago Tribune*, where he first photographed Obama—had some doubts of his own. As we talked things over on the president's train to DC right before inauguration, Pete expressed his worry that, as a campaign guy, I'd be catering to the day-to-day needs of West Wing communications, which was *not* what the Photo Office was supposed to do. He wanted to make sure I understood that White House photographers were first and foremost collectors for history—focused on posterity, not politics.

And, in accordance with the Presidential Records Act of 1978, a bill inspired by the misdeeds of one Richard M. Nixon, all notes and recordings—including all motion pictures—related to the presidency are preserved in perpetuity in the National Archives. For me, that meant every take, every frame, even every blooper, would be around forever—a *much* scarier prospect for video than still photography.

I admit I'd also enjoyed the supremacy of videographers on the campaign. I'd gotten used to telling the still photographers what to do instead of the other way around (to the extent that you can tell a photographer anything, that is; they're an obstinate bunch). I couldn't help but wonder if hoping that people will get "it" at some distant point in the future was less satisfying than setting the record straight in the present moment. But at least I had a job, which was good news to my very pregnant wife.

Like the other shape-shifting positions I'd taken since joining the Obama team, my duties in the Photo Office turned out to be multilayered. In addition to the archival footage I was responsible for providing, I'd be teaming up with New Media to supply them with backstage moments with POTUS for White House website productions, and working with White House TV to direct the *Weekly Addresses* and other official tapings.

Luckily, I didn't have to worry about Pete peering over my

shoulder at every turn. Like me, he preferred to work mostly on his own, and he was pretty hands-off as a manager. Even at the time I realized how rare it was to have such a big role in defining my job, though this freedom, in my case, turned out to be a mixed blessing. I was totally on my own; rather than rely on the list of accepted activities WHCA had filmed, I used my own judgment to decide what was and what wasn't appropriate to film, a time-consuming and occasionally scary experience.

The other members of the photo staff, who were all either photojournalists or magazine photo editors before coming to the White House, weren't grappling with the same issues. Though we shared some hardware and a bustling, noisy office,* the still photographers and I had very different responsibilities. After all, for all their surface similarities, photography and videography are extremely different disciplines (though I should perhaps point out that photos are no longer photos and films are no longer films). There's something about the frozen moment of a photo that opens it up to endless possibilities of interpretation, as if capturing the finite in totality can somehow subsume the infinite, whereas, as I argued earlier, a motion picture is absorbing and therefore more like a "real experience" with only one meaning, one possible interpretation. The core reason for this difference—and the reason for my caution—boils down to a single word: sound.

That's right: sound. The all-important audio track. Some might find this simplistic, but sound changes everything as sure as money did for Cyndi Lauper. The advent of sound in movies, many early film theoreticians argued, was a double-edged sword—it satisfied the audience's curiosity but also dumbed down the art. Once sound was added, a movie was no longer a fine art but a spectacle, some-

---

* I'm afraid I was the main source of noise; it was considered an initiation rite for an intern to sit at the computer crammed in the corner behind me.

thing to be taken in, not to be interpreted or even understood. The visual experimentation that characterized art films in the 1920s and early 1930s gave way to that persistent realism of movies today—and all because of sound.*

Every film student, or at least every film student from back in the day when people shot on film, understands the degree to which sound changes a movie. You always watch your dailies first as silent projections, allowing you to scrutinize every tiny detail on the screen, and only then do you sync up the sound. At first it's off and looks strange, but suddenly the sound lines up with the images and magically, just like that, everything on the screen seems to come alive.

There's just something amazing about audio. Who doesn't like music? People who don't own TVs are a dime a dozen and fond of boring others about their morally superior lifestyle choice. But anyone who says, "Eh, I just don't like music," should go on your no-fly list right away. Now, obviously I'm not trying to arrange our senses into some pseudo-hierarchy. Though they overlap, they all serve different purposes, and it's foolish to claim that one is more powerful than the other. But in the movies, only two senses signify, and those are sight and sound.†

In our species' adolescence, we were both predators and prey. Our close-together eyes let us peer into the night like a hunter, and our widespread ears could pick up on the twig snapping nearby and cue the group to impending danger. Movies work the same way. The click of the shoe on the sidewalk is where the fear in a noir comes from; it's why the dark is so scary. There is so much to listen to, always.

* In this respect, a Soviet peasant in the 1930s would possess a more sophisticated visual film grammar than the modern American (or Russian) viewer.
† Apologies to Smell-O-Vision stockowners . . .

We humans have very sensitive ears. Bad audio in a movie is an instant killer; it makes the whole movie unwatchable. (Ironically, most of what we define as unwatchable is actually unlistenable.) People will watch just about anything, but they'll react negatively to poorly recorded audio each and every time. One of my favorite maxims when I taught location sound at NYU was "bad video can look like a choice; bad audio will always sound like a mistake."

In the province of modern political media, visuals inform through data—that is, what you actually see—and sounds inform through emotion. Vision is text, and sound is subtext. That's why television journalism is the most rudimentary form of motion picture: the sound always corresponds exactly to what you see on the screen.* Chris Matthews talks about Obama, and a picture of Obama appears on the screen. What you hear is what you see, and what you see is what you get. There's no scary squeaky stair, no low rumble of the Force (Lucasfilm)—and that's a good thing, since the (supposed) objective of TV journalism is to tell the news at its simplest.

But as every filmmaker knows, when used more creatively, the audio track can be a powerful complement to the images on the screen. That's because the best audio doesn't come from the most state-of-the-art microphone or the crispest sound library. The best audio is written. Take a character like Mumbles in *Dick Tracy* or Kenny in *South Park*; those are audio jokes that are written ahead of time.

Political media takes advantage of that, albeit in a pretty base way. Campaign commercials excite our emotions with scary music and scratchy voices. One anti-Nixon ad made by the Humphrey

---

* Jean Renoir said that what is for the eye should never also be for the ear (but don't worry, I'm keeping my promise not to get too heavy with this stuff).

campaign was a far cry from the vérité experiments of Charles Guggenheim; the screen simply displayed the words "Vice President Spiro Agnew" to the soundtrack of a man laughing cruelly. Heavy stuff.

Audio considerations in documentaries demand a more delicate but no less writerly touch. The example I always used in my sound class was from the Maysles brothers' *Salesman*, a film that follows Bible salesmen selling their wares. In one scene, the Maysleses suggest the poverty of a family not by narration or even dialogue but through the ambient audio track. The man of the house, a tired-looking fellow in a faded undershirt, puts on a record when he sees he has company, clearly very proud of his selection. The scratchy horrible Muzak cover of the Beatles' "Yesterday" that comes on competes with the strained dialogue for the viewer's attention and beautifully encapsulates the sadness of the scene. A lesser filmmaker might've asked them to turn it down, but left alone, the music speaks volumes.

Understanding the complexity of the interplay between sounds and images, and being able to find both while on the location, are almost never part of TV cameramen's job descriptions. So when I staffed up for the general election, I hired people with backgrounds in film instead of journalism.

Anyway, when I made the move to the White House Photo Office, sound added all sorts of new considerations to my day-to-day decisions about what to film. Since I couldn't erase footage (and I took this stricture seriously), my camera sometimes felt like a ticking time bomb—although, to be honest, fear of the permanent record guided me less than my own instincts. Still, this was a constant, tireless process. Even when I had come to feel familiar and comfortable with the hallowed halls of 1600 Pennsylvania, I remained as cautious in my work as I was on day one.

People have asked if I would feel more comfortable with the sound off; why not just shoot some great b-roll? But that's not how I work, and that's not how video works, either. I think it's fairer not to go in at all than to go in without the sound. When people see me shooting (and I make sure they do see me), I want them to assume I'm rolling sound, so there are no unpleasant surprises later. The presence of a video camera should in general cue people that the sound is being recorded along with picture; after all, recording sound is a major part of what the camera does.*

These days, of course, there are cameras that look identical to still cameras but have microphones and can shoot HD video. The White House still has quite a few events that are only open to still photographers in the press, but one of these days, inevitably, a photographer will decide to roll sound, and . . . well, let's just say that one'll probably end in tears.

When determining what to shoot, I followed a simple rule: if people behaved differently than they would without the video camera present, then I'd prefer not to be there. I tried to shoot everything that seemed interesting unless I thought my camera would affect the situation one way or another. (Think of that now-classic bin Laden shot of the president and his chief national security advisers watching the raid go down in Pakistan; audio might've seriously compromised the high-security nature of that meeting.) I didn't dispute Jean Rouch's belief that the camera acts as a catalyst, by its nature always interfering, and this was why, around the president, when the stakes were so high, I tried not to be a distraction. Running this country seemed to be plenty difficult already.

Not that anyone was paying much attention to me. When Barack Obama was in the room, most people were way more

---

* Although you don't get as many suspicious looks as you do when you are a dedicated sound person with a boom mic.

focused on him than on the guy with the camera hovering in the background. When they forget the president's name, or their own name, or spontaneously break into song in his presence (FYSA I wouldn't mention this if it had only happened once!), it was demonstrably not for my benefit. But if I ever thought that someone would hedge on speaking to the president because I was filming the conversation, I'd put my camera down and walk away. I've been called the "ultimate fly on the wall," but I'd much rather be a gorilla in the corner.

I was always ducking out at the very beginning of meetings, or turning off the camera when I stumbled upon a private exchange with a national security adviser, which happens more often than you'd think in the cramped corridors of the West Wing. I didn't generally film one-on-one meetings for more than a few seconds, if at all. I'd normally wait in the Outer Oval and film the president greeting his visitor and walking into the Oval; I might follow them in for a second or two. (If the door closed and I wasn't already in the room, I did not go in, even if I really wanted to film the exchange. That was not a strict house rule, by the way, just one of my self-imposed standards.) There was always that moment in every meeting when the pleasantries fade into business, and when I sensed that change in the air, I usually bowed out. I stayed much longer at group meetings, especially Q&A-type situations.

I've sometimes thought of myself as the guy responsible for getting all the cutaways and transition shots for some future thousand-hour documentary on the Obama presidency. People will need to see the big speeches, but they'll also need these smaller moments to fill in the gaps and make the narrative flow. My job was all about transitions between the official and the unofficial, the public and the private, and these became both starker and more finely gradated after the inauguration. That's probably why the United Nations during the General Assembly was one of my favorite places to shoot, because it was both a public and private space. Private because world leaders and their staff wander about in secure areas, no press allowed; public because world leaders must be guarded even (especially) in the company of other world leaders. (This is where all the eye gazing takes place.)

But this all is theory. In practice, I was constantly using my own judgment, seeking information where I needed it. Knowing the exact right moment to leave was less a sixth sense than a marshaling of emotional intelligence with everything I knew—from context, from the schedule, from history classes. Constantly defining these boundaries could be stressful, but I soon became adept at this type of self-policing.

How much easier to be Pete, who just goes to everything! (See Souza, Pete, more Machine than Man). Because Pete was around the president more than anyone else, he was also better informed about the minute-to-minute minutiae. He could often tell me in advance if something was up. Once, he waved me out of a delicate situation in the Green Room. I was filming the president and a member of Congress right before an event; the Marine Band was already playing in the background. Pete tapped my arm and made a face to let me know that this wasn't going to be a pleasant exchange, and so I backed up. Again, this was not to eradicate a tape of BO dressing down a legislator from the permanent record— the archives are full of that sort of thing. It was more that I didn't want him to hold back (or rather I didn't want to influence *his* decision about whether he should hold back), and in a situation like that, in a room like that, I wanted to make sure POTUS's guests, much less used to life in front of the camera, were also as free to respond as they could be. I wanted *all* of our elected officials to conduct their duties as they saw fit without undue interference from the likes of me.

The only other time I received a caution was for a similar reason. POTUS was meeting with a group of local parish presidents at a Coast Guard station on the Gulf Coast. I used to start and stop filming these meetings, just capturing the moments that seemed interesting rather than rolling the whole time.

POTUS cleared his throat at the end of this meeting. "I just want to close by saying one thing . . ." This was usually a great cue to record remarks that would be considered and . . . conclusive, but Press Secretary Robert Gibbs gave me a small but certain signal to desist, one I'd never seen before. Again, it wasn't because the president was about to ask them to stop playing politics and work with him; we'd be happy to have that in the archive or in this book. It was that the president really needed the parish presidents to listen to him and be able to respond openly, without worrying about what the frazzled guy in the corner with the camera was doing.

In general, it was very rare that I was asked not to film something that I'd decided to shoot, and even rarer that the request would come from the president. I know it's a long march and that there's no reason to fret over every misstep, but I also never, ever forgot that official White House videographer is a new position and, as such, still delicate. One big screwup and the position could just vanish. And just as important, ending up as a footnote in history because I bungled something was not really what I was hoping for. So I was careful, sometimes to a fault, not to step on anyone's toes. Just a few weeks before I left the White House, in fact, I was filming in the kitchen outside the Ben Franklin Room in the State Department when Secretary Clinton glanced over at me from behind the espresso maker she was using and snapped, "You'd better not be filming that!" I immediately gasped out an apology and dropped the camera, only to have her burst out laughing and say, "My gosh, I was just kidding—it's only coffee!"

I stepped in it (or rather on it) once. I was traveling with the First Lady to Game One of the 2009 World Series in New York. I covered her rarely, but she and her staff were always great to work with and always supplied me with great footage. And with so much less security and fanfare, I always got amazing access. There was only one rule on this mission to Yankee Stadium, and it came not from the Secret Service but from the annals of baseball superstition—whatever you do, do *not* step on the baselines. Bad luck, apparently. Amid the rush and roar and general confusion, both Samantha Appleton, another presidential photographer (there she goes, right under the bus!), and I stepped clearly and indisputably on the first baseline as we accompanied FLOTUS to the mound.

*Moments before almost walking backward off a ledge at the Forbidden City.*
(*Official White House Photo by Pete Souza*)

The Yankees lost that night, and when I laughingly came clean to former OFA colleague and rabid Yankees fan Chino Wong, he actually called me some very rude things. The First Lady saw this coming: "Oh, man, you two are from New York, too, don't tell anybody," she said, amused and sympathetic, when we'd confessed our crime while watching my hometown team lose.

And that's what it is to be the official White House videographer, constantly forgiving yourself, for missing the shot, for leaving work a little early, for not getting in the room before the door closes, for stepping on the baseline or on a young farmer's seedling ("Arun, watch where you are going, man!" POTUS reprimanded me) . . . Four years is a long time, eight years is even longer, and there is always something else amazing coming down the pike.

# CHAPTER 14

# GOVERNMENT PRETTY

*In which I praise "Those Green Notebooks," make some rather*

*unfair comparisons, and fail to figure out a way to mention that*

*amazing art deco escalator in the Department of the Interior.*

ARUN is running down the lower cross hall of the Residence, out of breath.

> ME: Mr. President, Stephen Colbert left a copy of his book [*I Am America (And So Can You!)*] in the library; if you'd like it, I'll go grab it.
>
> POTUS: Wait, he did what?
>
> ME: Well, he stuck his book in the library shelf.
>
> POTUS: Why did he do that?
>
> ME (*looking slightly guilty since I'm the one who suggested Stephen do this so that I could have a funny shot to conclude my behind-the-scenes video*): He was, uh, being funny. Should I get it? I probably should.
>
> POTUS: Isn't it safe in the library? It's not like we don't have a lot of security.

Me: Yeah, but it isn't supposed to be in the library. The ushers will be mad, and they might get rid of it before you even see what it is. Maybe I could just run and grab it?

Potus: Why would they get rid of it?

Me: Well, because it's the White House, and they keep track of every . . .

Reggie: Enough, bring me the damn book! Man, they let anyone write a book these days.

Proof that Reggie's correct: They let me write this book, and I've never even been to Camp David. Some insider!

Even when Stephen Colbert wasn't around, our new life inside the White House was always at least a little strange and often completely surreal.* There were a million new rules and protocols governing where we could and couldn't eat (answer: not in the residence) and which furniture we could move to set up a shot (answer: NONE. EVER. If I moved an old chair or even a little vase more than a few inches, an usher was guaranteed to notice and be displeased).† And it wasn't just that your boss was now called "Mr. President"; now he actually *was* the president. The line between

---

* Right before the filming, I got to show the comedian war damage from 1812 and hear what turned out to be the equally hilarious other side to the cue-card fiasco in South Carolina during the campaign: Colbert's people were trying to keep BO's appearance secret from Hillary Clinton and John Edwards and had been calling him "the ham sandwich" or something like that whenever the other candidates were present.

† The ushers were the only people who truly frightened me—way more than the Secret Service guys and the rooftop snipers with their four-foot-long assault weapons—mostly because they had *no* equivalent on the campaign. It took me a long time to get to know them, even though I was around them all the time. Whether they're in their blue work shirts or their tuxedos, these men are true professionals, sticking with the house even when its occupants change. The best I ever felt in the service of the president was when one of the ushers told White House photographer, Samantha Appleton, that "the boss really likes that guy—he always relaxes when he's around."

wasting his time and blowing him off had become exceedingly thin.

President Obama, you see, is an intensely curious guy. This quality comes across far more clearly in backstage-type video (or in person) than it does in more scripted official appearances. I think this is something people like in their president, but it means that his staff must always be prepared for that extra question.* (My father is the same way, so I always think of it as a very parental quality.) I remember walking into the Outer Oval once, not expecting to stumble onto POTUS reading in Brian Mosteller's chair. "What's up?" he asked. I explained that I was there to get Reggie for an appointment at the Eisenhower Executive Office Building. I admit it sounded a little strange. "What kind of appointment?" he asked. After some hesitation, I told him we were scheduled to take our drug tests. "You have to do that *together?*" Here was a line of inquiry best curtailed by a staffer committed to protecting the boss's precious time.

In that hypercorrect atmosphere, I *loved* the surreal moments, lived for them. The president ordering General Odierno to shave Stephen Colbert's head? Awesome. Obama performing his inaugural oath so that Disney Imagineers could record the audio for the Magic Kingdom's Hall of Presidents exhibit? Yes, please. ("Are these holograms or robots?" the president asked. "Er, neither, sir. They're *animatronics*," the Disney guy said, just as he'd been trained to. Obama nodded and smiled indulgently. "Right," he said. "So they're robots.")

From time to time, the surreal and the practical overlapped, like the morning Reggie and I lined up all the president's ties in the

---

* In the small amount of time I spent around President Bush (number forty-three), he did not strike me as sharing this quality (although I did find him likable, authentic, and many other positive things).

Map Room and marked their labels with a Sharpie, indicating which ones were not suitable for TV owing to the moiré effect. (PSA for people who are on the national news every night: you, too, should think about this every once in a while. And yes, the president does actually pick out his own ties. Or I've been shut out of every single high-power consultancy tie-picking meeting. It's unlikely but not impossible. [See bin Laden, Osama.])

Tempting though it was, I didn't want to get distracted by the sideshows, or at least not by the wrong sideshows. I'd been given a rare opportunity to produce films from inside the White House—to let Americans look under the hood of their government—but I wasn't sure how I should go about doing it, at all, like not even a little bit.

Don't get me wrong: I was extremely excited to work in the White House. Just a few hours into the job I realized I was also excited to work for the *government*. I needed to jot something down, and the hardcover notebook someone handed me struck me as one of the most beautiful objects I'd ever beheld: the rough pea-green canvas, the narrow ruling, the stern sans serif font of the vague but evocative words "Federal Supply Service," which were followed by a federally interminable series of numbers. Government, I realized, had its own aesthetic, and a pretty nice one at that. English majors, I've been told, get all Hemingway when they scribble in their Moleskines.* In a similar fashion, those green federal supply notebooks inspired me. Whenever I used one to sketch out an idea, I felt a direct kinship with artists of yore who'd served their government and against all odds made beauty out of

---

* Though I majored in film theory, I've used quite a few Moleskines in my day! My wife prefers a specific brand of weird foreign-department-store notebook, smart and perennially hip; we're talking about aesthetics here, so I thought this was an appropriate departure.

*Government pretty: those green notebooks.* (Photo by
Arun Chaudhary)

bureaucracy. You know—musicians like John Philip Sousa, photographers like Dorothea Lange and Walker Evans, some serious
heavy hitters. Might I, simply by seeking inspiration in these slim
but sturdy little volumes, one day join their exalted ranks?

Given what I was actually doing—following the president
around all day with a video camera—Robert Drew seemed the
most obvious choice of role model for me, but he'd worked outside
of government, with its labyrinthine bureaucracies and outdated
word-processing tools. I'd landed right in the thick of it. And
government films . . . well, what could be more boring, less pretty?

If most people even have a concept of "government film," it
probably hews pretty closely to those scratchy, boring films we
remember from middle school science class, the ironically enter-

taining "ephemeral" films collected in Rick Prelinger's archives and stock footage churned out by corporations and special-interest groups.* You know, those generic movies about syphilis and/or sedimentary rocks. Whether anyone ever took these films seriously is an open question. Though modern filmmakers and admen have, with many knowing winks, exploited that aesthetic after the fact, on their own these films feel authorless, mass-produced, and anonymous.

This is not to say that there's no such thing as a good government-made movie. Some government movies are downright amazing, although the vast majority of these were made by outside professionals who subsequently returned to their vocations. (Coincidence? Hmm. . . . ) One of the best examples is Frank Capra. The perennial optimist behind classics like *Mr. Smith Goes to Washington* and *It's a Wonderful Life*, who volunteered for army service just four days after Pearl Harbor, directed the WWII Why We Fight information series.

John Ford, perhaps the most widely admired film director of all time, became a commissioned naval reservist in 1934 (he didn't like the looks of the European scene). He didn't just make the greatest Westerns, from *Stagecoach* to *The Searchers*; he was also a superstar of government film. Beginning in 1941, he made documentaries about defense preparations and actual battles, like *The Battle of Midway*, which contained live-action footage Ford had shot during the fighting (action, and how—he ended up with shrapnel in his shoulder—badass). When Ford's footage hit the average newsreel it became something quite out of the ordinary. In light

* Prelinger remains the gift that keeps on giving: the other day I was cutting a very quick and dirty film for Influenza Awareness Week, or whatever it's called ("get your shot" kind of stuff) and realized I could make it classy and also get a full night of sleep by simply downloading "Sneezes and Sniffles" from Prelinger, stealing the opening and the music, and bam! (As that guy who yells at his food says.)

of the popular success of Ford's documentaries, his unit was expanded to include training films, films of combat operations, and navigational films used for strategic intelligence. (Ford's unit also filmed the D-day invasion; it's a great tragedy of film history that this footage has been lost.)

I do not mean to compare myself to these two seminal directors. I could be inspired by their cinematic greatness even as I acknowledged that I was bringing a lower level of experience and craft to serve my country. I was more like famed government documentarian Pare Lorentz, who wasn't a successful filmmaker taking time off but rather a literature and film-theory guy, and sometime photographer, who made documentaries for the government during the Great Depression. After his words-and-picture book called *The Roosevelt Year* attracted FDR's notice and approval, Lorentz was commissioned to make a documentary about the Dust Bowl (*The Plow That Broke the Plains*) and another about the triumphs of the Tennessee Valley Authority (*The River*), both American classics.

For his sustained involvement in these and other New Deal documentaries, Lorentz came to be known unofficially as "FDR's filmmaker." I decided to aspire to a similar title with the current president. With Obama as my subject, I already had an ace in the hole (I'm a decent card player, so this analogy will stick better than the football/automobile ones everyone else seems to favor). Obama's unique temperament allowed me to shrink the distance between the camera and the man, and between the artist and the presidency, from fifty feet to five. The smallest camera in the world wouldn't have made a difference if the personality had been wrong, but since it was right, I knew I could make movies that were closer to the presidency than any that had come before. This would be a record of degree, not of precedent.* All I did was take the camera the last few yards down the field (wait, did I really just toss out another football metaphor?).

So not only had it all been done before, but my government-film heroes had set some insanely high standards. They'd achieved something magical: they'd made authentic art, managing to marry their unique sensibilities to the government aesthetic† in its very best sense, in the beautiful green notebook sense. Their movies had similar goals—either to educate citizens about the ravages of the Depression (and, concomitantly, the achievements of the New Deal), or to engage their sympathies in the war effort—but they were also highly individualistic and personal: you can see Capra's relentless optimism in Mr. Deeds as surely as in *Prelude to War* when he chooses to show scenes of college football games rather than rippling American flags. And the poet of the plains took incidents like the Battle of Midway and rendered them as large as Monument Valley. They won Academy Awards for their documentaries. The text Lorentz wrote for *The River*, when put into book form, was nominated for a Pulitzer Prize—in poetry! Talk about government pretty.

I didn't have classics like *Stagecoach* or *Mr. Smith Goes to Washington* under my belt (au contraire: I had a movie about a computer psychiatrist and a documentary about the history of eating), but

---

* If you have no idea what the difference is, don't worry; I didn't, either, until a representative of the *Guinness World Records* explained it to me at a UFO-themed bar in Columbia, South Carolina. He'd come to town to certify that the Oprah-led mass phone call/text to potential voters at the Gamecocks' Williams-Brice Stadium was the biggest the world had ever known—an example of a record of degree.

† By the way, I'm not trying to oversimplify here. Obviously not everybody makes the transition smoothly from filmmaking to government. Robert Flaherty and Jori Ivens, two of the original giants of documentary filmmaking, didn't find much success in Frank Capra's movie unit in World War II.

the people I had made movies with and for over two action-packed years on the campaign trail now found themselves at the highest levels of government, and they granted me a remarkable degree of creative freedom. This was another enormous and enormously important advantage—understanding, encouraging, and most of all indulgent coworkers. A sample "approval" conversation (with translations) went along these lines:

"I want to do X," I'd say.

"I'm not sure about X." (I'm not listening yet.)

"I'd really like to try X."

"Will you be able to do your job at the same time as X?" (Will someone ask me why you aren't doing your job?)

"Of course."

"Will you need anyone else to help with X?" (Trick question, see above. Also: Will this cost money?)

"Definitely not."

"I really can't wait to see X!" (We'll decide when you're done.)

But that kind of freedom is an obstacle as well as an opportunity. What exactly should I do? How could I rise to the challenges of documenting the presidency? In the White House, there were always, around the clock, a million things going on, and that was part of the problem. Without the campaign's competitive framework as a guide, I struggled to pick and choose. It was no longer a simple question of what needed to happen today to win votes; I had to decide what deserved to be preserved for history. When people on my team on the campaign would say, "But this is historic," they found a very unwilling partner in me. "Is it useful?" I would demand. "History is someone else's job." Well, now it was mine.

Although keeping up with the president's daily activities left me very little time to conceive or edit bigger projects, I saw a good opportunity in the summer of 2009 when, amid all the health-care town halls, the Obama family headed west to visit Yellowstone National Park, a reprise of a trip Obama had taken with his family when he was eleven. Award-winning documentarian and regular White House guest Ken Burns's epic miniseries on the national parks was about to come out; it was the perfect moment to make my own little documentary about presidents and their relationship to our great national parks.*

So after the first family had moved on, I stayed behind in Montana and Wyoming and shot b-roll of the parks, which I interlarded with footage from the National Archives and various presidential libraries of past presidents' trips, as well as interviews with Ken Burns, numerous park rangers, and my favorite bolo-wearing secretary of the interior, Ken Salazar. ("Can you make sure he wears the tie?" I asked his New Media director, Katelyn Sabochik.) We threw in some Recovery Act background, too; I was hoping matching the policies of the Great Depression and Great Recession might infuse a little magic into the movie.

The result was a nice overview of presidents in the parks, but something about the movie just didn't click for me. I'd done my best to imitate the styles Ford, Capra, and Lorentz had perfected. I'd both captured and excavated great footage and enjoyed the New Media intern's energetic editing and the excellent Brian McGee soundtrack. Still, the movie felt sort of boring and, well, *anonymous*.

I thought once again of my all-time favorite advocacy-movie-that-isn't-a-documentary, *A Hard Day's Night*. In his quest to portray

---

* Since Chester Arthur became the first president to visit it in 1883, Yellowstone in particular has had a long and storied history with presidents. (Trivia: Which president spent a summer as a park ranger at Yellowstone? Answer: Ford.)

*Access wasn't the issue. (Official White House Photo by Chuck Kennedy)*

the Beatles as individuals, a band, and a movement all at once, director Richard Lester employs an astonishing variety of techniques: from slapstick comedy to vérité documentary to that brand of avant-garde kookiness that's still the meat and potatoes of the music video. The Beatles were all things to all people, so it seemed fitting that the only movie worthy of them should likewise contain multitudes. The presidency, too, I saw, was many things at once—a man, an office, and an institution. It couldn't be captured in a single type of movie; the only plausible answer was "all of the above." We were still puzzling out the audience of WH.gov, where my films were shown. It didn't get nearly as much traffic as Barack Obama.com had during the campaign, though the proportion of crazy people seemed about the same. Just as in Iowa, I'd try everything and see what stuck to the wall.

I was off. My next project couldn't have been more different in content and tone from the national parks movie, but that, I told myself, was a good thing. Pete Souza, having already taken thousands of pictures in the Oval Office, became curious about the bowl of apples on POTUS's table. When he half-jokingly suggested I make a little movie about the provenance of these apples, he surely didn't expect I'd produce an over-the-top faux educational film to the beat of the Marine Corps Band playing a severe piece by Shostakovich.* But that's exactly what I did. The apples film, which would reach cult-classic status among White House interns, hardly fits with most stereotypes (such as they are) about government motion pictures, and that's precisely why it worked. When showing it to a group of interns, Jenn Poggi, the WHPO photo editor, introduced it as a glimpse into Arun's brain. It turns out that the inside of my brain doesn't look exactly like Ford's, Capra's, or Lorentz's—but it's mine, and that's the point.

I kept up the experiments. In November 2009, while the grand State Arrival of the Indians was taking place on the South Lawn (for those on the Bravo calendar, that *would* be the same night the Salahis gate-crashed), I was on my hands and knees in the West Wing, pretending to be a turkey for a video commemorating the annual Thanksgiving Turkey Pardoning. Anita Dunn, then the White House communications director, had assigned a real riddle: to make a video about the turkey pardoning without highlighting the death of the turkeys, or the turkeys at all. (The birds were staying at the Hay-Adams, a hotel that can safely be classed "fancy," and though the government wasn't footing the bill—the National Turkey Federation does—these opulent accommodations might

---

* Few outside the White House have seen the lighthearted short, alas. I made it for an educational section of the website called WH101, and because that site is still under construction, two years later, the apples movie remains unreleased.

*They say you barely notice the hidden camera on the South Lawn.*
*(Official White House Photo by Chuck Kennedy)*

still strike the wrong note during the Great Recession, I know it did for me.) So I decided to shoot the movie—one of my most watched that first year—from the point of view of the lucky turkey as he made his way through the West Wing to the Rose Garden for the pardoning ceremony.

As a fun side project, I set up a stop-motion camera in the First Lady's vegetable garden, programming the camera to take a picture every hour. This system worked well for the first two years, until an infestation of bugs invaded the entrails of the camera. I kept receiving requests for this footage, first for features on the garden, then for a how-to film the USDA put out about greenhouses, and finally from a White House chef who suspected a varmint of eating the kale. "Would you mind going through the night photos to see if you can spot any eyes in the leafy-greens section?"

It wasn't all animals and vegetables. On the momentous day the Health Care Bill was making the rounds in DC, collecting all the necessary signatures from the Speaker of the House and the president of the Senate, I decided to stick to its side for a good four hours of car trips and mini-events. I was so intent on filming the bill that several members of the press started to film me filming it on its final trip to the White House for the vice president and then the president to sign, not knowing what I was shooting.

In retrospect, and this is the point, I probably should've spent that day in the president's company. The passage of health care reform was indeed a BFD, but the same day as he signed the bill, he also had a full schedule including an Oval Office meeting with Netanyahu, the historical importance of which we don't know at present. Documenting history can sometimes be a defensive business. For instance, after the World Series with FLOTUS, we arrived back at the White House around midnight, only to discover that I had already missed the extra helicopter that was going to Dover Air Force Base where the president would pay his final respects to some fallen service members, and there was no room on Marine One, so by accompanying the First Lady to the baseball game, I had missed an event that was far more important and interesting than the Yankees' opening game loss to . . . crap, I no longer even remember who they were playing.

And while all of these mini-projects were definitely enjoyable, I was still having trouble finding a way to bring the public closer to the presidency itself. Eventually I decided to try to concentrate on the daily activities of the president and to try to avoid missing these moments. I had a large amount of amazing material and collected more every day, but I just didn't know quite what to do with it.

PART III

# HISTORIAN IMPERFECT

CHAPTER 15

# REINVENTING THE NEWSREEL—
# *WEST WING WEEK*

*In which I first mention the Black Mirado Warrior, the Air Force*

*One of pencils, and get trapped in the booth behind Tim McCarver*

*for a long time.*

In the summer of 2010, when WH staffer Carlos Odio was giving musician B.o.B. a tour of the West Wing, he was surprised by the lack of surprise the rapper evinced at everything Carlos proudly showed him. "Yeah, I saw that on *West Wing Week* already," B.o.B. kept saying. For me, there's no greater compliment than to know that the Web show I created has provided a general blueprint for anyone interested in seeing more of the White House (though frankly, the Aaron Sorkin show *West Wing* reproduces White House geography, especially the Oval and Outer Oval, with as decent accuracy as anyone does anything).*

* Case in point: White House visitors who've watched too much *West Wing* are always a bit taken aback by the real thing: "It's sort of small, right? Ew, and is that temporary carpet in that hall? Oh, ick." But in my opinion, that's what's great about the West Wing: that it's a mini-labyrinth filled with blood, sweat, tears and awesome green notebooks. After having seen countless state houses and palaces, I have to say the quiet industriousness of our White House does the nation credit. I

It isn't just the government edition of *Cribs*, though. *West Wing Week* is a four- to eight-minute video wrap-up of seven days in the life of the president, covering everything from major addresses and cabinet meetings to chance encounters in the hallway. It's where I put all the moments I captured that neither stood alone as raw clips nor lent themselves to larger topical pieces.

In my first year in Washington, I'd caught some hilarious backstage moments, like the time the president punched the Easter Bunny in his furry gut (don't worry, it was only Brian Mosteller), but I'd yet to find the right vehicle for the material.* A wrap-up video seemed to be just the thing, sort of a present-day updating of a project Pare Lorentz had attempted but never finished during the FDR administration. He'd spent years working on a massive database of FDR's presidential schedule, including films and audio reels of FDR speaking; still photographs of the president and other images from around the nation and abroad; shots of White House usher schedules, FDR's appointment calendars, and other documents—in an effort to give a greater context to the daily goings-on of the presidency.† I wanted to try something similar, but I knew that if I proposed an ongoing project I'd be surrendering the time, and therefore the opportunity, to do anything else. No more flying down Montana highways or cleaning insects out of the time-lapse camera in the garden.

---

always felt proud of its relative unfanciness when showing my counterpart videographers around.

\* I'd also had my share of missteps, like the time I was trapped behind Tim McCarver during the 2009 All-Star Game while he interviewed POTUS. The harder I tried to escape the tiny broadcast booth, the more painful my predicament became. It didn't help that my BlackBerry kept buzzing with messages from coworkers, friends, and complete strangers, all wondering if I knew I was popping up and down behind the president on national TV, and why I didn't just get out of there?

† Although Lorentz could never have imagined an online interactive multimedia exhibit of his work, his dream of matching this material to a timeline was realized long after his death by the talented archivists who maintain the Pare Lorentz Film Center at the FDR Library in Hyde Park, New York.

We'd done plenty of wrap-up videos on the campaign trail, but those were more manageable in both concept and execution because (a) there were more staffers to work on them and (b) they didn't need to be absolutely timely. Pennsylvania is still a state from one week to the next, so a video about a bus tour through Pennsylvania would still resonate with Pennsylvania voters even if it came out two weeks after the fact. And besides, the campaign narrative is itself so simple that it lends itself perfectly to the twenty-four-hour news cycle. Like I said, it can often feel like a particularly long baseball season.

But in an off year, it can be as difficult to keep up with the twenty-four-hour news cycle as it is to find content to fill it. Satellite and live-streaming technology have gotten more sophisticated, but that doesn't mean there's enough newsworthy content to put into circulation. Remember the contentious and heated discussions in the White House press briefing room and every major news network in August 2011 about the shocking scheduling conflict between the president's speech on the American Jobs Act and the umpteenth Republican debate? (I've heard many an administration official say incredulously to a member of the press, "Is this *actually* what you're asking me? *This* is what you want to know?") The material that survives, even if it wasn't trivial to begin with, can end up being trivialized by repetition.

The competition to get information out at lightning speeds isn't slowing down; when there's nothing new to throw up on the screen, the gaps must be filled with chatter, chatter, chatter. Pundits want to proclaim who "won the day," and, as the tech has grown more robust, even who "won the hour."*

---

* My wife-slash-ultimate test audience is a victim of this cruel system. We laugh about how she "rides the roller coaster." I don't need to have cable news blaring to keep up because I'll inevitably hear the daily back-and-forth from her anguished

I wanted to produce a Web show that would rise above this frenetic environment while still appealing to the modern appetite for up-to-the-minute newsiness (though I often think people are more afraid to miss something than they are interested in learning anything). During Transition, I'd had an idea for a regular show called *Step by Step with the President-elect*. (Marvin suggested *The Arundown*, which I mention only because it's awesome!) My schedule was so packed that it took me almost a week to edit the activities of a single day, so I decided to put together a behind-the-scenes short of that week's most interesting day, boil it down to a couple of minutes, and then release it the following week. For my first *Step by Step*, I picked a day on which POTUS-E rolled out a lot of National Security Staff and then traveled to Philly to meet with the nation's governors.

The problem—or one of the problems—with this approach was that, in the era of the twenty-four-hour news cycle, releasing the video a full week later made the material seem stale and irrelevant. I've no doubt this particular footage will make an invaluable addition to a long-format documentary made in the amazing year 21-whatever, but it wasn't strong enough to be released "a little bit later." So we shelved *Step by Step*, which was too bad because there's some really great stuff in it.

In the White House, I kept struggling with the question of how to release illuminating footage—for example, of the president filling out his census form ("What phone number should I use? Should I just put down White House main switchboard?"). Some of the difficulty was logistical. Technology had changed dramati-

lips. "OMG ARUN!" Laura will cry when I walk through the door. "If the president doesn't X, Y, or Z, it's game over! They'll impeach him!" And sometimes less than a day later, "Republicans are done for, like . . . forever, no longer a party! Listen to what I heard . . ." And she will then insert the first name of whatever newscaster was last on.

*Recording* The Arundown *in Transition HQ, Chicago.* (Photo by Alexandra Eaton/Presidential Transition Team)

cally even since the campaign, and with HD now standard every-where, even (or especially) on YouTube, the same types of files we'd uploaded in 2008 were exponentially larger by 2009. Thank God I didn't have to upload the speeches anymore—that job fell to the military—but occasionally I needed to pitch in to show every-one how to vandalize a hotel business center properly.

And I just had *no time*. You'll just have to trust me that living by the president's schedule is tough. Even without the natural disas-ters and national-security flashpoints, duties keep on getting added to the docket. If the president meets with a trade association, or delivers a video message to a group of ironmongers, or personally congratulates the winner of a professional sports league, then every subsequent president must do the same until the end of time. (And the press, by the way, with its Correspondents' Dinner and News Photographers Association Dinner, and so on, is no less guilty of these impositions, despite their firsthand knowledge of the rigors.)*

The conventional practice, as we've discussed, was to post footage immediately after the many events I was still supposed to film, but with a crowded schedule and no deputy to review it, I could no longer post raw video in a timely manner. And because of all my overlapping commitments, I could never count on how many minutes or hours a day I'd be able to devote to putting together a wrap-up show. But after months of toying with different ideas, I realized that a week of the president's schedule had just enough shake in it to get a weekly wrap-up done, which is to say, I knew it would take between eight and eleven hours to edit one of these films from stem to stern and I'd need at minimum a week to squeeze that many hours out of the already overcrowded schedule. By covering Friday to Thursday, I could theoretically edit all the material into a coherent five- to eight-minute film. That's to say, barely enough time—but the fact that it was even possible excited me.

Deciding to go with the week-by-week overview wasn't just a function of my crowded schedule. I also thought the week was a more natural time frame than the day. We measure our own lives by the week—what I did this week; what I have planned for next week. Even before organized labor brought us the weekend, folks had split their days into weeks, and, like movie scenes organized into sequences, this longer parcel of time could hold more of the real story than the trivial day. I think this weekly structure is a big reason *West Wing Week*, unlike *Step-by-Step*, took off from the

* So I'm taking this opportunity to beg you, America, please don't ask the president to speak at your next function. He's busy already.

beginning. It makes the events feel immediate even when many of them have already been broadcast ad nauseam on the news.

I've also found that people appreciate the longer view, and maybe a deceleration of the pace. There's something so nice about slow news—maybe it could join slow food and become a full-on movement? I once saw Robert MacNeil speak when I was younger, and I clearly remember one comment he made that feels even more important these days. He said something to the effect of "People think I'm a little boring, and I'm okay with that because the news should be a little boring."

So, with that in mind—not to be boring, but to be a little more *classic*—I specifically avoided modern news formats when trying to figure out how my project should look and feel. I took visual inspiration from old newsreels, specifically the March of Time series that was produced between 1931 and 1951, my tacit tribute to a time when the nightly news was slower and more serious, with a hint of that old-school WPA-style government aesthetic exemplified by my beloved green notebooks.

I also included a number of bright-colored, goofy *Rocky and Bullwinkle*–inspired elements in the titling and editing to make it playful. The very act of summarization—of making something very big very small—is inherently funny. That's why wrap-up videos lend themselves so well to snarky videos about celebrity activity, like those top five lists on *Entertainment Tonight*. I wanted to acknowledge this humor without poking fun at the subjects themselves, and even in episodes that dealt with the most serious topics I tried to maintain a light touch.

When to release the videos was the next big question. The *Weekly Address* already had Saturday morning reserved as a matter of long-standing tradition. We also wanted to take Web-viewing habits into account and release it during the workweek since, as I have mentioned, people mostly consume Web media at work. If work computers are the new TVs, you definitely want your movie coming out while people are in front of them. We eventually settled on Friday: the perfect time for a nice summing-up of the week that people could consume with their morning coffee and congealed egg-and-cheese sandwich.

It was less easy to figure out how to pack so much information into such a compact time frame. I eventually settled on voice-over narration for two reasons: One, I simply didn't have enough time to edit together a more complex, vérité-style piece every single week; it just wouldn't be possible. The second reason was that I thought it was important for there to be a steady audio track. A person should be able to watch over her lunch break while unwrapping her food and checking her e-mail and still know what was going on with the president that week.

All that was left was to name it, and that happened at thirty thousand feet with the assistance of Josh Earnest (whose smooth Kansas City accent made him the perfect narrator), Jon Lovett, a Mirado Black Warrior pencil, and some AF-1 stationery. "I like alliteration," Lovett said, and he jotted down five quick ideas, including *West Wing Week*.

"But doesn't it sort of sound like the show *West Wing*?" someone protested.

"I believe that section of the White House was named before the popular high-budget network drama was released," I retorted, really liking the sound of it, and also thinking that if someone looking for *West Wing* NBC found *West Wing Week*, they would likely not be displeased, in fact quite the opposite (although I admit I could've lived with *The Arundown*, still a solid title; thank you, Marvin, for not forcing me to think of it myself).

And so off I went. Actually, it wasn't that simple. By calling the show *West Wing Week*, we were committing to making one every single week, which was scary but also part of the point. Josh and Macon encouraged a training period, so for two weeks I just wrote sample scripts to see how long it came out naturally, just how much I could fit. I spent the next two weeks making sample episodes that would never be broadcast just to see if I could really pull it off every single week. How many hours did this process take? I missed the first deadline by a full weekend, but the second faux-episode, which clocked in at about seven minutes, was in good-enough shape to go out on the scheduled timetable. For the sixty-two weeks that followed, I never missed a deadline. And it was tough: I'd spend some—okay, many—Thursday nights in my undershirt, muttering profanities in the empty halls of the EEOB at 3:00 a.m. And if we were traveling on a Thursday, I'd have to edit in helicopters and vans and motorcades, just like in the good old campaign. And believe me, there were some weeks when I would've preferred to do something else, *anything* else, but the regularity was part of the story, too. (Or okay, I did miss the dead-line once, but that was because I was in Iraq—a good reason, right? Nevertheless, people were downright cranky when it went up eight hours behind schedule.)

Owing to the arbitrariness of Internet running time (not to mention the wonderful creative freedom I was given), I was left to determine the length of the episodes. When I tried to cut the first *West Wing Week*, the final product ended up at about eight min-utes. It felt too long, but I couldn't figure out how to shorten it without omitting some of the necessary highlights. I thought the ideal length was around four minutes, like a longish pop song. As time went on, I got better at nipping and tucking, at packing more material into less time. Eventually the average running time did dip to four minutes, but I reserved the right to let each episode find its own natural length. On some particularly big weeks, I needed eight minutes to do the material justice.*

In other ways, too, the shows evolved, and I had my fair share of misfires, as one does. The birth of *West Wing Week* coincided almost exactly with BP's Deepwater Horizon oil spill. I had put a backstage scene in *West Wing Week* of POTUS talking to some local fishermen about what he was doing. He told them, "I can't dive down there and suck the oil up with a straw but I can put good smart people in place to help like Thad [Allen] here." I thought it was honest humble and put it in. By the time reporters were done parsing this, the game of telephone had gotten so out of control that Gibbs called me into his office (the only time this happened, by the way) and just said, "Arun . . . Superman? Really?" Somehow, the quotation had been incorrectly interpreted to have POTUS petulantly saying that he "wasn't Superman and he couldn't suck up the oil."

Also, early on, I had the notion that it was important to begin each episode with a quirky PSA from a cabinet secretary or other recognizable administration official, as in, "Welcome to *West Wing Week*, your guide to everything that's happening at 1600 Pennsylvania Avenue—but first, a word from Transportation secretary Ray LaHood."† Then the luminary would recite a government-funny bit I'd written. Though I was very attached to these add-ons, which had the right vaudeville feel to me, they were a pain to schedule, resulted in some uneven performances (to put it as

---

* I've noticed this same pattern on Web fiction shows like *Web Therapy*, a post-*Friends* vehicle for Lisa Kudrow. While most episodes are around four minutes, the "important" ones can run as long as eight. Interestingly, they're trying to make *Web Therapy* into a full-length TV show by slapping these vignettes together; we'll see if it works. It definitely wouldn't for *West Wing Week*.

† Secretary LaHood always turned in a solid performance; he never let me down.

politely as I can), and often led to hurt feelings between me and the agency communications staffers I was coordinating with, who'd invariably change my jokes, which I'd then invariably change back. These little PSAs, though entertaining, were ultimately too much trouble. We scrapped them.

In their place we put a summary of the episode, a suggestion from Lauren Paige that I'd initially rejected—"How can you summarize a summary show without getting too annoyingly M. C. Escherish?" I'd asked. Soon enough I saw the benefits of her idea, which created a space for all the shots that didn't fit cleanly elsewhere and helped define the scope of the experience for the viewer.

Once I had a format that worked, *West Wing Week* evolved into its own quasi-institution. These days, *West Wing Week* and the *Weekly Address* are the only WhiteHouse.gov programs that come out on a strict schedule. The White House produces many other series, but they're all released when they're finished; only the *Weekly Address* and *West Wing Week* resemble McLuhan's lightbulbs, empty spaces that need to be filled. I believed that the only person capable of filling this particular space is a White House videographer, and I fervently hoped that my position would become a permanent slot that had to be filled rather than a job made up just for me.

Soon enough, I no longer had to write separate memos justifying when and why I'd be filming somewhere. "This is for *West Wing Week*" became an accepted blanket statement that allowed me to concentrate on a comprehensive historical approach.

Just how comprehensive is it? Fairly. The president does far too many things in any given week to fit them all into a four-minute show, but I tried to hit a cross section that represented the different scales of events at the White House and on the road. Regular *West Wing Week* viewers should have a pretty good idea of what their president was up to over the last week, and a decent sense of the geography he inhabits.

So do people watch *West Wing Week?* It's a success but not a runaway-train success. Its numbers conform to a steady plateau growth model that's far more reminiscent of traditional television than the quixotic quest for online viralness. Basically, every time an episode deals with an issue that a specific online audience cares about—like Darfur, or the passage of health care reform, or the withdrawal from Iraq—we get a good number of new viewers, and then retain a certain percentage of them in subsequent weeks. (Again, this is much more like traditional television watching trends than any online viewing patterns, viral or otherwise; paging Mr. Nielsen . . . )

Lots of people reload *West Wing Week* into their own players, meaning that it gets around. The White House New Media team has staffers devoted to metrics, but the Photo Office, with its historical mission, does not.* I'm less concerned with parsing exactly who watches it from week to week (Washington insiders versus Duluth housewives or whatever) than with producing material that appeals equally to two distinct groups: this week's audience and the audience of posterity. I wrote and edited each *West Wing Week* with the idea that POTUS meeting Elena Kagan right before he signs her commission on the Supreme Court will be fascinating to watch this week and even more fascinating to watch in the future. ("Let's make sure they spelled your name right," President Obama said to Kagan as they examined her certificate in the Oval Office, "it could be really embarrassing.")

---

* Though New Media staffers would occasionally pump out a report about how we were doing; they were the ones who first noticed that we had a spike in views whenever the VP made an appearance. Joe Biden—White House movie gold. Traveling with him on Amtrak is still one of the highlights of my WH tenure.

I really can't say how far into the future I mean. We don't know if the Internet is forever, but right now it certainly seems that way. And you can't always predict what your stuff will look like later in the style of famed Nazi architect in chief Albert Speer, who designed buildings that would ruin in a certain way. Things on the Internet are more like tattoos of ex-girlfriends' names than stadiums. You're stuck with them forever, so you'd best make them good.

And speaking of forever. Immediately following the general election, we had to decide whether to leave our anti-Hillary spots on our YouTube channel. In the end, we left them, both because expunging them seemed ridiculous and because none of them seemed all that damning after the campaign. On some level, though, their presence on the website is an unfortunate holdover of her now much-changed relationship with Obama. Now I look forward to filming moments of her and BO, like when they made fun of Chief of Protocol Capricia Marshall at Buckingham Palace, playing off each other like two old comedians: "She is in protocol heaven," HRC said. "She just loves all this stuff!" POTUS: "This is the Super Bowl of protocol isn't it?"

This was a far cry from the campaign, even or especially Unity Day, a.k.a. the worst day (for me) ever. Tensions had never been higher. Katie Lillie spilled milk on me on the plane (she denies this), and when Obama got on, he grimaced at me: "Does this mean you're going to smell like milk all day?" as I kept trying to get an elusive shot of HRC and BO together.

There is a third audience that is just as important, the internal audience. This is a lesson I've had to learn a number of times. On the campaign Joe asked me to write up a summary of what we filmed every day: speeches, OTRs (off-the-record—a stupid name because they're not), DTCs (direct-to-cameras), the whole nine.

But very quickly, what started out as a simple sheet for New Media and Paid Media folks to know what footage and pictures were available, became almost like an internal campaign newsletter with a large following. I started to include colorful detail from events, funny quotations, links, and relevant pictures; these "road reports," as I called them, provided a strong morale boost for those working hard but rarely getting to participate in events with the candidate. Scott Goodstein called it the campaign zine.*

*West Wing Week* became much the same. Staffers would always tell me that their parents had seen them on *West Wing Week*. (This definitely fits the Photo Office mission; it's the video equivalent of the famous jumbo prints up all over the White House complex.) I'd see an extra spring in staffers' steps when I'd arrive to film an event they'd organized. "Oh, man, is this going to be on *West Wing Week?*" You bet. And I'll be honest, it's not like demand was so high that I couldn't fulfill special requests on occasion. Congressman André Carson (D-IN) once asked me on AF-1, "So what's it going to take to get on *West Wing Week?*" I turned the camera on. "Just that, sir." But all joking aside, the videos are a great tool for the White House to project transparency, even internally, and a way for staffers working on disparate tasks to maintain a sense of common purpose.

And the internal audience is always the first to let you know there is something missing. Remember Government Funny? Let's call this one Government Passive-Aggressive. "I noticed you weren't able to cover the conference on Wednesday. Not a big deal—only two million people are without enough food to eat because of it . . .

---

* Since it retained its original purpose, there were occasional dustups with advance team members who thought their sites were portrayed harshly in the report. "Did you really have to say the room looked like a Marriott conference room had thrown up on itself?" I actually did; I was trying to steer the ad folks away from ugly footage.

glad the Boy Scouts made it in." Sometimes I've even gotten some frowny-face emoticons sent over, with no other text in the e-mail.

There have been some interesting—and extremely flattering—*West Wing Week* imitations. There is the *Bay State Brief*, following the governor of Massachusetts, and *School Days*, by the Department of Education. I helped advise the folks making *School Days* and in our discussion quickly discovered that like so much else in life, *West Wing Week* is not easily reverse-engineered. Secretary Duncan's videographer may have more time to edit, but he may also have fewer interesting public events to film. As a result, *School Days* covers the highlights of the secretary's schedule by the month, not the week. Another formula I could imagine working would be covering a full week of Secretary Duncan's schedule, but only doing this once a month (though they didn't take all my advice, including my idea of having former basketball star Arne sink a three-pointer from a different high school gym on every episode).

Mitt Romney has a characteristically stiff attempt that comes out periodically on his YouTube channel. And Leader Cantor, who, as I've mentioned, doesn't exactly ooze winning authenticity, has begun making wrap-up videos documenting sections of his schedule in the Capitol. These products feature stills and voice-over rather than video, probably partly to ease production hassle, but they also mitigate the effects of Cantor's authenticity deficit.

Not that I'm claiming *West Wing Week* is anything like a perfect product, or that I'm a perfect historian. *West Wing Week* tends to highlight my chatterbox nature and you can frequently hear me talk through my shots. For example, on the president's tour of Westminster Abbey in the spring of 2011, he paused midway through reading out Sir Isaac Newton's achievements as listed on his headstone. POTUS looked over at the camera and nodded at me: "Physics, calculus, I'm just saying . . ."

The next thing you hear is the loud agreement of a nasal camera operator (me): "Yeah, Newton was pretty good, an impressive guy."

I'm not particularly proud of stepping on this little moment, but I *am* proud that the administration will continue to produce *West Wing Week* after I leave. Especially at a place like the White House, people all seem irreplaceable right up until the moment they're replaced. Of course, it's different when you have an established job like Joe Biden's or Rahm Emanuel's; you have a Secret Service name before you even report to work. My biggest success as the first White House videographer is having a successor at all, and I can only hope that, not too many administrations from now, a member of the Secret Service will murmur, "We have Hitchcock in the support van," into his earpiece. (Oh, and I'm talking about the pudgy English thriller director, not former Council of Economic Advisers chief of staff Adam Hitchcock, in case anyone was confused.)

# CHAPTER 16

# THE TWO PS—PROPAGANDA
# AND THE PRESS

*In which I go negative on turkey sandwiches yet again, get asked*

*to leave the elevator, and accept that sometimes friends fight.*

**F**ame is not one of the perks (or drawbacks) of the third best job in the White House. Despite the considerable amount of time I've spent at the edges of cable news frames, I ride the Metro without exciting the attention of the paparazzi. In fact, only once have I ever been recognized. A young lady tapped me on the shoulder: "Hey, you're the official White House videographer!"

The way she used my exact title should have tipped me off, but I stopped and smiled, prepared to be generous with my time and advice. "Yes, that's right."

"I was the camera person on that video you were interviewed for about *West Wing Week* two days ago."

My face fell. "Oh, that hit job? You guys made *West Wing Week* look kind of evil."

"Hey, it wasn't my deal," she said. "I'm just a student who volunteered to help out and borrowed the camera." The DIY spirit had been turned around on me, but students with borrowed equipment moonlighting for local news were not the only ones trying to figure out what I was doing. From the get-go, journalists were downright suspicious of this weekly recap. Telling the world what POTUS was up to was their job. Now some guy with a video camera was going to try to do that job, only from the inside? Attacks and misinterpretations were par for the course for a couple of months.

For the most part, I'd enjoyed a good relationship with journalists since joining the campaign. In all the ways that have been documented in countless boys-on-the-bus-type books, including *The Boys on the Bus* (which it was always embarrassing to see being read on the bus), our enforced proximity basically left me no choice but to get to know the traveling press corps quite well, and I liked them. I had a lot in common with them, came from a similar background. We did favors for one another when we had trouble with our gear. Sometimes there were hurt feelings about seats on the campaign bus, or the last turkey wrap, or someone would complain about bandwidth hogging, but these people were a big part of my world. If I was getting dinner or a drink before editing, chances were it was with one of them.

After the primaries, our team and mobile studio swelled for the general. Since we no longer fit on the bus, we started traveling in our own van in the motorcade.* Now that we weren't spending as much time with the reporters and TV cameramen, the heady camaraderie of the early days dissipated, and even though we still occasionally shared planes on the big foreign trips, I would never be quite as close to the press again. We still covered the same events, and while POTUS was in public I worked alongside the

---

* The volunteer drivers would often call us the "fun" group, which pleased us.

journalists and cameramen. But POTUS was a quick in and out, and that meant I was, too. There was no more time for swapping audio over a leisurely turkey sandwich at the turkey sandwich table.

Still, I can't help but wistfully recall that long ago night in January 2009 when we left Chicago and landed in Washington. Obama needed me to take some photos with the pilots and staff of the plane, but I didn't have a flash. "Don't worry," the press photographers said. From the sidelines they flashed their flashes over and over and over, giving me enough light to get the shots. Memories!

Everything changed as soon as we got to the White House. The press had questions and complaints about access right from the start. When POTUS reswore his inaugural oath in the Map Room, members of the White House press corps—the select group of TV and print journalists stationed in cubicles inside the West Wing who exclusively cover all manner of goings-on inside the White House—reacted angrily when only the Print Pool (i.e., no photos allowed) was permitted inside. And in the months that followed, as the Photo Office began to distribute an unprecedented number of official White House photos, making use of social media and Flickr, the press photographers began to complain that Pete Souza was getting sole access to photograph events that they'd always been invited to shoot and was distributing pictures that they had always been *paid* to distribute.

Occasionally I was the target of this ire. The first time I really took note was in a *Politico* article about a bill signing, something very mundane about tourism; the only remarkable thing about it, I thought, was that if she saw my footage in thirty years, a certain congresswoman might be embarrassed by the way she had badgered the president of the United States about giving her one of the signing pens. So I was surprised when, a few days later, the article

cried foul on my presence at this signing, though the only difference between this one and countless other minor bill-signings was
that *someone* was filming this one. The video we released of the
event (or nonevent, as the case may be) very obviously used no
editing tricks. It was a very simple moment that I had simply
recorded, but suddenly I was branded a manipulative mastermind
who had brought his big bag of tricks to the White House. It didn't
help that shortly afterward Gibbs identified me in a press briefing
as the guy who'd gotten to interview Elena Kagan right before the
announcement of her nomination when the press corps had not,
which only added fuel to the fire. (In this particular case, it wasn't
even true—New Media video director Jason Djang had been the
one to land this plum assignment.)

The cry in the wilderness turned into a steady howl of hate for
several months after *West Wing Week* debuted. Members of the
press corps weren't the only ones who didn't know what to make
of the show. The battle over whether *West Wing Week* was inherently good or inherently evil (never anything in between) was discussed in the lowest levels of the Internet, that is, the comment
boards. We got, "These provide great insight into the presidency
and we should use them in schools." We also got, "These people
get creepier by the minute. I wonder how long it will be before
these videos become part of the curriculum in our schools (Lonely
Conservative.com)."

The real trouble was a matter not of content but of precedent.
The press corps worried that their traditional access was going
to be crowded out, and many wrongly assumed it already had
been. They tried to understand my role, which was still being
invented, in the old terms ("I thought he was supposed to be the
new Scott?"). I was the same old Arun, and my personal relationships with most of these folks were still good. People do not, how-

ever, make it into a body as prestigious, high-pressure, and territorial as the White House press corps without a certain sensitivity to gradations of power. And for this group, access *is* power.

The growing fear that my pretty much unfettered access to events on the president's schedule would diminish what the press would and could cover surfaced in a series of almost-identical articles that came out soon after *West Wing Week* premiered. (I'd always know when one of these articles was about to come out because a photographer would suddenly start shooting Pete and me instead of POTUS.) "The administration has narrowed access by the mainstream media to an unprecedented extent," said ABC News White House correspondent Ann Compton, who has covered seven administrations. "Access here has shriveled." She and other correspondents clearly viewed my intrusions as emblematic of a larger problem.* Luckily, not everyone was in a state of panic; Caren Bohn, a Reuters reporter and now president of the White House Correspondents' Association, told *Politico*, "The WHPC does not have a problem with anything the White House wants to do to get its message out," as long as *West Wing Week* was not curtailing media access to the president's schedule.

And there were other objections as well. Outlets as venerable as the *Washington Post* expressed concerns that viewers would confuse *West Wing Week* with the news, which I then maintained was unlikely, and which has not in fact happened. That's yet another reason I added those deliberately whimsical newsreel touches—to make absolutely certain that no one would mistake my weekly videos for journalism.

I kept finding it strange that my attempt to show a more

---

* In the next episode of *West Wing Week*, I featured a shot of Compton palling around with POTUS at the Correspondents' Dinner just to show her that there were no hurt feelings.

*Pete Souza and I work on the beach on the Gulf Coast.*
*Whenever they are taking your picture, it means an*
*article about you is about to run.* (AP Photo)

human, unscripted side of the minutely choreographed existence that is the presidency narrowed so many eyes. Some people actually seemed to believe that I was a rank propagandist, twisting reality before our rightful storytellers, the journalists, could judge it for themselves. One ABC correspondent claimed that my job "mocks the work of the press." But to me, the two things have nothing to do with each other. I'm not a journalist and have never claimed to be one; I'm a documentarian. When POTUS walks into a room, the reporter has to be front and center to get the text of whatever is happening. I have the freedom to take the long view. I can shoot the president slipping out a doorway backstage; I can show what it was like to be there, to go beyond what people ordinarily see on TV.

Many think of the presidency as nonstop glamour, a succession of fancy hotels and palaces and state dinners, but I soon came to see it more as a long slog through freight elevators, loading docks, and other less than fragrant byways. I once mentioned to POTUS that I thought people might be surprised to learn that the presidency smells like stale beer. He smiled at his wife and quipped, "As long as the president himself doesn't smell like stale beer, it's all fine."

The way I see it, my job is to make the fantastic mundane, to humanize what might otherwise seem intimidating and institutional. This, in my view, is the opposite of most stereotypes about propaganda—that vague, catchall pejorative in my line of work; for these purposes, let's define it crudely as using deceptive and/or manipulative techniques to puff up a person or institution. Rather than obscuring or distorting it, my work presented a super-important part of our government in a way almost anyone could absorb.* And no matter what the writers of sensational headlines say, *West Wing Week* isn't propaganda if for no other reason than because I made it, and I didn't intend it to be (pace Barthes) and

---

* The state-run media accusations really bother me, especially since I saw some of the real stuff straight out of North Korea recently, and though you'd think a collection of factory visits is a collection of factory visits, *West Wing Week* has a dramatically different tone, scope, and intent than "Kim Jong Il Gave On-the-Spot Guidance to Various Fields of the National Economy." Our undertakings couldn't be *more* different, as far as I'm concerned. Still, though, I admit that my detractors do sometimes get to me. After I saw a photo of a Libyan State TV journalist trapped in the lobby of the State TV building by an angry mob, I actually had a nightmare about it that night. Another time aboard Air Force One, I eavesdropped on a conversation about how state-run TV centers were command and control centers, and therefore fair targets in wartime. When I asked him about it later, National Security secretary Nate Tibbits joked that I could be considered a "command and control" center and thus targeted.

made very conscious choices to avoid it. I intended to record the presidency for history, but also to make the presidency more human.

"Propaganda" is just another one of those words that gets thrown around in this supercharged political atmosphere, but I think it's another thing that we know when we see it. To qualify as propaganda, in my opinion, there must be an element of dishonesty. Here's an example courtesy of Ron Brownstein's book, *The Power and the Glitter*, about Hollywood and Washington. In the California governor's race of 1936 Hollywood executives targeted Upton Sinclair to punish him for proposing tax increases on them. They made a newsreel attacking Sinclair and showed in theaters as if it were a factual document. This was a full decade before LBJ made those false newspaper headlines about Coke Stevenson, so this exact trick can clearly work over and over. But in all my time working for Barack Obama, I have never been asked to construct—nor have I ever attempted—any such falsity, and I admit that before joining the campaign, I expected this sort of thing would happen, and almost looked forward to it.

As it is, I like to think my fidelity to the truth is equal to or even above what most journalists practice, since I don't get caught up in every last tempest in a teacup (as discussed, the never-ending news cycle requires Washington to be roiled on an hourly basis). It's a sad state of affairs when the government is keeping the news media honest and not the other way around, but that's occasionally how I feel when reviewing the president's schedule for any given week; the press only covers the tiniest fraction of his activities, which makes all those "state-run media" accusations even more grating. I honestly believe that *West Wing Week* is as useful to the hardened reporter as to average citizens. This is the kind of perspective I strived to offer, and it is also, I think, the exact thing that is near impossible for deadline journalists to deliver.

What history offers that news does not, even or especially when delivered fresh to your in-box every morning, is context. Take the *West Wing Week* that covered the night bin Laden was killed. The president's week contained far more than that operation, but you wouldn't know it from the news reports. That week Obama interacted with the military in a range of other situations: awarding a posthumous medal to the families of two soldiers, starting a bicycle race for disabled vets. But however revealing, very few of these events merited mentions on the nightly news in a week that held such an event of international importance. Once again, it was my job to fill in the gaps, to offset the marquee with the mundane.

Still, whatever it was I was making, the press wanted to make clear that it wasn't the same thing they were making (just to be triple-clear—I certainly never claimed it was). The old chumminess all but vanished. Once, during a meeting of the UN General Assembly in NYC, I arrived late to cover the opening of the bilat with Kyrgyzstan. I made a dash for the nearest elevator, which happened to be the one the White House press corps was taking. Although the elevator was pretty crowded, I correctly judged that there was enough room for me to squeeze in. But as I slid inside, a photographer I'm friendly with held up his palm and said, "Sorry, but you've gotta use the staff elevator." We all laughed, except that he was serious and so I left, slightly wounded.

My fragile psyche aside, what was really at stake here wasn't my intentions, which I don't think many in the press corps ever really doubted. I always had to remind myself that for the most part, these weren't really my friends. They were just folks I worked near (not with), and everybody had a job to do. Hearing a wire photographer apologize to his bosses for missing a shot reminded me that everyone was under just as much pressure to succeed at their job as I was.

Another issue is that technology that has been folded (relatively) smoothly into politics has wreaked a truly chaotic transformation in journalism. Reporters on the ground, especially at the White House, are far too busy to think through new models of journalism much. (I can certainly relate. Never having a free moment to plan any additional projects, much less how I might pursue them, was a constant source of aggravation for me in that pressure cooker.)

But it's disingenuous to suggest, as some journalists have, that there are First Amendment issues at play when the White House begins to use that transformative technology to tell its own story. The reality is simple, really. Once upon a time, when the press was the only way to get a message out, the government counted on the press, relied on them. But these days, technical innovations have greatly reduced the government's reliance on them. An Ethernet cable or even an AirCard can now do the work of a whole satellite truck. Once, on a riser, a cameraman gazed at my live-stream setup, which fit inside a small backpack, with envy. "Man," he said, "if I'd had one of those back in '96, my back wouldn't have given out and I wouldn't have spent the last fifteen years on all these painkillers."

Even in 2008, a campaign no longer really needed the national press, and especially the networks, to reach a large portion of the American people quickly. One AP photographer explained to me that the "protective pool"—the permanent coverage of the president or candidate by the established press—was necessary so that photos like his could reach millions of people, but this was revealed as plain condescension when you looked at the viewing stats on BarackObama.com. Anyone with a laptop could break news these days; we no longer needed the national media to help us along. But technology, or rather technological limitations, has always been the root cause of much of what we take for granted as the "way things are." I read in the *New York Times* that the Iowa caucuses were moved to January in 1972 so the old mimeograph machines they used would have enough time to get ballots ready for the convention—in May.

There had never been a reason to have the networks film the *Weekly Address*, and yet no one ever cried foul on that score (or not too much; Commander Bean said he had a couple of conversations); members of the press just took it as a given. Still, there was plenty of proof of the fraught relationship between access and technology. For example, two weeks after Obama's speech announcing the successful mission against bin Laden, the press latched on to an unlikely follow-up: "Obama's Reenactment of Bin Laden Speech for Press Photos Stirs Controversy." The pseudo-controversy, as a Reuters wire photographer revealed, was that these photos were staged after, and not during, the speech.

But this has been the practice since the Reagan administration. Wire photographers typically take their photos of live speeches from the White House seconds after the speech is concluded, to ensure that the loud clicking of shutters doesn't interfere with the audio of the speech or catch the president's eye line and distract him mid-speech. (Pete used to shoot those situations carefully with the live view on his camera to keep very quiet; video cameras like mine luckily don't make anything like shutter noise, just the faintest electric hum.) I don't know how previous presidents felt about these fixed tableaux, but BO hated them. Like I said, he's never enjoyed any type of playacting.

Anyway, after the stink about the bin Laden speech, reporters long familiar with this practice started objecting to the ethics of these reenactments. It seemed like a tough problem, except that technology offered an extremely straightforward solution to it. During the address itself, a remote silent camera could take a picture for all news agencies to share, even if adopting such an obvious innovation would surely be met with more cries of "no access!"

So now, instead of the reenactments, a pool photographer comes into the speech and puts a remote camera in what we call a "blimp"—a device that muffles the sounds—and photographs the speech while it's going on. When Pete explained the new setup to POTUS right before a taping of the *Weekly Address* that would serve as a trial run for the new system, he shrugged and nodded. "You guys are always crawling around anyway," he said. "One more camera can't possibly bother me," and it didn't.

Doug Mills, a staff photographer for the *New York Times*, put it in perspective in an article about the situation: "We are taking one step forward—we get live coverage—and four steps backward—we will lose four photographers from the room." He continued, "We clearly lose out in terms of perspective. There will be no wide shots or risk taking, for that matter."

As usual, the thing that suffers is the art. Poor art.

During one of the administration's first "pool sprays"—an access opportunity when the press pool rush into a room to shoot for a few seconds—what seemed like the entire White House press corps came barreling into the Oval Office. In the crush, a boom-mic operator accidentally swept everything off of the president's desk: folders, papers, even a glass of water. When the sound person stuttered out apologies, the president cracked a smile. "Don't worry about it," he said. "It's just the Resolute Desk." Since I'd been stationed in the Oval Office before the crowds showed up, I managed to film the whole *Three Stooges* exchange.

As with so many parts of governance, the problem here was logistical. Most rooms in the West Wing are much smaller than the Oval, and the press corps consists of a minimum of eight or nine people, and winnowing it down always involves more hurt

*Would you want forty-nine different reporters covering your son's bris?*
*(Official White House Photo by Pete Souza)*

feelings than a junior-high dance; most of the time, the headcount goes into the dozens. The White House briefing room is designed to accommodate the crowds (but even that gets cramped), but is it really appropriate to bring such a swarm to a small or sensitive event? Would you want forty-nine different reporters covering your son's bris? No, when the people reporting on the story become the story, then it's time to make some changes.

I'm just one guy with a handheld camera, and my presence has *not* spurred any limitations of access. On the contrary, I've provided an additional perspective, one that has never before existed, and one that I think is valuable for citizens and journalists alike. I am not, I repeat, not a journalist. I shoot different things, in different ways, from a different point of view. Eventually, my friends-turned-competitors seemed to realize this, as eventually the articles trashing *West Wing Week* stopped, replaced by references to it and clips from it in print and on TV. My hope was always that *West Wing Week* would be as insightful for members of the press corps as it was for citizens, not as a messaging competition with the fourth estate.

But then, the journalists, photographers, and cameramen who've had the opportunity to observe the president at close quarters for the last three years could already tell you what I hope every episode of *West Wing Week* reveals, which is that Barack Obama is exactly the same on and off camera, backstage and behind the podium, in official and casual settings. And it's a good thing our cameras all capture that rare and important quality.

# CHAPTER 17

# THE BUBBLE

*In which I mention Afghanistan without admitting that I wasn't*

*on that trip, fall in love with a small joke about Kyrgyzstan, and*

*introduce the world to Herman Cheung, the official Canadian*

*videographer.*

One late night in May 2008, on a trip to South Dakota, a big group of us—both staffers and journalists—decided to head out to see Mount Rushmore instead of retiring to the hotel. After we were on the press bus ready to roll, though, Obama caught wind of our plan and decided to come along, and why not? It did sound pretty fun. But in the scattered conversations outside the bus, I could detect the mixed emotions of the people who'd never seen the monument before. We all knew that nothing was quite the same inside the bubble. Sure, it'd be cool to visit this historic site with (possibly) the next president of the United States, ask him whether he could imagine himself up there one day, and so on, but lots of us just wanted to escape the bubble for an hour or two, and with the VIP on board, that wasn't going to happen.

The bubble. That's the term for the immediate staff and

elaborate paraphernalia that constantly surround the president. The composition of the bubble stays basically the same, whether the commander in chief is going to get a burger with Russian president Medvedev in Arlington, or speak with troops at Bagram Air Base in Afghanistan. Life in the bubble has its up and downs— ease of work being the chief benefit, myopia the chief danger.

As the spaces get smaller, so does the bubble. The White House complex itself holds a few buildings. Air Force One carries a limited number of people; Marine One, the president's helicopter, is an even harder ride to score. The most coveted spot of all is on what we call an elevator movement; making an elevator manifest is as tough as it gets, especially after Secret Service and nuclear code-carriers are accounted for. Oh, and don't forget Pete, usually the last face I see before the doors slide shut and I dash toward the stairs. Getting booted from the elevator almost resulted in my having a heart attack at the statue of Christ the Redeemer in Rio de Janeiro. While the president, First Family, and Pete Souza took an elevator to the summit, I ran up all 220 steps to the closed-press section to film the calm before the storm of camera clicks and bright lights. But by the time I got there, I was so exhausted (and sweaty) that I could barely turn the camera on, much less get a good steady shot. I was breathing so loudly that Pete turned to tell me to shut up, took one look at my condition, and decided to leave me to my wheezing misery.

And so the audio of the First Family admiring the twinkling lights of Rio contains loud evidence of my athletic shortcomings. I knew exactly what would happen afterward, when we met up with the press in the gift shop—the usual comic exchange between POTUS and the guy behind the cash register, POTUS opening up his wallet to pay, the cash-register guy saying no, no, of course not, how could you even *think* of paying? (This exact same conversation goes down every single time BO ventures out, by the way; the Christ the Redeemer clerk was by no means uniquely generous. Yet another thing to feel imprisoned by, not being able to use your money anywhere.)

For the filmmaker in particular, the bubble offers some unmatched opportunities. The world is like a movie set that builds itself around you with someone else worrying about location, transportation, art direction, and casting. The set is seemingly seamless. There's always food (usually with ranch dressing), and someone to tell you exactly where you're supposed to be. To pick up on the wedding theme again: It's like showing up at thousands of weddings just for the toasts. You'd think the world was made of nothing but lace and lilies, or, in this case, of serious Bruckheimer props, helicopters, flags, the whole nine yards. Government should really plan destination weddings.

At its heart, the bubble is really designed for the POTUS and his staff to be able to work twenty-four hours a day with minimal distractions. The taxpayers are getting their money's worth for sure. Since it holds everyone necessary and no more, you can get a lot of questions answered very quickly inside the bubble. Question about Kyrgyzstan? Ask the Central Asia adviser! Need to spell Kyrgyzstan? Ask a speechwriter!

Air Force One nicely encapsulates the bubble at its most refined and efficient. People might think of the president's personal 747 as this gigantic luxury lounge with wings, but it's much closer to a mobile office, with a computer lab to look up the capital of Kyrgyzstan, photocopiers to make an info packet about Kyrgyzstan, and national security advisers to direct a response to an event in Kyrgyzstan should one arise while the president is thirty thousand feet above the ground. Of course, all of these essentials are where the beds would go in a real luxury jet. But in AF-1, there's only one

*Sitting in for the boss on Air Force One. (Official White House Photo by Pete Souza)*

bed, the president's. Everyone else uses chairs or scrambles for floor space; some of my favorite footage is from long night flights where people found unusual sleep spots, tucked behind chairs and under tables. I'm not saying Air Force One is schlocky; by no means. Every last detail is top-notch, down to the Mirado Black Warrior pencils. (So much more than a pencil, more of a graphite-based writing instrument.) But everything is designed for maximum work efficiency, not comfort.

Although Internet may be a little slower on the plane, there is not a single aspect of the filmmaking process that I couldn't manage on AF-1. WHCA keeps some lights onboard in case we decide to shoot a direct-to-camera. In fact, more often than not, preparing for a long trip was about organizing oneself to get on the plane to *begin* work, rather than finishing it before takeoff.

This setup had its ups and downs, of course. I sort of missed the campaign days, when we'd break cloud cover and go beyond even the faintest wireless signal (see the Slider Principle) and experience a rare sense of release. We often still edited on the plane, but because we couldn't post until landing, the sense of urgency was inversely proportional to the length of the flight.

But on AF-1, it was all work, all the time. I spent one flight to Prague editing *West Wing Week* and simultaneously uploading some footage I'd shot that morning. I was hunkered down in the plane's conference room until about an hour before landing. "I guess it's too late to sleep," I remarked to Robert Gibbs, who'd been diligently plugging away at his computer all night, reading European coverage ahead of the trip.

He looked at the clock and hit his forehead. "Dammit! I was watching you! I figured you'd turn in with at least three hours left." This is a rookie move; you should never, ever rely on another bubble inhabitant—unless it's the president himself—to make sure you are safe. You're really just securing companionship for when you both get left behind. And getting left behind is the worst.

Once, in Pittsburgh, I was running late and didn't make it to my vehicle until the motorcade had already departed for the airport. It was one of the most bewildering moments of my life. There I was, in a major American city with a BlackBerry, a cell phone, and an AirCard-equipped laptop, and for a solid ten minutes I had absolutely no idea what to do with myself. Luckily, advance man Peter Weeks found me and spirited me to the airport just in time.

Because that's the whole problem, or one of them, with the bubble: If you stay inside it for too long, you get soft at the edges. You very quickly stop doing the things you're asked not to do. The morning after the election, I spent a dazed fifteen minutes waiting inside the elevator in my apartment building before realizing that I really ought to hit the button myself. (Of course, this "let the

Secret Service do it" stuff isn't an indicator of luxury but just another security precaution.)

I can only imagine what it's like for a party nominee or a POTUS to readjust to life back outside the bubble, as it's so truly all-encompassing. A special phone rings in the Photo Office whenever POTUS goes anywhere. Every time he enters a new room, people are apprised of his movements. You don't even have to pick it up. "He must be headed into the residence to make that phone call . . . he must be back in the Oval." What happens when the center of the bubble suddenly becomes a regular person again, or does the bubble protect against that very eventuality? Did John McCain have to drive himself home from his concession speech, or is he rich enough that he's long lived in a different kind of bubble that excludes driving anyway?

For the filmmaker, this Nerf-like atmosphere is both an obstacle and an opportunity. I'll grant that being able to drop pieces of equipment willy-nilly in the madcap dash of production and knowing they won't get lost or stolen feels quite cushy for an indie filmmaker who learned the hard way on the streets of NYC. But the Secret Service perimeter definitely has its downsides. I remember an out-of-breath agent running up to me at an event in New Mexico. "Did you tell your camerawoman to get a 'panoramic shot' of the event site from up there?" He pointed to a ridge that overlooked the beautiful canyon location. I nodded hesitantly. "Not very smart to send someone with flashing glass up on a sunny ridge without telling us." He didn't have to add, "You ought to know better," because I ought to have. Whenever I asked them ahead of time, there was very little the Secret Service agents weren't willing to figure out. They are very accommodating that way, just as when the president wants to do something slightly off book, like visit the Mexican border on a whim or play soccer with some kids in a favela of Rio de Janeiro.

This back-and-forth between creative and secure is likely unique to the American presidency. Just like the military used to be in charge of all the president's AV needs, more often than not, other countries use members of their security services or state-run television people. There are very few other creative youngsters in these positions (if you are willing to call me creative and a youngster; it'd be easier if I could show you some side by sides of me alongside these grizzled bureaucrats).* There are, of course, exceptions. Medvedev's videographer is a sprightly fellow who I'll put out there as the only other official videographer with distinctive clothing choices. At the G-20 in Toronto, he donned a head-to-toe denim suit.

You get a good look at people on foreign trips when the "official videographers" are lined up at the G-20 or any bilateral situation normal to foreign affairs. Often to cover these events, I had to stand with my counterpart from the other country. The foreign government with a position most similar to mine is, perhaps not surprisingly, Canada, and Prime Minister Stephen Harper's videographer, Herman Cheung, was my only foreign colleague with whom I correspond regularly (we're Facebook friends!) to swap success and failure stories. "How did you get them to light the Oval Office so nicely?" he asked once. As I know from personal experience, PM Harper's office in Ottawa resembles a cave. "It's all natural light down here, Herman. Sorry, man, we don't go for castles so much in the States."

---

* This looks and feels like surveillance more than documentary, although one supposes that distinction is diminishing with the 24/7 recording from so many different sources, whether they be CCTV or the latest Droid phone.

*The moment of hesitation on the tarmac in Cleveland (me, not him). (Official White House Photo by Chuck Kennedy)*

Once Herman e-mailed me the front page of a paper in Canada that showed President Obama just after he had dropped his Black-Berry on a tarmac. On one side of the frame I stare at the Black-Berry, clearly telegraphing my dilemma: to pick up the BlackBerry or film the president grabbing it himself. "What'd you do?" he wrote.

It was nice to have someone out there like Herman who totally gets it. It's the kind of decision that he would have to make, but the Chinese military videographers who I get embedded with would not. They'd keep rolling no matter what. It reminds me a bit of a story I heard at NYU. A Soviet cameraman in the Second World War dropped a rolling camera to run and pull a wounded soldier out of harm's way. The fallen camera captured the whole scene in

16mm. He was promptly awarded a medal for his courage, and kicked out of the Film Guild for his negligence.

I like to think that I would be the first to rush and save someone, but I haven't really been put in that situation yet. In the case of the fallen BlackBerry, I started to move to pick it up and then stopped and filmed it, just in case you are keeping score, neither being helpful nor even getting the shot.

Just another decision one makes in the bubble, where even the highest-ranked inhabitants face the practical disadvantages of a world totally created for the commander in chief. Unless you're the guy who never gets to leave the bubble, you're always entering and exiting the bubble with all the inconveniences that entails. In bubble life there was always something to keep track of that doesn't really fit with anything we'd learned before or since. Take clothes, for instance. Say everyone inside the bubble wakes up in Zanesville, Ohio, and the morning schedule is a coffee event in town, then a quick motorcade ride to the airport, then a flight that lands in Detroit at noon. This compressed schedule doesn't have enough wiggle room to go back to the hotel and pick up suitcases. And dragging luggage around in the motorcade all morning, which would slow down AF-1's departure, was likewise not an option. So more often than not, we'd have to take out the clothes we would be wearing the next day the night before, then give the rest of our luggage to the people responsible for putting it on the plane. This sounds simple enough if you didn't have a hundred other things on your mind, in which case you might, like my campaign deputy, Sharon Barnes, forget your pants. Former White House photographer Samantha Appleton was always prepared for this contingency, and to avoid Sharon's fate of spending a morning in the motorcade wearing borrowed boxer shorts, she always puts on the next day's outfit the night before just to make sure she has all essential elements in place.

Especially because you never know who will be in the staff van on any given day. It might be the senior senator from wherever, Melinda Gates, or even famed astronaut Buzz Aldrin. Even if you have all your clothes with you, it's hard to stay out of trouble all the time. In this case the pugnacious Space Hero became noticeably angry when he thought speechwriter Jon Lovett had compared him to Barbra Streisand. "Do you think that's funny?" he said in a menacing voice after a long pause. Jon was very surprised because, in fact, I was the one who'd made the offhand comparison, but there was a lot of context, and *he* was the one who'd brought Babs up (something about a literary agent) in a discussion with Mr. Lovett. I could not be more sorry for the incident (especially after a YouTube clip of Buzz punching a guy out surfaced; both Jon and myself are too delicate for such an encounter).

Comical mix-ups of all sorts are fairly common intra-bubble occurrences, like the time Kat Westergaard almost got a ride in John McCain's motorcade (all those vans look alike!), or the time an Obama press bus followed Speaker Nancy Pelosi's motorcade. But there are also less amusing side effects of staying in the bubble for too long. I had a good deal of trouble keeping track of my world outside, or my health, or big milestones in the life of my child. Exactly eighteen hours after my son was born, I was back behind the camera, directing the *Weekly Address*. (When I showed the president the pictures I'd taken in the hospital the night before, he commended the baby's handsome features, then added, "But why'd you have to take such weird artsy pictures of the poor little guy? He's just doing his thing.") My son took his first steps when I was at that G-20 in Canada hanging with Herman, and so on and so forth—my wife would be happy to provide a list of such grievances.

I also lost touch with certain aspects of popular culture to an extreme, embarrassing degree. I bought only two albums, totally mainstream stuff that I heard on rental car radios and will immediately drive a stake through the hearts of many in my life—and downloaded another one illegally (this they respect)—in my four-plus years with the Obama team (I won't say which to protect the guilty, me): Amy Winehouse's *Back to Black*, Guns N' Roses' *Chinese Democracy* (the *Waterworld* of crappy rock albums), and *Recovery* by Eminem (which, if considered as a comeback record, should still not be mentioned alongside *Chinese Democracy*). During Transition, I smiled and nodded as my intern would switch among Pandora stations I'd never heard of.

Films, too. The only movie I've seen in the theater in the past three years was *The King's Speech*, which provides a nice (if approximate) illustration of how I spent my days. If the part of the king were altered slightly so that instead of a pathologically shy stutterer he was a fantastically gifted speaker and writer (I'll avoid trying to cast this, no way to pass the Daily Show Test on that one), and Ralph Macchio played the Geoffrey Rush character, then the scene would *almost* resemble a *Weekly Address* taping.

And though I'm often flip about it, I do think this is the most insidious part of the bubble: the self-bubble if you will—the tendency to begin viewing everything through the extremely narrow lens of the political world. And from a filmmaking perspective, the worst aspect of the bubble for the filmmaker is never getting to hear, or to film, the other side of the story. This isn't to say that I don't know what's happening outside the bubble. I have a Twitter account and a cable box, too. But more often than not, when it comes to events in the world outside, there's usually nothing for me to film except flickering television screens. It takes enormous discipline to get proper b-roll and transition material in an environment like the bubble, one that is conducive to "amazing shots!" but not thorough filmmaking.*

And it has always been in these moments of grabbing that extra shot of b-roll that I get myself in trouble. Trying to get the shot of a motorcade leaving the Capitol and then trying to enter that same motorcade more often than not resulted in a moonlight stroll through Washington. And of course, the one time I decided to linger in the Oval after a phone call I had filmed to get some insert shots of the phone receiver, I got into a spot of trouble. "What are you filming so close?" the president asked from behind me. I turned around to explain that I was going to give New Media some editing options (it was for a project for them) and saw him frowning at me. "You need a haircut, Arun. I mean, you really, *really* need a haircut." Pete Souza took this opportunity to pile on: "Yeah, it's getting a little crazy—you should probably shave, too." Ah, to be that proverbial fly on the wall!

---

* D. A. Pennebaker told me the same thing happened to him while working on *Primary*. He regretted not getting a chance to shoot Kennedy's plane parked in a very conspicuous corner of the airport as a campaign tactic.

# CHAPTER 18

# THE OTHER HALF OF THE STORY

*In which I get called "sir" an awful lot, learn about the smart shrimp of Nicaragua, and drink one metric crap ton of Gatorade.*

You don't necessarily need the president around to manufacture a surreal moment. In August 2010, I was on board the drillship in the Gulf of Mexico at the site of the Deepwater Horizon oil spill. I was decked out in an oversize red jumpsuit, undersize orange hard hat, and steel-toed boots that I tripped over every time I had to scramble down a ladder.

I was there to make a movie about the plugging of the BP spill with high-pressure mud, which turned out, cinematically at least, to be a total anticlimax. (Not sure exactly what I was expecting.) After having to shave (for the regulator mask—it wasn't like a date or anything), become certified to use a respirator, ride two helicopters, and change into that ridiculous red outfit, I went on board with an AP photographer and reporter to witness the "static kill" operation at the well site. If all went well, the leak—which had already been significantly slowed—would be more or less fully

Dispatches *was shorthand for smaller planes, fewer ties. On the ground in Sudan, here.* (Photo by Kristina Johnson)

plugged. Still, however kick-ass it sounded, the experience was not very visual. We all just stood there and watched machinery chugging away while other hard-hatted men peered at gauges, nodding until they appeared satisfied.

"Looks to be holding pretty well," one sun-wrinkled engineer told us. Then there was a pause, a long one. The Coast Guard officer on my left jabbed me in the side. "You should say something," he hissed urgently in my ear. "You know, on behalf of your boss."

My boss—oh, right. Okay then, well . . . I tilted my camera down awkwardly and cleared my throat. "Uh, congratulations, you know, and, uh, thank you so much," I said. "What you've done here is—well, it's pretty great. We've all really been rooting for you, you know, especially around work and stuff." I paused, struggled, but somehow everyone seemed happy with my pronouncement and went back to work.

As the first White House videographer, I wanted to tell the whole story of the Obama administration, even if that sometimes meant showing up places without the president. This moment in the Gulf of Mexico was exactly the sort of event I couldn't cover in a typical installment of *West Wing Week*, which hewed closely to the president's schedule. But the BP oil spill was one of the major events of Obama's first two years in office. (And it also coincided almost to the week with the birth of *West Wing Week*. The timing was so uncanny, in fact, that quite a few people assumed the video series had been created as part of the administration's response to the spill.)*

Especially because the BP oil spill was a domestic—read non-national security—crisis, it seemed like an invaluable opportunity to capture a range of aspects of the president's involvement—from the phone calls he placed in the Oval to the many in-person visits he made to the affected sites to updates in the Situation Room.†

But pieces will always be missing. The president can't always be everywhere his policies are having an impact. And while I was determined not to be distracted from providing a backstage glimpse into his world, the filmmaker in me often yearned to run after some of these outside-the-bubble events just as I'd run after

---

* Whoa. That was dangerously close to a non-denial denial. Let me be clear: it was *not* created in response to the disaster.

† I'm no Pete Souza, who has total access to everything all the time. The only place I always had to ask permission before entering was the Situation Room. So being in there for these updates was a treat. We didn't release any Situation Room footage in *West Wing Week* until a meeting on Afghanistan. Ben Rhodes, the deputy national security adviser for strategic communications, and I braced ourselves for an uproar in response to our releasing motion picture of the Situation Room, but no one really batted an eyelash.

the health care bill as it was carted around the District. I just didn't realize they'd all be in such hot places.

Surprisingly, though I'd been mulling over these issues for many months, it was Pete Souza who first suggested the movie about the BP oil spill in the summer of 2010. Pete, a White House veteran who was a stickler for precedent, told me that this sort of thing had in fact been done before. In October 1981, White House photographers had gone to Egypt to photograph Anwar Sadat's funeral even though neither President Reagan nor Vice President Bush had been able to attend. And early in 2010, I'd traveled with a State Department tech delegation to film their visit to Haiti the week after the catastrophic earthquake struck.

So we agreed that I should make movies about relevant milestones, good and bad, of the Obama administration, with and without Obama in the frame. It was my idea to brand these short films *West Wing Week: Dispatches*, my feeble homage to Michael Herr's classic book of Vietnam reportage of the same name. (When I told Deputy National Security Adviser for Strategic Communications Ben Rhodes the name, he immediately guessed the origin. Props to a fellow Tisch grad.)

My goal was twofold. First, I wanted to make more of these movies going forward—creating a lightbulb, as it were. But I also had to keep up with the rigorous *West Wing Week* schedule no matter what. Even with these new projects, I didn't want there to be a gap in the regular coverage; I was determined to stick to the promise I'd made when I was first sketching out the idea for *West Wing Week*, which, in any event, Deputy Press Secretary and *WWW* narrator Josh Earnest never let me forget. So to keep the momentum going even during one of the president's rare vacations, I'd make short movies featuring letters people sent to the president. We called these placeholder films *Mailbag Day* and always kept a few questions and answers in reserve. "How many chimneys does the WH have?" and that sort of thing. (Researching this one provided a great excuse to clamber on the roof of the WH with photographer Chuck Kennedy.)

But this time, when POTUS went on a short vacation, I went to the Gulf Coast.* This was going to be great, I thought. For once *I'm* in control. We'll be able to make a movie the way a movie should be made. I'll get up at 5:00 a.m., not to wait in an idling motorcade but to cruise to the Louisiana coast with ample time to get a nice sunrise shot. Oh, crap. That reminded me that to drive to the Louisiana coast, I'd need a car and also a driver's license. We were talking about the bubble, right? Forget weight and eyesight and all that health crap, the real thing that I never caught up on was the paperwork. Laura (the wife) helped to keep most of my affairs relatively in order (if I hadn't been married, I'm sure I would've left the White House to live in a trailer by ol' debtors' pond), but the one thing she couldn't keep track of was my driver's license.

By the time my Gulf trip rolled around, my NY license was so expired that I had to retake the road test—that very afternoon. Crap, crap, crap. After I was done with my stress meltdown, trip director Marvin Nicholson lent me his green Volvo station wagon to take the test in (another piece of missing paperwork was the proof of registration for our car, sigh) and offered an invaluable last-minute tip. "You gotta really hit the brakes; don't just tap them." For all my neuroses, I passed the test and returned to the EEOB to find that my colleagues in the Photo Office had plastered Sweet Sixteen banners all over the room to mock me.

---

* I never went on vacation with POTUS, not even to Hawaii, not even during the campaign; I just never wanted to. It seemed like crossing the line into becoming-a-noodge territory and never felt right to me. During the campaign, I had other people cover these events when it was my responsibility to make sure we had the senator covered in case he needed to make a statement.

And though I was excited to set out on my own for a bit, I quickly learned that there are advantages and disadvantages to filming movies outside the bubble. True, I was now the center of my own hierarchy, but without the organizing principles of the bubble, that hierarchy was awfully messy and un-hierarchic. And without a ready-made tableau laid out before me twenty-four hours a day, the work process was more creatively demanding—and also a good deal less convenient. Another thing I noticed the first hour: when the president vanished, so did my veil of invisibility. All of a sudden, the magic was gone, and people started noticing me and my video camera, and not always welcoming our intrusions. (There is *nothing* creepier than having to say, "Uh, I work for the government" to a complete stranger.)

But though I quickly learned that the president's videographer sticks out a lot more when *not* traveling with the president, my status did have certain perks, as when I was making my way to Iraq to film the last day of the combat mission there. "Sir, the plane is loaded," an airman with a clipboard told me. "Oh, great, when are we leaving?" I asked, setting my camera for very low-light situations we'd encounter between Kuwait City and Iraq. "Whenever you want, sir. This is your flight." Later that same day, a smiling security guard tried to bar my entrance to the U.S. embassy in Baghdad. "I don't know what you are fishing for in there," he said firmly, "but there is zero percent chance you are bringing that camera on these grounds." Then I produced my credentials and just like that he changed his tune. "Oh, damn, I see," he said, and ushered me—and my offending camera—inside. Sounds like I'm showing off (and of course I am), but I'm telling you because this was significantly different than normal bubble life. I won't lie, it was kind of nice.

And when the president wasn't around, you were still safe, but safe meant something different. For instance, people would open the helicopter door so you could get the best possible shot, even if this videographer happened to be terrified of heights and wanted the door shut tightly. "It's okay, you can lean all the way out," the Coast Guard gunner told me as she double-checked my safety belt. "I doubt you'd even fall out without this." I looked out into the ocean and imagined a hundred different ways I could die. But if courage is the outward display of calm, I passed. I bravely crept to the edge and got some nice shots of the well site. "Okay," the gunner said. "We have time for you to do it one or two more times before we land." Gulp. "Imagine doing this with drug dealers shooting at you," she cheerfully added. No, thanks. And when that same helicopter took off after dark, an amazing procedure was instituted where the crew members wore night vision goggles and essentially tossed me from person to person and then into the running chopper. It was totally foolproof safety-wise, but definitely wasn't the way you help POTUS into Marine One.

But White House credentials can also be unhelpful, even beyond the (very) occasional impromptu speech or phobia confrontation. There was the time my BlackBerry rang at a Coast Guard command center in Alabama, and I stared at it in confusion. The only person who ever called my BlackBerry was Deputy Director of Oval Office Operations (or Double D of the Triple O) Brian Mosteller, and this wasn't his number or even a Washington area code. "Hi, is this Arooon Cha-hardary?" a voice asked.

"Uh, this is Arun. Who is this?"

"Hi, yes. This is X and I'm an attorney with BP. We heard you're making an Internet video for the White House website and just wanted to check in with you about some particulars . . ." Again: No, thanks.

And for all the jokes I could crack about the horrors of

commercial travel, it's true that it takes a long time to get from place to place when you're driving yourself. On the six-hour schlep from Pensacola to Louisiana, I also realized that transportation time was actually the entire key to *West Wing Week*'s existence. When I was driving I was not editing. All that transport time I'd taken for granted was now not on the table unless I could somehow get the band back together. I was very lucky that my colleague from the primary, Jessica Slider, an editing maestra who had taken a job at the Department of Veterans Affairs, was able to join me on the trip thanks to some aggressive lobbying of White House New Media director Macon Philips. That way, I could shoot b-roll out the window while we drove down the highway, and she could edit till the wee hours in hotel rooms with MSNBC blaring in the background. Just like old times.

But getting the other side of the story isn't all stopping by the side of the road for scenic panorama shots. Everyone on the president's official schedule is generally vetted beforehand, both for security reasons and to avoid embarrassing revelations with the local press. At the very least these stories are distractions, so it's just easier to check people out before the fact.* Still, when you're out on your own, nothing comes at you thoroughly researched, or researched at all. Sometimes you find out right away, from the interviewee himself. "Well, I sailed down to Nicaragua so I could fish those great white shrimp they've got down there," one guy told me. "I'm telling you, you can really match wits with those Nicaraguan shrimp. The red shrimp around here are just dumb. So yeah, I might've done some time in prison for that . . ." This guy might've been the nicest person on the Gulf Coast, but he clearly wasn't going to be the best spokesman for the cleanup efforts.

---

* This is the cheerful flip side of campaign opposition research because the people doing the vetting are often researching success stories.

Sometimes you find out later, like late on the Thursday night before we were set to release the Gulf Coast movie, when we learned that a volunteer boat captain had a slightly shady incident in his past. He also, alas, had a fantastic quote about the pride he took in the cleanup effort: "The cynics, they all say, 'Where'd the oil go?' I tell them we cleaned it up. That's where it went—right into these sacks here." And he indicated the scores of white trash bags that contained the oil-soaked boom that was sponging up what little surface oil remained on the Florida coast. Having to excise this great speech from the film at the last minute left the scene totally gutted, but what can you do?

Speaking of gutted, for these dispatches, the surrealism threshold was much lower than on a normal *West Wing Week*, precisely because they came out at irregular intervals. So while it's an absolute fact that at the National Oceanic and Atmospheric Administration (NOAA) facility in Mississippi a human nose can be trained to smell tainted seafood to a degree no technology can match, I couldn't include this truly astonishing fact in my movie.* Although I believe this activity has the ring of truth in a vacuum, it kind of comes across as an improbable Scooby-Doo reveal out of context.

I was shocked that NOAA hadn't already made a movie about this amazing human sensory skill, but since they allowed the press to tell their story, and only in terms of the environmental disaster, it made it sound a little too convenient, and a little less true. More government agencies should produce content like *West Wing Week*— that is to say, day-to-day coverage of the nuts-and-bolts, behind-the-scenes stuff, and not simply material that's prompted by massive disasters. Running a country is a fascinating process, and the government should be making these types of films all the time, and

---

* Before you go freaking out and spitting out your Po' Boy, be assured (a) a machine *also* tests it and (b) the human sniffer is better, no fooling.

*A rare day in boots while filming in Kuwait.* (U.S. Navy photo)

not only that, but the films should be good enough that people actually want to watch them. I think fish sniffing is just the tip of the iceberg of things the population would have more faith in their government if they only knew.

My Gulf spill movie was a success—one of my most-watched videos to date at that point—so I lobbied to make more *Dispatches.* Less than a month after my long drives down the interstates of Alabama and Mississippi, I went to Iraq to film the change of command there. On the ground in Baghdad, I was treated like a VIP until the actual VP showed up, at which point I was dropped from an armored car to a bus. But unlike the real VIPs, I got to see things that never made the nightly news, like USDA specialists helping to modernize Iraqi farms, more notable for the fact that a tremendous number of journalists were in town to cover the transition.

In Iraq I got to see and appreciate the U.S. military in action, and a few months later, in Sudan (or rather Sudan when I arrived; South Sudan as you read this), I had the opportunity to observe the miraculous work of the U.S. diplomatic corps—yet another fascinating (and indispensable) aspect of government service that the public rarely got to see. And something I hope we will see more of in terms of regular programming, not just crisis response.

Sudan was probably the most meaningful trip I took, and the highlight of my tenure in the White House. (Mental note: always send postcards from Darfur.) I spent the two-week referendum on secession trailing the president's special envoy, General Scott Gration—and let me tell you, no one, and I mean no one, who watches General Gration at work can doubt the importance of good government. And it's impossible to watch the hard-fought birth of a new nation without an immense amount of emotion. There were no butter sculptures here, just long lines of people at the polls, many of whom had walked for hours to get there. The hope and optimism that were evident throughout the countryside of South Sudan made a compelling contrast with the bustling apathy of Khartoum and the entrenched misery of Darfur. It was a lot to take in.

And believe it or not, it was seeing General Gration in action, and not the dinner party with George Clooney, that made the trip so amazing for me. ("Sir, Arun just got back from Sudan," an aide in the Outer Oval said when I showed up to give POTUS some shirts from the successful referendum. "Yeah, I saw your picture with Clooney and the jet set," the president replied with one of his wry grins. I didn't feel the need to detail the rather unglamorous condition of the New York Hotel in "there is no downtown" Juba, which did, it should be noted, have ample parking, just as the rusting billboard advertised.)

*NGO chic. (Why am I the only one holding a bottle?)* (Photo by Kristina Johnson)

The general was the ideal no-nonsense character for this type of project. Whether he was telling it like it is to UN officials ("this is *constructive* criticism"), NGO representatives ("look, of *course* it's good to feed people but you are screwing this up!"), or the local government ("no, I'm pretty sure that clinic we built was around here somewhere, why don't you show me?"), he proved that good policy makes good movies.

Through sheer force of personality, General Gration created a bubble of sorts that was not unlike the president's in the rigorousness of his schedule, but which allowed me enough freedom to wander from a garden meeting with a local politician along the Blue Nile to a UN vehicle for a little b-roll. Kicked out of a peace talk on Darfur? Visit the Sky Lounge and get some scenic shots of the perma-'70s city that is Khartoum. There are never any casual interludes of that sort when you're traveling with the president. It makes me think that there could be a sustainable model for this kind of work in government agencies somehow, but lending out the president's guy is definitely not the easiest way to go about it, or so I had to remind myself as I nodded off on a couch while General Gration conferred with President Carter. (Don't worry. I used what little footage I got of this moment as if I'd been alert the whole time.)

In the end, though I believe that the *Dispatches* series is probably the best filmmaking I've done at the White House, the work model was simply not sustainable for a one-man-band operation like myself, even with the support of the World's Finest Broadcast Communications Support!! (WHCA's slogan, as printed on their lens cloths.) And sneaking off while the president was on vacation was a fallacy for two reasons: one, because even I needed a real vacation every once in a while, as my wife kept reminding me; and two, because the president is never really on vacation. Keeping up with his schedule and monitoring events in the world outside was just too much for one filmmaker.

As I edited in an Ambien-induced haze in a hotel in Khartoum (I would wake up with gum inexplicably jammed into my external hard drive and Jimmy Carter's name spelled with a pound sign), my BlackBerry buzzed with the news that Congresswoman Gabrielle Giffords had been shot in Tucson. On the other side of the planet as I was, I couldn't capture the backstage moments at the memorial service; I could only watch it at WH.gov (weirdly, one of the very few sites not censored in Sudan) a few days later. No one recorded the time Obama spent with Gabby's relatives and closest congressional friends, Congresswoman Wasserman Schultz and Senator Gillibrand, and her husband, astronaut Mark Kelly, in motion pictures. I missed the rewriting of the speech that I knew would be happening in the conference room on Air Force One, as well as those special moments right before a big speech: the closing of the eyes and the bowing of the head that still photography can only capture as static before and after shots. The movement is what's missing.

CONCLUSION

# "YOU MIGHT WANT TO PUT ON SOME PANTS"

On a quiet Sunday night in early May 2011, I was sitting in my pajamas at the computer, reviewing the president's schedule for the coming week, when I got a seemingly routine message from the White House. The president would be making a statement in a few hours, and I needed to get over there.*

"What's up," I wearily wrote communications staffer Ben Finkenbinder, who was responsible for corralling the press to such events. It was almost 9:00 p.m., and after a long weekend of parenting I was ready to wind down. (Childless readers, this is the equivalent of 11:45 p.m.; not late-late, but getting there.) "Do I really need to put on my pants for this?"

"You should definitely put on your pants," he wrote back immediately.

---

* As colleague Samantha Appleton later noted, there was nothing routine about making a statement on a Sunday night, and I should have been on my game right away.

That was the first I heard about the killing of bin Laden—just about two hours before the rest of the nation, and probably well after a lot of connected journalists who would've already had their pants on to feel the buzzing of their BlackBerries.

That night, I didn't stop with my pants; I put on a whole suit. But weirdly, as I made my way to the Oval to scope the situation, I was surprised to see that pretty much everyone else was dressed down. Like, extremely. Staffers were in workout clothes, or barely disguised pajamas. The on-duty network TV cameraman was donning a well-worn Washington Caps hockey jersey. Finkenbinder was also wearing Caps gear; they'd both rushed straight over to the White House from the game.

As a jeans, sneakers, and polo–clad Reggie Love noted with surprise, the president and I were pretty much the only ones on campus dressed up that night. Even on this unusual day, this was unusual. I wish I'd gotten the Casual Sundays memo, as Reggie's outfit conformed with my favorite White House dress code, a style that would come to be known, at first colloquially and then semi-officially, as Disaster Casual: clothing that's generically corporate enough for polite society but still appropriate for wading along an oil-drenched beach, or filling sandbags on a levy, or showing up on seconds' notice for any other catastrophe that may strike in the course of following a president.

In a way, the night of bin Laden's death was just another day at the office. I went through my usual routine, filming the bustle of national security staffers in and out of the Outer Oval Office; VP Biden in his Sunday blazer—okay, so he was fairly dressed up, too, but he's Joe Biden—calling congressional leadership to tell them the news; the descent of frantic journalists into the East Room, where the president made his statement; and the president's solemn walk down the colonnade with his chief of staff and the vice president. These were all scenes that I'd shot before, more or less, but of course this night had that extra glow of "super history" to it. I mean, everything a president does is important, but OBL is *big*.

The secrecy was in and of itself a huge deal. Usually you hear something—hints, whispers, speculations. The First Lady didn't even know what was about to go down, so as you can imagine, I wasn't in the loop, either. I wasn't tucked next to Pete Souza in the Situation Room while the mission went down, smoothly panning from Secretary Clinton to Admiral Mullen; no, I was in my pajamas. I've no doubt that this footage would be fascinating, but the contextual footage I'd shot in the week leading up to the big event was just as telling; let me make the case.

You can play along at home by watching *West Wing Week: A Good Day for America*. (I actually had to change the original title for national security reasons. Um, awesome.) As I've said, it's all about the context. I filmed the president on a trip with such far-flung stops as Joplin, Missouri, where he inspected tornado damage; and Cape Canaveral, where he went to witness the launch of the second-to-last space shuttle at NASA (which was later scrubbed), and Miami to deliver a commencement address at Miami Dade College—all of which becomes more interesting when you realize that he was making this momentous decision in those in-between moments. The loading up of the limos—one of my stock shots from almost every day—to go to the traditionally lighthearted White House Correspondents' Dinner also takes on new weight in this context. Over the course of this week, you also see an American president dealing with his greatest responsibility, the military, in various incarnations, from ordering the mission in Pakistan to awarding a posthumous Medal of Honor to starting a bike race for wounded warriors.

On my way home after the announcement, as I pushed through

the drunken college students thronging Pennsylvania Avenue, I thought of how carefully I'd filmed that night, and how carefully I'd pick through the footage the next morning. And even though the OBL footage promised to be infinitely more interesting than any of the umpteen congressional caucus awards dinners I'd filmed, I also had to confront a growing sense of weariness—even on that of all nights. Maybe, just maybe, I was getting a little burned out. I'd been at this job for four-plus years by that point. I'd seen countless world leaders, and observed some high-level decision-making, and logged an incredible amount of filmmaking experience. But was I doing the job justice? Was I still bringing it each and every day?

While it was always a privilege, filming Barack Obama around the clock for four years sometimes felt like meditation and sometimes even like a cruel joke. In the winter of 2011, just before the averted government shutdown, I filmed POTUS, Speaker of the House John Boehner, and Senate Majority Leader Harry Reid over and over again as they held the exact same meeting at the exact same table day after day after day, until eventually I ran out of angles. In a more general way, that's how I started to feel over my last few months at the White House: out of angles. Even if my health hadn't been deteriorating at a rapid clip, I was getting ready to play in different genres and focus on different subjects.

And in cabinet meetings as in life, I believe that knowing when to go is an important skill. The adrenaline of working in a place like the White House can be addictive. There's always the next factory trip, the next international drama, the next battle royale with Congress. But after bin Laden, I knew nothing that big would come down the pike for a long, long time.

I also thought that my legacy, such as it was, was pretty secure. I like to think I've helped establish a new standard for videos coming out of the White House, a new degree of intimacy between the president and the rest of us. So even if I didn't film the brilliant Betty White birthday video, I imagine that I did pave the road to that video with countless diners, bowling alleys, and NASCAR races. And so, once it became clear that *West Wing Week* was established enough to continue without me, I decided to start crafting my exit strategy. (Okay, so this is actually pure spin. I may have dramatically declared at a meeting that *WWW* would have to be buried with me; how could it possible continue without my stamp of authorship? Only to be talked down by . . . everybody.)

Another big reason I decided to leave the White House was because, after observing big historic events for so long, I was ready to have a more direct impact on them. Just a few weeks before the OBL killing, we were in the presidential palace in Chile, which was, of all the places that I've been with Barack Obama, the one that felt the most haunted by history. There was even a door reserved for Salvador Allende, the martyred president deposed by Augusto Pinochet, that no one was allowed to use in deference to Allende's memory. President Obama and his national security adviser were sitting in an ornate dining room discussing the situation in Libya while I wandered around trying to figure out what to film. Then suddenly it occurred to me that I didn't just have opinions on what to film; I had opinions on the subject at hand.

A few seconds later, the president paused to frown at a jagged piece of electronics on the table—most likely from a telephone or other conferencing device that was just ever-so-slightly suspicious—and then rose to his feet and moved it out of the room. "That should be in a movie," I thought to myself, a reminder that my need to tell stories had survived a hundred state dinners.

That same week, I got an e-mail from my old NYU officemate, Jay Anania. He'd attached some clipping of my exploits and written, "All of this is so amazing! I'd love to catch up with you and talk about it, but in the meantime, when are you making a movie-movie? I want to hear about that."

He was right. It was time to start looking forward, to plot my own future stories, and what was going to come next. Even in politics, I was spending all my time perfecting the techniques of 2008 rather than taking the time to envision future techniques. Repeating the past never bears much fruit.

In the context of Obama's reelection campaign, for example, I know that the most remembered videos of 2012 couldn't even have been envisioned in 2008, and the most successful ones won't be informed by them.* But at this point in the Republican primary, I can safely say that the videos of 2012 haven't had much of an authentic ring to them. The percentage of MSG-laden negative ads has reached new heights, and attempts to "do the Obama thing" (see in particular the Romney campaign's Mitt on the Road series or Bump in the Road) feel hollow and derivative. They can't even say the word "road."

Of course, a lot of that has to do with the futility of reverse engineering. You wouldn't be able to use this book to reverse engineer a presidential victory. This book is not a V-2 rocket, and you couldn't, say, turn Bill Clinton into Al Gore the way you can make the V-2 into NASA's workhorse the Saturn V rocket or even the way you can get German scientists to turn the V-2 into the Saturn V (or whatever we made them do with it). I mention this because Washington, DC, is a town hell-bent on reverse engineering, in full disconnect with the American inventive spirit.

---

* This isn't to imply that Obama '08 was the only game in town, then or now; two other '08 veterans have continued to make interesting contributions to political video: Mike Huckabee has been making these nostalgic (if fairly misinformed) cartoons, and that Palin show on TLC was nothing short of amazing.

Politicians share this obsession with sports commentators. They're always seeking that magic potion, the secret to someone else's success. I call it Bob Costas syndrome, the idea that examining a successful person's biography somehow reveals patterns that others can replicate with similar results. But whether you're a gold-medal slalomist from rural Idaho or the first African-American president of the United States, no two paths to success are the same, and any attempts to copy or even establish a previous pattern will likely fall flat.*

And while I'm extremely alarmed by all the corporate money pouring into campaigns, it's not a cash discrepancy that makes for such bad political media.† I do worry that campaigns of the future will use technology as a means to save money on the real videographer, and one cameraman who knows what he's doing will be replaced by twenty nifty HD cameras for twenty trackers. This is both a shame and a waste, for can't anyone with a cell phone be a tracker? Well, maybe not. I've been in a thousand rooms with ten thousand phones and every single bystander misses the shot every single time. And if I could only assemble all the blurry photos and videos that spectators shoot of the motorcade whizzing by! That monkey had better luck with the self-portrait.

---

* A great example: In the aftermath of the 2008 blowout, Republicans realized they had a New Media gap. Their response was merely to parrot and outdo what had come before, that is, we need more tweets than the Democrats. In the spring of 2010, they even held a Final Four–style tournament to improve their New Media presence (I swear I'm not making this up), but this is a classic example of working hard rather than smart, which on the Internet is a major no-no. It's almost like hiring a post office's worth of employees to send out a mass e-mail. Not that I'm looking to pick a fight with post office employees; I think they're wonderful and wish everyone would just get off their back.

† Factoid: In England, they don't have campaign commercials, and the average cost of running for Parliament is a mere 18,000 pounds (a little more than $28,000), though of course in England they also have a royal family and we're sort of over that.

In 2012, new frontiers on online video have been opened left and right. Not only did Herman Cain form a SuperPAC with no seeming aim other than to produce high art ads involving dying fish and, well, Herman Cain, but before bowing out, Rick Santorum managed to almost enter will.i.am territory with his fan-created hit "Game On." The milestones aren't only relegated to American presidential politics. The year 2012 has seen both a high ranked Syrian minister defect from his country and a 600-pound man (coincidentally named Robert Gibbs) plead for help, both via YouTube. The bottom line is that it's increasingly legit to conduct "serious" business online, and more and more people are taking society up on that proposition.

But more isn't always better, and it's certainly not what the public wants. The nexus of politics, media, art, and entertainment that we saw emerge in 2008 wasn't just driven by the Internet, but by a new public hunger for transparency, an offshoot of the same distrust of government that gave birth to the Tea Party. People wanted more accountability from their government, and the video camera provided a direct portal to it.

No matter who is president in 2016, I know that I for one will still be curious. I'll still peruse press pool reports and try to imagine exactly what's going on inside the bubble on any given day. I already love being able to get a real inside-look-from-the-outside on WH.gov, but it's true that, more than a year after I put the White House in my rearview, I feel a twinge whenever breaking news flashes across my screen, or POTUS visits a new country, though (I tell myself) it's a little less painful every time.

The discipline I've taken away from this experience has no match. My four years with Obama were transformative for me as an artist. I went from being a dawdler and dreamer to cranking out videos week after week no matter what. Perhaps, it's a little self-indulgent to need the office of the presidency to get down to work, but, well, here we are. The president summed it up best late at night on the campaign plane when we were the only ones up. "You're a responsible son of a gun," he said, shaking his head, "but you wouldn't know it by looking at you."

I also like to think that the Office of the President has grown a little with me, that I've helped to equip it with the infrastructure necessary to keep up with the clamor of the day while at the same time preserving history right as it's happening. No less important, I've been able to advocate for the rules of traditional filmmaking in one of the epicenters of the "new way" of doing things.

And, the through line of it all, the ideal in both traditions and innovation that I've learned weaves through both art and politics? Practicality trumps dogma every time.

I was trying to explain this to General Gration, as we circled in a chopper over Darfur. "It used to take me awhile to finish movies, but we'll have this Sudan movie up on the WH site by the end of next week, guaranteed. The president always says, 'Don't make the perfect the enemy of the good,' and I've tried to apply that to my filmmaking."

The general grinned and shook his head. "The best piece of advice you'll ever get from President Obama," he said, "is 'if you ain't doing it, it ain't getting done.'"

I've now adopted that credo as well, and I'm ready to start getting it done.

# NOTES ON SOURCES

In this book I've tried to tell the story that is uniquely mine to tell, not least of all (but certainly not most) so that I could rely a good deal on my own memory, which is at least slightly better than average.

I was able to catch up with some busy people to fill in the gaps, many of whom I acknowledge in the acknowledgments but David Axelrod, David Plouffe, and John Del Cecado were able to show me another view of the New Media story of 2008 than I was privy to. Stephen Geer and Chris Hughes were invaluable sources of wisdom when it came to understanding the New Media story I actually did experience but didn't quite understand. Reggie Love and Josh Earnest also helped fill in some of my more murky recollections.

I name most of my written sources in the text of the book itself, a rare and important exception was *Documentary: A History of the Non Fiction Film* by Erik Barnouw, a book that will be familiar to anyone who has a film education of any kind.

I also mention learning about government documentarian Pare Lorentz. The entire span of my knowledge of PL is based on two books. Lorentz's autobiography, *FDR's Moviemaker* and *Pare Lorentz and the Documentary Film* by Robert L. Snyder (1968).

On the filmic end of things I was also able to speak with documentarians Albert Maysles, D. A. Pennebaker, and Chris Hegedus.

# ACKNOWLEDGMENTS

In the last five years, more than anything else, I feel as if I've been indulged: by colleagues, by superiors, and even occasionally the president of the United States. They had no real reason to, other than that they did, and their trust has driven me to try to succeed as best I can.

This book was no different, so I must single out the most indulgent force in my life, that of the lovely and talented Laura Moser, who's not so coincidentally my wife, and who slaved away on the words you just read. "Indulgent" is really the only word applicable when sometimes all I sent was a note in all-caps accompanied by a YouTube clip of a bear eating hot dogs. She untangled and elevated my words beyond what I thought possible (and secretly cut things that I haven't noticed yet, I'm sure). Robin Bellinger added her characteristic enthusiasm as well as her unmatched command of the language while helping us make an impossible deadline.

While it's be impossible to mention all the people who have made my story possible by name, I'd be remiss in not thanking Kate Albright-Hanna and Joe Rospars for taking that initial chance on me. The two Davids, Plouffe and Axelrod, who not only took the chance but have been invaluable in filling in gaps in this narrative. Reggie Love, Marvin Nicholson, Chris Hughes, and Eugene Kang, too, thanks! Stephen Geer, who not only offered his eagle eyes on drafts, but let me steal several jokes for this book, of which I have only used one. I challenge you to find it. Dan Stroker and Katie Stanton also helped on new media matters.

People who I've no idea why they answer my e-mails: famed documentarians Al Maysles, D. A. Pennebaker, and Chris Hegedus, and dear friend Livia Bloom, who put me in touch with them; unparalleled expert in this realm Larry Sabato, and curator of the Museum of the Moving Image David Schwartz, all of whom in brief conversations gave me more material than I could possibly include in this book. Likewise, big thanks to Bill Allman, the White House curator, who took time out to speak to me despite losing his voice.

Definitely not forgetting: Paul Golob, the editorial director of Times Books, and my fearless editor, Serena Jones, who both indulgently looked the other way when several deadlines arrived and passed. And to Bridget Wagner, who had an idea.

Special thanks to the folks at my two new homes away from home: Revolution Messaging, where Scott Goodstein and his staff generously let me write on their conference table, and the School of Media and Public Affairs at the George Washington University, where Frank Sesno, Nina Seavey, and Dan Reed forced me to actually think through my notions long enough to teach them to others. (Thanks Emilie Frank and Sara Firestone for the research help!)

Finally, I'd like to thank my family and friends who remain my family and friends, for no real reason, and to apologize to Leo, it's been great to catch up.

Deeply grateful,
Arun Chaudhary
Washington, DC, 2012

# INDEX

Page numbers in *Italics* refer to illustrations.

# ABOUT THE AUTHOR

ARUN CHAUDHARY served as the first official White House videographer from 2009 to 2011 and was also a key member of Obama's New Media team during the 2008 campaign. He previously worked in film in New York and was a member of the NYU Graduate Film Department faculty. He received his MFA in filmmaking from NYU and his BA in film theory from Cornell University. Chaudhary has been profiled by the *New York Times*, the BBC, *National Journal*, *Politico*, *Fortune*, and many political websites. He lives in Washington, DC, with his wife and son.